Living Faith, Hope and Love

Living Faith, Hope and Love

✦

A Memoir

Mary O'Brien Callaghan

iUniverse, Inc.
New York Lincoln Shanghai

Living Faith, Hope and Love
A Memoir

iUniverse books may be ordered through booksellers or by contacting:

iUniverse
2021 Pine Lake Road, Suite 100
Lincoln, NE 68512
www.iuniverse.com
1-800-Authors (1-800-288-4677)

ISBN-13: 978-0-595-36553-1 (pbk)
ISBN-13: 978-0-595-80984-4 (ebk)
ISBN-10: 0-595-36553-1 (pbk)
ISBN-10: 0-595-80984-7 (ebk)

Printed in the United States of America

Contents

Prelude

I word-processed and edited the memoir you are about to read with much help from my eldest and youngest sisters, Margaret and Bridget. Mother never got to finish writing her memoir but I think you will find what she did write both interesting and inspiring. She also never gave her story a title although years ago she said that if anyone wrote the story of her life it would have to be titled something alliterative and ironic; her favorite title was *Shit and Shinola*. But that was in the days when she was knee deep in diapers and childcare. Another title idea came from the reaction some unsuspecting soul had when she found out Mother had so many children (I think it was 15 at the time). The lady blurted out, "You must be Catholic or crazy!" Mother's response was typical: "Well, I'm a little of both."

Catholic Or Crazy, Shit and Shinola, Martyr But Certainly Not a Virgin, But Don't Ever Call Me Boring, and *Some Day You're Gonna Miss Me, Baby* would describe some aspects of Mother's personality and some of what she experienced and at times felt, but none of the titles comes close to fitting what she actually wrote so I took up the task of coming up with a title. A writer friend and mentor of mine, Steven Dunning, always said, "Name everything you give birth to."

A number of factors went into the title you see on the cover. The week before she died, I spent a night with Mother at the house on Warwick. I had heard that she wasn't being very cooperative: she had refused to do the pace maker procedure or to go to a care facility, was reluctant to take her many medications, and was suggesting we engage hospice care. She also knew that another episode of pneumonia would be the end for her. I figured I would spend most of the time trying to handle her agitations and to give her as much comfort and help as I could.

The opposite happened. She asked me to read some passages out loud to her: a beautiful essay on prayer by an Anglican monk (his name escapes me) and several passages from the Bible, one of which I chose for the memorial service we did in Oswego (the gospel in which Jesus describes how the apostles will grieve after He is gone but that in the end the experience will be like the distress a mother goes through in giving birth and the joy that will follow). We said the rosary together and then had an amazing conversation about death.

"You know, John, I don't want to die. Even though I'm in my mid-eighties and have had a full life, I'm not ready to die. Something in me wants to keep going. There are weddings to attend, grandchildren and great grandchildren to welcome into this world. I'm worried about your father. This is all very hard on him."

"And you haven't finished your memoir yet. You've just gotten to the Manor Road part—many juicy details to come."

"That too. I really have to do something about that. Anyway, everything is in God's hands and we have to accept his will. You know, 'Thy will be done…' and all that. I should be ashamed of myself. I've had more blessings in my life than most people, even though at times I wasn't very appreciative. Beautiful children. A loving husband. Great parents. All kinds of hidden blessings. You could say my life is *full*-filled. But I don't think anyone goes to the other side willingly—maybe Mother Teresa."

And one week later she was back in the hospital, a second bout of pneumonia, but fighting the good fight. Once again I was sitting there at her bedside, only this time at Beaumont, listening to her account of Fr. Rick's visit that early afternoon. She became agitated for a moment and then said, "I'm exhausted. The medication knocks me out." She then went into a deep sleep at around 3:30. At 5:30 Mary and Bridget stopped by, took one look at Mother, and became very concerned. Mary said, "She might be in a coma," and went to get the nurse.

After some prodding, the nurse got Mother to wake up. Mother was at first disoriented. The nurse began to check her out by asking a series of questions.

"What year is it, Mrs. Callaghan?"

"199…No, no…2003."

"Where are you?"

"Detroit, uh, no…Beaumont, the bowels of Beaumont."

"Who's the president of the United States?"

"Bush. The bastard."

"How are you feeling, Mrs. Callaghan?"

"Awful. Please, no more medicine. I am weary to the bottom of my soul. Please, no more medicine, no more…"

Less than twenty-four hours later, we had just finished the rosary and Dad a reading of the *Magnificat*—"My Soul Doth Magnify the Lord"—and Mother breathed her last. Many of her children, her grandchildren, her sons and daughters-in-law had the privilege of being present, standing by her bedside, each one touched in a special way by this very special person. We would none of us be the same again.

Three themes keep emerging from the text she created. First is faith: her faith in God; in her parents, relatives, friends and teachers; and in Jack Callaghan. Hope sits right along side of that faith. As often as events and circumstances tested her faith, she never gave up, always hoping for and expecting the best. And I can echo St. Paul by saying the best of all was her love, her infinite capacity to care for her parents, her husband, her children and grandchildren, her friends, and just about everyone who met her. She thought about and shopped for Christmas and birthday gifts every day and was able to purchase something that fit each individual just right. She was equally interested in telling you what she thought and in what you had to say (unless it was political). And even though she had her "moments," she was a keen observer and an empathetic listener.

I'm sure each reader who knew her could give an example of any one of these themes, but during the conversation I mentioned above, I told her I'd never understood how she survived the time just after moving to Manor Road, when she was taking care of three grandchildren, Uncle Jim and Nana Callaghan along with 19 other people in the house. Her answer was candid: "I was not a happy camper, but what can I say? I loved your father." Her faith, hope, and love were not just ideals preached in a catechism, but virtues deep within her soul that evolved, that she nourished, and that radiated out from her being to our minds, bodies and souls.

A memoir is a unique form of writing—it transcends history, goes beyond autobiography—because it attends to narrative more than it does to exactness of detail or chronology. The narrative allows for the writer's voice to come through loud and clear and makes that writer's *persona* present to the reader in a way neither historical fiction nor autobiography could ever accomplish.

Mary O'Brien Callaghan is no longer with us in body. But she certainly is with us in her spirit and in her words. As you read her story, she is there right along side of you, that expressive, sonorous voice resonating in your head, full of humor, compassion, and, above all else, full of love for her God, for her husband, and for you. And if you open that third eye of your imagination, you'll also be able to *see* her—as a stunning little girl, beribboned hair, decked out in all her fancy outfits, those brown eyes never missing a trick, the joy of Nana and Big Paul's life; as a schoolgirl bubbling with curiosity and talent; as a young teenager in love for the first time; as a high-schooler full of song, dance, scholarship and, yes, romance; as a college girl full of passion for her music and her man; as a young wife and mother, coping with experiences for which she had no forewarning nor preparation; a maturing mother overwhelmed at times by a burgeoning family, a world war, a move to a large industrial city, continuously surrounded by an endless array of soiled diapers, clothes, dishes, and floors; and as a friend to neighbors and their children, to nuns and priests at church and school, to her husband's colleagues, and to anyone who came to the door, including Jehovah Witnesses.

True, the memoir is not finished. What you remember and what others are able to tell you can fill in the gaps. What was left unsaid or untold inheres in the text that came before the interruption because the spirit of love for her husband and family and of faith in her God and in her Church that permeated her life and that rings throughout these pages continued into the Manor Road and Warwick years. It was a life fulfilled. We are blessed to have been a part of it.

PART I
OSWEGO

1

Birth in Oswego

People would say to me, "Where are you from?" And I would reply, "Oswego, New York." Some would ask, "Where is that?" And I would answer, "North of Syracuse, New York on Lake Ontario, population 22,000." Others would respond differently, "Oh, Oswego, that town you pass through on Route 104..." Still others would say, "I've heard of Oswego. Isn't that where there are as many bars as people and everyone is Irish?" Fortunately, this last comment is true hyperbole.

The Oswego River runs into Lake Ontario and Oswego County built a canal there. It was part of the Erie Canal system and many of the Irish immigrants, who had helped build it, remained to make their homes where the canal ended on the rocky banks of Lake Ontario. The Oswego River flows north into Lake Ontario, separating the town into two natural parts, Eastside and Westside. I come from the Westside; Jack from the Eastside. Two big bridges connect the two sides, one on the north end of town, the other on the south. On the Westside is the State University of New York (SUNY) at Oswego, overlooking the lake. Oswego is a beautiful area, surrounded by delightful, scenic routes. An Oswego resident is always aware of the lake; one can smell it, feel the breezes and, in winter, shiver in the extreme cold. (Jerry Seinfeld attended SUNY at Oswego and left after one winter). In the heat of summer, however, there is always a gentle breeze to cool a sweaty brow.

Some Historical Facts: The Iroquois Indians frequented the area and were the most dominant tribe. On the present eastside of Oswego is Fort Ontario, now an historical site that dates back to the 18th century. In 1756 during the French and Indian War, the English made a valiant effort to defend the fort but lost possession for a brief time to the French, who had entered the area through the St. Lawrence Seaway.

Later on in history, the people who lived in my cousin Larry's house sheltered and hid a number of escaping slaves on their way to Canada before and during the Civil War. At the turn of the century Oswego enjoyed both economic growth and a population increase. Residents around 1913 on a lovely Sunday would promenade around the fort on the shore of Lake Ontario. I always imagined it like "Sunday in the Park," the painting by George Serat: the long dresses, the fancy hats, parasols. I doubt, however, if there were any monkeys.

Jack was born October 5, 1916 in Pious Hollow on Oswego's Eastside. He was impatient to appear on the scene so arrived before the doctor got there. His father Edward (Fishy) and mother Margaret Hogan Callaghan named him John Foster and were proud of their third child.

Two years later on the other side of town in the upstairs bedroom in unseasonable 35-degree weather, with the hearths lit and the heat on I, Mary Margaret O'Brien, was born. My mother Margaret Conway O'Brien had an extremely difficult delivery. My father Paul Joseph O'Brien was present when I was born on August 19, 1918, two months before the Armistice that ended World War I. I was to be their only child.

Before I was born, my father and his family made their home on 315 West 3rd Street in Oswego. It was a large Victorian house, front door right, sweeping porch on the left of the dining room, which was the entrance most people used. The dining room had a lovely bay window where Grandpa sat in a huge rocking chair. There was a plate rail bordering the room with many plates, on their edges, leaning against the wall. To the left was a huge kitchen where the real action took place. Rolls, cookies, pies, cakes—the oven was always lit. The back door led into a deep yard full of grape vines, so very fragrant in the fall. They used the back stairs (off the dining room) more often than the front stairs.

At noon, my dad or his brother Bill, whose blond hair and blue eyes contrasted with my father's dark hair and brown eyes, would take a break from school and trudge six blocks from the pub, bringing a pail of beer to the Kingsford Foundry where Grandpa worked. He needed something with which to wash down his lunch. Many years later my cousin Larry O'Brien (Bill's son) bought the Kingsford property where his grandfather had labored. By the way, before they lived on West 3rd, the O'Briens lived on Varick Street. Next door to them lived the Callaghan family, which included my future father-in-law, Fishy Callaghan.

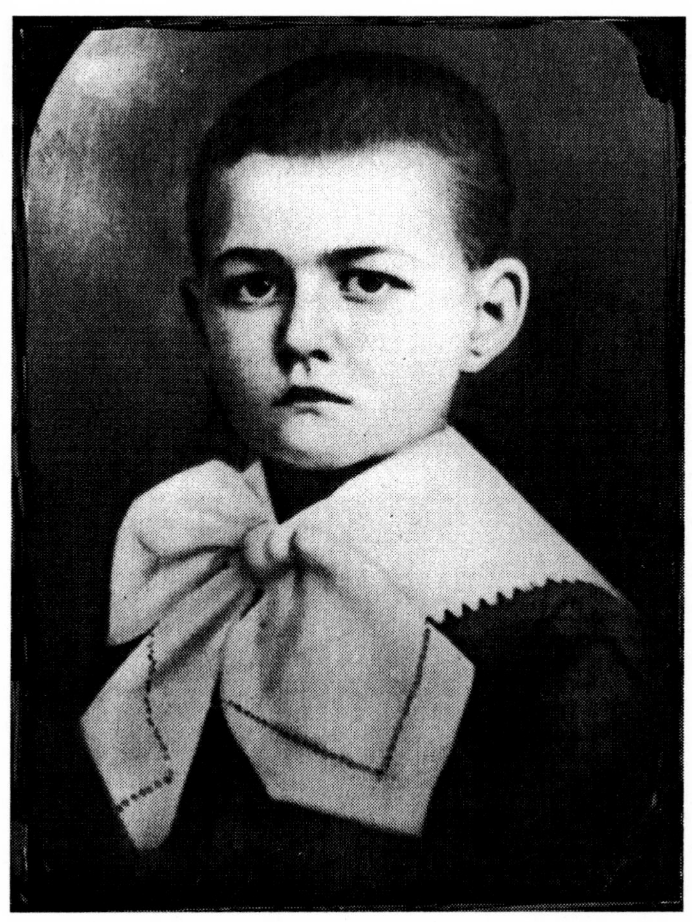

My dad as an altar boy around the time he and his brother brought daily pails of beer to their father's work at Kingsford Foundry.

2

The Aunties

Since I was an only child, my aunties were special to me. When you came to their door, their greetings were amazing. Ann, Helen, Mae and Agnes would surround you and make oohing and aahing sounds and gave little pats on the back and I felt warm, loved and welcomed. Not only that, they laughed hysterically at every statement I made, which convinced me that I was a very funny person, and it encouraged me to consider myself a comedian.

Mae was four feet with dark brown eyes; she wore glasses, size 4 shoes, and was very talented. My mother said, "With an education she could have been outstanding." One day, before she was married, my mother was visiting with Mae. Mae said, "I am going to make you a dress." She walked around mother a few times and that was that. Lo and behold, a week later Mae appeared with a beautiful garment, a lovely fabric that fit perfectly. Mother was amazed. Mae was very vivacious and fun to be near. When my father had his restaurant, she supplied pies, cakes, cookies and bread. When anyone was ill, she was the nurse on the spot. Mae had once been "Miss Oswego," a beauty contest she had won.

Mae married Harry Baker. They talked baby talk to each other. He was six feet, four inches. He was Uncle Sam at a Halloween party I had when I was seven. In retrospect, I think it was the adults who wanted the party and used the occasion as a ruse. I know the next morning one of the jardinières was smashed and I learned the culprit was Uncle Sam. Uncle Harry was an electrician, but his reputation was not good. Rumors of his lack of expertise were known around town. Mother asked him to hang two chandeliers in our large dining room. When he finished the work, they were beautiful to behold, their many layers of prisms sparkling. There was a hitch, however; in order to turn them on, one had to get on a ladder to achieve this. And it had to be a 12-foot tall ladder because of the high ceilings. They were seldom lit except for the holidays, but they were elegant anyway.

Uncle Harry collected stamps. What he *didn't* collect was money. And it became one of Uncle Bill's main projects to rescue Harry from ruin. Harry was pleasant and amiable and I think he and Mae loved each other. They sure did a lot of billing and cooing. Out of nowhere Uncle Harry suddenly got a job with the government in Panama (as in Panama Canal). We accompanied them to their boat. That was the first time I saw New York harbor in all its glory. We even boarded the boat. The hustle and bustle, the farewell kissing—flowers being delivered to the staterooms, champagne glasses lifted in farewell—I was nine and it was most exciting for me!

One time when Mae was visiting Oswego and Harry was supposedly in Panama, he suddenly showed up at the door and another exciting event occurred—four foot Mae leaped up in the air and with her tiny fist socked him in the kisser. Now it was Harry's turn to be surprised. Great memory. Ann, Helen, Agnes and Grandma had great visits to Panama and returned with many treasures, one or two of which I still have.

In the end, Mae and Harry ended up at 315 West Third, alcoholic and penniless. Uncle Bill, however, was always to the rescue. Bit by bit the teak furniture and Persian rugs disappeared. Fewer and fewer people visited. Then the call came in the night and Mae was gone to God. Harry went into a hotel room with his worthless stamps in tow. 315 West third exits no more, the victim of city renovation so today, if you wanted to, you couldn't drive past it.

Agnes took me for long walks on West 5th road and in Kingsford Woods and taught me the names of trees and flowers, which were always abundant there. She taught special education and married George States in 1929. He was an architect for Shell in New York City. They were late coming down the aisle at their wedding and Father McGloughlin was furious and let all attending know about it. It put a pall on the ceremony. It was the first time I heard such terms as "aelceon lace," "tulle," "satin train"—the color "firecracker." The reception was "up home," with places for everyone except Grandma, which was typical because Grandma never had much time to sit.

The bride and groom moved to Closter, New Jersey, and Uncle George commuted. The town was a lovely hamlet. A block from where they lived was a lovely pond, and when I visited I would frolic in the cool soothing water. That was the summer I brushed my bangs aside and played the piano with the latest sheet music. In those days you could pick the latest tunes in the Five and Ten-Cent Store where there was a piano and a player more than willing to help. "42nd Street," "Shadow Song," "Only a Rose," "I Love You So Much"—That summer I was introduced to L.M. Montgomery, a woman novelist, and to this day I would like to visit Prince Edward Island.

I heard Mother tell someone that Agnes and George had trouble on their honeymoon but that Dr. Burden had stretched her. Sounded good to me. Agnes taught special children. When she retired, they moved back to Oswego—she ended up known as the cat lady. She was sort of pussy-cattish herself. They said whenever she returned to New Jersey after a visit home, she never left empty handed; also that when she was a cashier at dad's restaurant, they always came out a little short.

No children came from Mae or Agnes or Helen, but my dad's brother, Frank, had two, Francis and Betty. Frank was tall, flabby faced, and very pleasant, presenting me with a quarter every time we met. I wouldn't call him lazy, just laid back. Ann and Helen told a story about Frank—nothing specific—but it wasn't acceptable behavior and Grandma made Frank get on his knees and vow to reform. I suspect he had been drinking. I know that Ann and Helen were deeply moved by witnessing the event. I used to hand wrestle with Francis when I was at Grandma's house. I liked him and thought him OK, but he eventually became schizophrenic—poor guy!

Betty was quite the gal. In her eighties she had sand in her shoes and traveled quite a bit. Betty's mother, a true witch, disowned her for marrying a non-Catholic. She had a great marriage, though, and received her masters and C.P.A. when she was over forty. I forgave her for being active in the Republican Party. She had four children, the last entering the world when Betty was fifty. The last time I saw her she was over eighty with great legs encased in groovy boots. OK, I admit it. I was jealous!

Helen was the youngest in my dad's family. She was sweet, kind, and gentle, with a delightful giggle and an endearing laugh. Her eyes were slightly crossed and a true blue. She married late and lived on a farm and had no children. She worked at the lumberyard for Uncle Bill. She told me that on her way home from school she used to pass Dr. Mary Walker who dressed like a man and who was famous for her work on the battlefields during the Civil War. Helen loved to go to church to pray, but never for ecumenical fellowship. She and Ann were sincere in their belief that only Catholics could go to heaven.

Here I am, the only child (far right) with the O'Brien family (Dad is 3rd from the right, Grandma Dehm 2nd from left).

3

The O'Briens

Paul O'Brien had one child, a daughter, *moi*! Bill O'Brien married Louise Fitzgibbons. Bill was the youngest O'Brien boy and had four children. Louise dated my father at one time and told my mother before she married dad that Paul didn't have a "lazy bone in his body." Uncle Bill and Aunt Louise's children, Ellen, Jean, Larry and Ruth, felt close to our family; my mother was very fond of Louise and about once a month had a good phone chat covering many subjects—mostly in-law talk.

Since I was an only child and lived in a neighborhood with few children, I had very little acquaintance with "little people." The first baby boy I ever saw was a friend's little brother. There also was a little girl, a distant relative of Mother's, Sally Carson, a duplicate of Shirley Temple. One day I got to see a baby two days old: Aunt Louise had a little girl, Ruth. We went to visit them and beheld the beatific vision of mother and newborn child in the upstairs bedroom.

Ruth grew to be a lovely woman, with a pithy sense of humor. She would say, "Patience is a virtue and I ain't got none." She became a social worker. Her mother (Aunt Louise) would go to the linen closet and find it empty. Ruth had given the goods away to the needy. She met Jim Brennan, married and had four children: Ellie, Jim, Bill and Tim.

I am two months older than Ellen. We shared the same homeroom in high school. I remember before the Regents Exams, Ellen attended daily Mass, lighting many vigil candles in hopes for a good grade. Ellen was a lovely actress. She had a quality, a flair for playing a role, and a true stage presence. She once visited me in college and we saw Nazimova in "Doll's House." Extraordinary performance! In high school she was in "Little Women," "The Man Who Came to Dinner," etc.; her performances never any evidence of the amateur—a true professional! I loved visiting at their home; the adults ate in the dining room, the children by themselves in a booth. It was fun being with my peers, but I also was wondering what was going on in the dining room and what I was missing. Louise had an endless supply of juice and cookies. My Uncle Bill was very handsome with the bluest of blue eyes. He loved to sing "*Du, Du, Du, Du, Bist Mein Herzen.*" Their mother was 100% Bavarian and used to pay a dollar a week for her sons to learn German from Johanna whom we called Aunt Anna. My dad used a lot of German phrases. One phrase when translated meant, "There is gold in the mouth of the morning" which he truly believed because he was a noisy early riser, with poems and joyous sounds. This made it a little hard on mother and me who were slower at greeting the day.

Jean was beautiful, blonde and deeply thoughtful, a true Christian woman with a daughter, Maura, and sons Martin and Brian. She is very well read, taught English in the high school, and married Martin O'Toole from Boston.

Larry had his father's blue eyes. When he was a little boy, my mother at Christmas time would explain to Mr. Wells at the Men's Store about these eyes and did they have a sweater worthy enough. This was fun for me because he was the only boy on the shopping list. OK, I confess. I always liked the boys! Larry studied piano. He was always interested in music. He went to Holy Cross and was in the Navy during World War II in the Pacific. He married Margaret O'Brien and had eight children: Mary, Larry, Patrick, Margaret, Katie, William, Carrie and Christopher. They live in a great pre-Civil War home on the city's eastside with a huge porch overlooking Lake Ontario. As I mentioned before, it had been a shelter for the blacks during the Civil War. The lower level of the house has a huge hearth where the slaves hid until a boat docked and, in the middle of the night, they stole aboard and took off for Canada.

Since Larry was the only boy, he had an interesting sideline as a rescuer of inebriated relatives. I'd like to hear his memories. He was there for so many people throughout the years. During my father's many gall bladder episodes in his mid-eighties, Larry was there to help the aunties clean things up; in the middle of the night when one of the attacks was so severe that my father tumbled off the bed, Larry was there in no time. He also did such things as pay some of Ann O'Brien's unpaid bills. It's one of the many reasons that I am so very proud of him. He certainly followed in his own father's ways. At Uncle Bill's wake a woman started to weep and said how Bill had saved her from financial ruin. Another woman spoke up about Bill concealing her debts. The story moved me greatly. I was very proud of my Uncle Bill as I am very proud of his son now. My father thought Larry was the best, and I say "Amen" to that! He was the brother I never had. As in any family we shared laughter; we shared tears.

The brothers, Bill and Paul, shared one irritating trend. They refused to shop for themselves. And they were suspicious of new fads. Bill's favorite sweater was ancient and Aunt Louise one year was gathering garments for the Salvation Army. She decided to discard this sweater. One cool evening not long after, Bill was searching in the closet for the sweater; he looked so sad when she told him that she called the Salvation Army and, lo and behold, they searched and found it and returned it. The story had a very happy ending. In later years I shopped for my father and I was his size, a 42 short. I tried on different clothes and if they fit me I bought them and he loved them. I admit it was fun to be in a men's store trying on suit coats, and people looking startled. In the old days you could call a store and ask for things on approval. You could try them on at leisure, compare, return or keep—Ah! Those were the dear old days. Sometimes we had difficulty charging because the store confused us with Ann O'Brien who was always in arrears big time.

My O'Brien cousins (Uncle Bill and Aunt Louise's children): left to right—Ellen, Jean, Larry, and Ruth.

4

Aunt Ann

Now we come to Aunt Ann who was a middle child and a rascal. My mother said she had the most beautiful head of hair, a mahogany shade. She was tiny, with big brown eyes. Her sister, my Aunt Mae, once said, "When *I* die and have to give an accounting of *my* stewardship, hypocrisy won't be one of *my* sins." She meant, not like Aunt Ann. Even though she was voted most likely to succeed in school, Ann was very religious and desperately wanted to be a nun. Being poor, however, she had no dowry. Limited education and menstrual cycles prevented her from achieving her goal. I think the Church was better off for it. When we used to fast before receiving communion, she worried—rain (on the way to church)—if it touched her lips, would it break her fast? She always worked as a sacristan for the priests.

Grandpa was very fierce with any beaus that came to 315. Mike O'Mara courted Ann. She let him drive her to Novenas. Some evenings she had him mop the floors or do some menial job and by the time he finished, it was too late to go to the movies. She always lied about her age. One time as she was being whisked into emergency, the doctor asked her age. Her nephew Larry who accompanied her said, "Sixty-Five" and she yelled out "Fifty-Five!" Larry said the tombstones in all the cemeteries were lies, and my mother said it was OK with her for then she too would be younger.

One time Ann was living with Agnes and got quite ill. She was not recuperating at all. They had to carry her everywhere she went. This lasted for months. On surveying the scene Bill sent her back to the hospital where she received "therapy". This was in the 50's and "therapy" at that time was a word not in our vocabulary. She bought a wreck of a car and was determined to drive but couldn't pass all her many road tests. This I'm sure benefited humanity.

Ann was very irksome when she would call Aunt Louise or Mother and say in a spooky voice, "Oh, Margaret, I'm so upset. I had a frightening dream last night. It was so real." Sometimes she dreamed my father was dead, or that my mother was dying or went to Hell or was in a terrible accident. Mother and Louise tried to ignore these calls, which were sporadic, but secretly the dreams really disturbed them. Ann was also a wheeler-dealer and a schemer. She had life-like statues wherever she lived and king-sized vigil lights. When she lived at 315, these contrasted with Mae's Buddhas from Panama. It was quite a sight to encounter in some room a large, inscrutable, fat-bellied Buddha side by side with a longhaired Jesus, pointing to his Sacred Heart.

I'm willing to admit collecting is in my blood also.

Anyway, Ann's affair with Mike O'Mara ended because Mike was worn to a frazzle, mopping floors and missing so many nine o'clock movies at the Strand Theater. Ann hated her bosoms and for a while kept them bound together. She wanted to enter the convent so badly but consoled herself by being a sacristan in the third order Carmelite and by fasting on Fridays and Saturdays. Her rosary was always near by and when we did group recitation she would let Helen, Daddy or me have a decade and kept cutting us off over part of the "...Holy Mary, Mother of God..." which irked me and made me feel at times non-Christian.

After Mother died, Ann and Helen came to live with Dad. They took wonderful care of their brother. On cold days they heated the newspaper on the radiator before he read it. He was always clean and spiffy. They saw to that. Of course, he always had been clean and spiffy. Mother would wear Chanel No. 5, dabbing a drop on each ear before going to church; often Dad would emerge from the bathroom splashed with English Leather, which overpowered the Chanel. Anyway, my aunties took great care of him. The girls would spat from time to time with Helen eventually saying, "I don't care. I'm entitled to my own opinion."

One of the priests in Oswego was building a church in Scriba, a community close to town. There are seven Catholic churches in Oswego, a town of 22,000. One could say there was not a great need for another church. Yet Ann O'Brien got on the phone and solicited for the project. The church was to be called Sacred Heart, which inspired her to ask, "Won't you please give to the Sacred Heart?" She was very terse to denials, intimating that people who did not give to the Sacred Heart were doomed.

One time she called the office of a Mr. Caruso who was in charge of car racing on the East Side. His secretary answered the call. Ann gave her spiel. The secretary asked Mr. Caruso. She returned and told Ann Mr. Caruso would donate $200. Ann was horrified at the amount and said, "You tell Mr. Caruso that he is a successful man, but God gives and takes away. I'll wait for his answer. I'll give him another chance." Five minutes later with Ann still seething on the other end of the line, the secretary got on the line and said Mr. Caruso said to change that to $400. Every few months Ann presented Father Segrue with checks of hefty amounts.

One night at a dinner party a man next to me asked, "Are you related to Ann O'Brien?" On admitting to Mr. Hosmer Culkin, who was district attorney for the city of Oswego, that I was indeed related to Ann O'Brien, he said, "I turned her down once on money for the church because I sincerely thought it wasn't needed, and she scolded me for being so unfeelingly stingy."

One Easter when she was 95, she ordered $300 worth of lilies for St. Peter's church. St. Peter's was a German church and Grandma O'Brien was related to a Bishop Fidelis Dehm from Bavaria whose image is honored in stain glass in the German church in Syracuse. Most of the seven O'Brien children were baptized at St. Peters, which catered to the people of German heritage. Ann O'Brien was involved in decorations of this little church. Larry, of course, ended up paying for that escapade!

Ann was in the hospital in her mid-90's and, when cousin Ellen visited her, she found Ann very upset. Ann confessed that she had borrowed money over the phone and couldn't pay it back and had received word that the lenders were most upset with her and planned action. Ann told Ellen that she was afraid they would come into her hospital room and usher her away in a paddy wagon and whisk her off to jail. And guess who came through for her? In the meantime, Ann treated Larry with utter disdain and when he visited and picked up some papers near where she was sitting, she gave his wrist a good slap.

In 1928 Al Smith, a Catholic, was running against Herbert Hoover for the presidency. On election night, the aunties and others came to our house to listen to the results on the Atwater Kent Radio, which was as big as an icebox. I was ten years old and was allowed to stay up. At that time I had never attended any live dramas, but that night I did. As the returns became more ominous, Ann started a slow soft keen which became louder and louder. When she realized it was all over for Al Smith, she did a whirling dervish dance, threw herself on the floor, and pounded it with her little fists. In later years I told Ann how impressed I was with her performance, but she denied it ever happened!

Once many years later, we were visiting 162 West Third when the girls were caring for my father. Ann showed me a pretty tablecloth, which she had placed on the table. "Mary, Mary, this is Battenburg lace."

"Um, nice," I said, my mind on other things.

About five minutes later she repeated the remark.

This time, I said, "Lovely."

Five minutes later, she said, "You know, Mary, your name is on it."

"That's nice," I said.

After a long pause, Miss Ann said with vehemence, "*Maybe…*" Anyway, Jean (O'Brien) O'Toole has it now.

Whenever I danced in a big stage show, Ann would send me Sweet Peas. They had a dainty scent and soft pastel shades. One time when they were presented to me, I received a signal for an encore so I held them in my hand and danced with them. They were so light and fragrant—a lovely memory!

Ann visited us when our son Jim was born. He was about three weeks old. To our horror she squeezed him, twirled him, tossed him, ran with him from room to room—and he survived! I also remember a yellow daffodil cake came my way from Ann, an angel cake with pale yellow frosting. One dozen eggs and lots of labor were involved (before cake mixes). What a thoughtless wretch I was, with a casual "Thanks" for such a thoughtful effort. She always said, "Mary, Mary, quite contrary." I guess she was right.

5

My Mother and Dad

When Mother and Dad came back from their honeymoon, Dad said, "Well, that's over," not a very good remark to make and not forgotten either. Also not forgotten was Grandma saying to Dad, "Now your goose is cooked!" One day before she was engaged, my mother was walking in the park when a woman her age approached her and said, "I hope I don't cry at your wedding." One of my dad's old flames, I guess. Mother and Dad had their wedding reception at 162 West Third Street. He had bought the two-story Victorian home and had a piano installed there for his talented bride.

162 West Third

In the cool evening with a soothing breeze from the lake, Mother, the one who was told so many times of her "gorgeous pansy eyes," would curl up in the gray wicker rocker, lemonade by her side, and wait for her Paul to come home from the restaurant. There in the protective shadow of the vine, the Dutchman's pipe, she would eavesdrop on the conversations of people as they passed by on their way to the movies or just on an evening stroll. "A red house! Why would anyone paint his house red? Can you imagine Irish Catholics live there!" It's true. We were the only family of that origin around. Dad had broken the barrier.

Dad worked hours and hours and Mother sat at the bay window waiting and waiting. His chef would go on a spree, his cashier wouldn't show up, or no waiters would appear so he would be cook, dishwasher, and waiter. He greeted everyone with a cheery hello and meant it. Holidays or convention times were full of stress. He used to fascinate me as a child with his rings. For a few months he would have a signet, then an onyx would appear, then a diamond. My favorite was a ruby set in rich gold. When I was older, he told me that he would loan money to people and the rings were security. He used to wear common pins on his lapel because someone told him they brought good luck, but years later someone told him only gays wore them so he abandoned the project.

My mother visited the restaurant as a customer only and sometimes Dad sent up her meals to her. She was a great dreamer, mad for her Paul. She suffered from mental fatigue only. Dad was twenty-four when he purchased the house and lived there until he died on his 92nd birthday.

Believe me when I tell you, Paul and Margaret O'Brien were true lovers so when five years of marriage elapsed and no baby had arrived, Mother decided to take Lydia Pinkham pills and to pray novenas to St. Joseph—and it worked. But she admitted she never again took the pills or made a novena to St. Joseph after I was born.

As the date approached, she was more and more enthroned in the chair in the bay window. One day she started to leak—she never said anything because she thought she had lost control of her bladder. This condition lasted four day. Then the labor began. The doctor said she had a dry birth. No hospital. After an endless, excruciating labor, I appeared. The day I was born was a Monday. The weather was so cold they had to turn on the heat and build a fire in the hearth in the bedroom. A nurse came and stayed a couple of weeks until Mother got her strength back. She nursed me so I had a great start.

Christmas holidays were magical "up home" at my O'Brien grandparents. My grandfather's name was Dennis. Grandpa was one of ten children. His mother's maiden name was Gillespie. His father was on his way home from work on

Christmas Eve to his large family when he was robbed, beaten and thrown into the canal. I don't have to tell you how depressed Dennis was at Christmas time. Being the oldest, Dennis looked out for his nine brothers and sisters (Julia, Nellie, and Jim are some of the names). Julia became a nun, Nellie a housekeeper, and Jim, tall and handsome, was in the cavalry of the New York City Police Department. These three were the only ones I got to know.

As a child, I was not aware of Grandpa's sad memories, but I was aware of the preparations. Off the dining room was a tiny room full of mysterious treasures. At holiday time it was buzzing with activity, with lots of tissue paper rustling, a mysterious, exciting room. At Christmas the great Christmas tree stood in the front hall with Christmas lights glowing within metal reflectors. Angel hair was artistically festooned throughout the tree and it was covered with fragile ornaments. These are available in some states even today.

When I knew Grandpa, he had white hair and a white mustache, which tickled me when I kissed him. He was very strict and I heard he tore his shirt in a fit of pique because it wasn't ironed perfectly. He had eye problems. I remember visiting him in the hospital after he had cataract surgery. When I was very small, I said, "Grandpa, when I am naughty Daddy says I act just like you." He turned red and said, "What's that?" I don't think Mother and Dad ever forgave me for that one! He did like me, though. He always liked to relate the story of my first social event at the age of four. Althea Wagg had a birthday party. She lived a few houses away; after the event Mrs. Wagg called my mother and said that after she had served the cake and ice cream, I demanded, "Where's the meat and 'tatoes?"

Since my mother only had distant relatives, "up home" was the center of my life. The attic was beyond enchanting with trunks galore and a strong scent of cedar. With my hand in one of my auntie's hands, we went up to that wondrous attic. The trunks and chests were full of laces, yards of fabric, satin tulle, soft wools, etc. Presiding over all of this was Fluffy, a big white angora cat.

Mr. Matthews had a livery stable in Oswego. He was of German descent and had a handlebar moustache. The stables were on East Fifth Street, a few blocks from the main road, Bridge Street. He and his wife had six children when this story begins. Their children had already been raised. The house and stables were near the Catholic church, St. Paul's. St. Paul's was the hub of all social life, with Masses, devotions, choir, and parish plays. (There was no radio or movies at the turn of the century). Mrs. Matthews received an urgent letter from a nephew in New York City on Mulberry Street. He had lost a son and now his wife.

At the turn of the century in New York City at that time, the big killer was consumption. That must have been the cause of their deaths. Her nephew had a daughter, two years old; her name was Margaret (she had been baptized at St. Patrick's Church on Mulberry Street)—very frail and abused by the people who cared for her while her nephew worked on the railroad. What could he do? Would she take pity on him and care for this child until she regained her health? Mrs. Matthews after consulting with her husband wrote, "Yes, of course."

The day came when they were to meet the train and the little girl whom they had never seen. After the train stopped chugging, who should emerge but a tiny two-year-old girl who was dressed in mourning: black shoes, dress, coat and hat, all black—so fragile. So pale! The whiteness of her pallor accented even more the shade of her attire. The neighborhood became quite interested in this waif. The pastor, Fr. Barry, would pass by the house, pat her curly head, and say, "Little girl, I pray for you every day."

Mrs. Matthews was strict and braided Margaret's hair tightly. Margaret Conway used to find ribbon and hide it in the umbrella rack at the front door, and as she went out the door to go to school, she retrieved her ribbon and put bows on each braid. As she returned from school, off came the ribbons, and they were returned to their hiding place.

My Mother (Margaret Conway) as a little girl, bowing at a piano recital.

Margaret got hold of a record that was popular at the time. Early 1900's and the title was "Come, Take a Dip with Me"; the men's chorus begins with the preceding phrase, followed by women singing, "You Bet We Will." When Mrs. Matthews heard it, she ripped it from the turnstile and smashed it. Such scandal!

Margaret was a practical joker and loved to remove a chair, as one was about to sit in it. For this antic, she was sent to her room. Sometimes she walked in her sleep and was found in peculiar places. One night they could not find her and after a search, they heard a voice; she was on the roof, having climbed a ladder in her sleep! When they approached her and called her name, she replied, "Don't bother me. I'm peeling potatoes."

Mr. Matthews would have her kiss him: first a kiss on one cheek, then on the other, which she complied with. Then he would say, "Now the lips." Nothing doing! The stable beside the house was a source of great fun. Sliding down the piles of hay, petting the horses, pretending in the carriage, gave her lovely memories.

Music was a priority at St. Paul's. The pastor had brought from Belgium to Oswego a fine organist, Professor Wiegand and his family. They lived across the street from the Matthews. People considered them different because they walked in the middle of the road, European style. The professor called Margaret, "Maggie Matches" and always said, "You drink all the water and I'll drink all the wine." This was a fact in more ways than one.

The Matthews had a married son who was childless and wanted to adopt Margaret. Francis Conway, her father, wrote and said, "Never." She was, however, known as Margaret Matthews. She had a Boston Bull Terrier to whom she was devoted.

When she was about seven, she was told to be cheerful because her father was coming to see her. The family made many preparations to welcome him. When he arrived at the house, Margaret was not to be found. Yet eventually found she was—covered with clothes in a corner of a closet. Screaming and sobbing, she was coaxed out and she flung herself away from them and wiggled under the bed still screeching. A weeping Francis Conway left, never to return.

A new organist replaced Professor Wiegand. He too was from Belgium, eighteen years old, handsome and greatly gifted. He lived across the street too and taught Margaret piano. She had a blithe, facile touch and she gave sensitive interpretations. These lessons came in handy when as a young woman she went to different homes teaching piano at fifty cents a lesson.

Mrs. Matthews died when Margaret was eighteen years old. She had a choice of living with one of the Matthews' daughters, Kitty, who was married to George

Donahue, or she could live with Maggie, who had married a Murphy. She lived a while with the Donahues who had a large family, but George was too fond of the bottle. When things became unbearable, she went to stay with the Murphys who fought incessantly. She alternated between the two until she married. Her boyfriend, Paul O'Brien, was confused because he never knew where to pick her up, one house being on the west side of town, the other on the east side.

Her girlfriend, Kitty Fleischman, introduced her to Paul O'Brien one cold afternoon at the corner of West First and Bridge Streets. Margaret dated him occasionally. Kitty liked him very much and extolled his virtues and promoted him generally. Margaret thought him conceited, boastful and just not her type! One evening she attended a movie, a new form of entertainment, which was just becoming available in Oswego; sitting in front of her was Paul O'Brien and a date! She heard an alarm go off in her head and a few days later she decided he was the one for her. They did some serious smooching on Kitty's Donahue's couch and after they married, the two had a new couch delivered to Kitty's house. The "used" couch was discarded immediately.

Margaret liked to say, "God takes care of an orphan." And He did. Paul had a successful restaurant and bought a house on 162 West Third Street, which was a real coup, as all the neighbors were WASPS. He broke the barrier, and now an Irish Catholic family was in their midst. He had their wedding reception catered at the new house. He was quoted as saying, "Everything will be 50/50." And this, my dears, was in 1913. What a guy! He also told Margaret she was his balance wheel.

My father was a good student with a special love for math and a lifetime fascination with words. As a boy, he had a paper route, and he was an altar boy. His family was poor and he told me one day someone gave a present to him: a bag of candy. He told me he rushed home, ran to his room, opened the bag and started to take a piece, but a voice in him said, "You must share this good fortune," so he went downstairs and said, "Hey, everybody, come see what I've got."

Mother said he always worked. Even at a young age (too young), he worked in a bar that his uncle ran. In January of his senior year, Miss Murphy called him out of the classroom and introduced him to a man from the railroad. The man wanted to hire her best student to do payroll for the company. He was to start that very day. So Paul, whose family needed the money, made the first big mistake of his life. He took the job and never graduated from high school. Aunt Louise said he didn't have a lazy bone in his body, and she was right.

After leaving the railroad, he worked in Minetto at a shade cloth factory. The job of management was available after a while. He worked overtime to impress everyone. One morning the notice on the bulletin board announced the new manager: the boss' nephew. Paul couldn't believe it. He went to the boss and said, "I deserve that position. I worked hard and assumed the job would be mine." The boss said, "Well, you've learned one thing, Mr. O'Brien. It's foolish in this life to assume anything." Paul got his hat and walked off immediately.

He then went into the restaurant business and he loved it. He loved people and he loved food. He worked long hours—sometimes the chef was drunk and Dad would cook, or he had to replace the cashier who was stealing from the till. He became a very successful businessman.

6

My Childhood

While she was pregnant, Mother sat around much of the time. A plumber came during this period to do about a week's worth of work. One day when Mother was sitting on the porch, he asked her, "You are always sitting. Don't you ever do any work?" She never liked him after that. His name was Fishy Callaghan.

I think I was a big baby, at least in my baby pictures I'm not frail! When I was three, Mother put me in an experimental nursery school at the college at the edge of town. This was unusual because it was 1921.

One of my first memories was getting on the streetcar two blocks from my house on Bridge Street, the main drag in Oswego. I had an enamel lunch box with two handles. I remember opening it up and putting my nose in it to smell grape jelly sandwiches.

Mother said that when I was taken out in a carriage as a baby, I waved to men only! Dad read to me every night, mostly "Uncle Wiggly" books. One night he skipped a few lines because he and Mother wanted to take in the nine o'clock movie, but I protested and he had to read the lines he was trying to skip.

When I was three I bumped my mouth on the bathtub and lost a tooth. At four while riding my bike, I fell in the driveway and lost another tooth. I remained in this condition until I was eight. I have photos where the photographer painted in the two teeth. I was always breathing through my mouth. My mother didn't care to see me gaping like that all the time, so off we went to a specialist in Syracuse. Ever after, when a doctor looked in my throat, he marveled at the surgeon's artistry.

When I was a little girl, people sat on their porches of a summer evening. I was a visitor to all on the block. One day I spied a flower box and thought how happy Mother would be if I picked some flowers for her. Dr. Calish whose box I depleted lived only two houses away. He called me in one day and said there were hop toads in the flower box; he advised me to stay away so I wouldn't get warts. I remember one time visiting all the neighbors and announcing to all that it was my birthday and wasn't it just wonderful!

Mother and Dad once slipped off to the seven o'clock Mass at St. Joseph's Church which was nearby and left me sleeping. When church let out, it was raining. As they approached home, they were appalled to find me strutting up and down the street in the rain with an open umbrella and completely naked. Lady Godiva of West Third Street!

My first birthday party was at Althea Waggs when I was five years old. Althea lived next to the Baptist church at the corner. She had golden hair and true blue eyes and we used to sit on the top step of church after sunset and say, just after the first star would appear:

> "The evening came upon us.
> Star light, star bright,
> I wish I may, I wish I might
> Have the wish I wish tonight."

Then we would silently make our wishes. We performed this ritual often—two little girls, one golden haired, the other black haired, with their arms entwined—a lovely memory.

I was such a sassy brat. I went to confession often saying how I sassed my parents. Why did I act this way? When was I going to stop? Why was I such a brat and especially at holidays? Why, why? Dad would say, "Enough of your lip! Enough of your guff!" One day I must have been seven and I said something obnoxious. He picked up a stick or broom. We were in the kitchen. As he approached me, Mother screamed, "Paul, Paul, not her back; Paul, not her arms, not her legs...Paul, please!" Poor Dad, he wanted to give me a good wallop and to tell you the truth I wanted him to. He threw down his weapon, grabbed me by the arm and said, "Well, young lady, you will have to go down to the dungeon." He brought me down the stairs into the cellar, opened the door to the fruit cellar, pushed me in, and locked the door.

It was dark, damp and very cobwebby. A few jars of tomatoes and peaches were on the shelves. A broken chair was in the corner, waiting to be fixed. It was really wonderful and I felt sorry for Dad for not giving me my first whack. I was quiet for a while; then I cried, "Please, please let me out. I promise to be good!" I said this over and over while pelting the door with my fists. Pretty soon he came down and released me. I'm sorry to say it didn't help my character at all!

Getting ready for church is another of my early memories. Dad and I were shiny, sparkly dressed. Mother had all sorts of rituals and it seemed forever but eventually after a last minute search for her Missal she would be ready: a vision in hat, gloves, high-heels, and perfectly scented. Dad had been an altar boy as a youth so after Mass he would sing the entire *Pater Noster* for us before lunch! At first the church was small with an ornate, white altar but then the parish built a new church using wondrous fieldstones. This new edifice was and is so very beautiful with hand-painted Stations of the Cross and hand-carved statues from Germany. I especially admired the statue of St. Rose of Lima that, if you stared long enough, seemed to smile right at you. There was also a side nook with a small altar and a painting of St. Joseph with just room enough for two kneelers. I used to love to go in there to kneel and pray to St. Joseph. The statue figure had thick white hair and cuddled a one-year-old Jesus.

Behind the main altar was an exquisite stained glass window depicting Mary's Assumption under which began an inscription of the "Hail, Holy Queen" that traveled around the entire church. On either side of the altar were choir stalls and on the Gospel side was an enormous pulpit that soared above a little child like myself. Even though the priest was up so high and seemed very remote, I remember wonderful talks. I didn't understand them but they were given with such vigor and force that I was impressed.

I grew to love St. Mary's church. Early in my days at the parish school, I was chosen one May to crown the Blessed Mother. Mother made an appropriate outfit for me and I carried a basket that contained the dear coronation crown (my father provided a french fry basket for Mother to cover with satin and ribbons). At the appointed time, I ascended the ladder behind the statue—it seemed very high but probably was not—and plopped the crown on her head. Everyone sang "Bring Flowers of the Rarest" and it was a lovely moment for me. Afterwards Mother was furious because Sister had immediately re-attached the crown. Mother thought it looked adorable the way I had cocked it over the statue's left eye! Was there a pattern here that I would forever be doing things a little off kilter? I hope not.

May Coronation

I remember preparing for my First Communion. I was very excited to receive Our Lord but when I came back from Communion, I felt nothing—nothing! I was crushed. I was sure I would feel His presence. Everyone had said, "This is your happiest day!" Not for me—and I felt unworthy. I also remember Sister telling us about a bad girl who as she stuck her tongue out to receive the Host was horrified to see it take wing and refuse to enter her mouth—I confess to this day I feel it could happen to me.

In fourth grade I come home thrilled with the singing of carols at the program before Christmas vacation. As ever anxious to share with my mother, I looked for her to find her nowhere. I called her name and no one answered. I sat in the breakfast room. It was extremely still without her presence for she was always there. The phone rang and it was Mother saying she and Dad were at Grandma's house and that Grandma was dying. Dying! I was full of the idea of Jesus' birth. I remember standing in the breakfast room a long time and for the first time in my life beseeching the Lord to have mercy on my grandmother.

There was a pump organ in Sister Vivian's room and Jane McCormack (my darling friend to this day) and I alternated playing hymns. I also remember we had processions on Holy Thursday and during Forty Hours devotions. The girls marched with their white dresses and veils behind the priest holding the monstrance that was covered with a canopy. What a thrill—I remember singing, "Jerusalem, My Happy Home" loud and clear.

In fourth grade Mr. Lally, our music director, came to our room and auditioned the girls. He chose Jane McCormack and me. He already had a boy choir that was doubly interesting to us because of what they would sing (my favorite, "*Veni, Jesu*") and because of the fact that we could study them for future boy friend material! One day Sister Evangelista called me aside and asked me to ask my mother if I could walk in procession with Julia Carr, the only black girl in our school. Sister wanted a written acceptance and Mother gladly wrote an OK note that I returned to Sister. On the playground the next day I announced to Julia, "I'm to be your partner in the procession."

"Oh, sorry, I already promised Jane McCormack."

One day that year I needed supplies (maybe yes, maybe no) and Sister Alicia took me to the magic door on the first floor. She bent over and searched in her voluminous pockets that seemed to reach the floor for her many jingling keys. We entered into that vast room with row on row of supplies stacked to the ceiling. The scent of shellac and pencils and paper was great. I bought some paper; however, on leaving the room I spied a painting of Saint Therese the Little Flower dressed in Carmelite garb, holding roses. I loved the idea of her being in heaven from doing good works on earth and of her rose petals falling from the sky. The painting pictured her with her arms folded across her breast and one day I went to communion with my arms clasped thusly. After Mass, Sister pulled me aside and bawled me out and said, "Never, never do that again…"

So Sister knew my love for Saint Therese, but the price was beyond my reach. So we worked out a deal. I paid ten cents a week. So at that very moment I started two things early in my life: I purchased my first religious work of art and established my first charge. I gave that painting to my daughter Teresa who now has the picture in her home today. I have bought a lot of religious art in my day but so far no Buddhas! I nearly bought discarded sanctuary lamps once but fortunately changed my mind (a woman's privilege). A friend of son-in-law Vincent told him that the first time he came to our house he was so surrounded with religious art he nearly genuflected!

I absolutely loved the nuns. I loved their deep pockets filled with all sorts of mysteries, their keys jangling, their rosaries bouncing on their habits, and they smelled so wonderful. I loved it when they bent over me to check my papers in school. I once saw a picture of a Sister of Charity with her stiff white wimple reminding me of stout sails out on the sea, and I thought, *I will be a nun, a Sister of Charity.* Then a boy came into our school from New York City (more on that later) and everything faded into the sunset and I thought of no one else. My vocation was over.

It was right around that time at St. Mary's that I heard some homilies and sermons from two Doctors of Divinity, Fr. Moore and Fr. Dwyer. Fr. Moore was most interested in elementary school children and spent many hours with us. Some of the parishioners thought too much time. Every Friday at 10:30 Fr. Moore talked to our class. I watched the clock in anticipation of his arrival. This wonderful time lasted during our 7th and 8th grades. He explained the ritual of the Mass to us. He taught us how to read our missals, how to follow the liturgical year. He brought the vestments and holy vessels out and explained to us each garment and each holy instrument. He even had us research such things as how many times the word "peace" appeared in the liturgy. He certainly enhanced our prayer life and our appreciation of the Mass and all the holy sacraments. I am eternally grateful to him. God bless his soul!

One time I remember Fr. Moore saying that one couldn't achieve heaven without being baptized. At that time I was studying piano in Syracuse with a Russian Jew whom I loved deeply. I was very upset at the idea and asked Father in class why this wonderful person wouldn't be welcomed in heaven. He calmed me down by telling me the different types of Baptism: of desire and fire besides baptism of water. His response gave me great consolation.

My mother was always sitting in the bay window in the front room when I came home from school. I mean *always*! When my father skipped up the street at noon and again at six o'clock, she was waiting for him, sitting in the bay window. She claimed she suffered from mental fatigue. There was never a flurry of activity in housekeeping matters, but the home was serene and very clean. I guess she didn't allow us to mess it up. Her baking and meals were wonderful; when she made a special cake, she would say, "It is too coarse, don't you think? The frosting could be better..." Those comments would continue until we would smother her with compliments—and we weren't exaggerating!

As a child, sleeping and waking were always delightful for me. Mother would stand at the foot of the bed and say, "Good night, sweet dreams," quietly leave, shutting the door. One night when I was in my teens she just said, "Good night" and I kept saying "Good night" and just as she exited she said, "Oh, yes, sweet dreams."

In the morning Daddy would rush in and put up the shades and say, "It's a peach of a day" or "There is gold in the mouth of the morning." Sometimes he said it in German. I even remember on a Saturday morning in high school years Mother would wake me by singing, "Lazy Mary, will you get up?" and I would sing, "What will you give me if I get up?" Mother responded, "I'll give you Jack Callaghan, if you get up, if you get up." And so forth. My response, of course: "Oh, yes, Mother, I well get up this morning."

Fall and spring held difficult episodes. Mother did spring and fall cleaning. She acted as if it were Dad's and my fault that she had to endure this disruption in the tranquility of her life. The beating of rugs on the clothesline and washing of windows was fun for me. I would help Dad on the outside; Mother would be on the inside tap-tapping on each pane to show Dad where he had missed a spot. They had about thirty windows to do, but when they were finished, the sparkling panes of glass gave us a feeling of serenity.

Dad and I were home together one day while Mother was at the hairdressers. A strange thing happened. Mother appeared not looking like Mother at all! Even Dad was upset. She had gotten her hair bobbed. That ample heavy dark brown hair was gone! But I have to admit that she looked adorable.

A few times when I was young, Mother went on a grapefruit diet, which was Ok with Dad and me until she made us do the diet with her! Talk about unfair...

After Dad bought a big green Chrysler with green plush upholstery and vases on either side of the back, Mother and I would go to Syracuse to shop and go to the Loews' State Theater. There was a huge organ that they used for community singing during the intermissions. There was vaudeville, Jack Benny, The Duncan Sisters. Their skit was one girl dressed as a black girl who kept saying, "I's Topsy, I is, and I'm wicked." She would roll her eyes and do a great dance. Her partner had lots of golden hair and she declared in a sweet voice, "I'm little Eva and I'm the sweetest girl in the world." She would do a most dignified dance. Let me tell you, I loved that act and stayed to see it over and over again.

The theater appointments to a little girl like me were gorgeous: huge oriental vases, real birds in cages and parrots on perches, lounges with exotic plants and ferns everywhere you looked and such exquisite lamps! It was a real thrill.

Believe it or not, Fran Brown and I took a train up to Syracuse to hear Schumann Heink sing. She was not young and at the time I didn't know she was desperate for money and had to do the circuits. Here was this elderly woman in an old brown dress singing German Lieder and ending the show in her still beautiful contralto, singing Brahms's "Lullaby" in German and English. We were so deeply moved, we wept. You could take a train from Oswego to Syracuse in those days. The glamour by 1930 was fading in the formerly elegant cars. Who says life in a hick town can't be exciting?

Dad loved to bring home coconuts, figs, dates, and nuts in their shells. And oranges were a treat to find in your stocking on Christmas morning. Dad would take a nail and hammer a hole in the coconut and drain the white milk from it and share it with us. Then Mother would grate the coconut for a cake. "No, Mother, it is not too heavy...Yes, Mother, it's the best one yet..." And it always was!

I remember Wednesday was Dad's day to pick up the *Saturday Evening Post* and his weekly supply of cigars. The *Post* at that time used to run serials and he was especially fond of Zane Grey stories. Sunday was the best, though. After church we always had the big roast beef dinner. One day Mother refused her cut of meat from his hands. She said he always gave her the choicest cut of meat and me the next and saved the lesser cut for himself and she would tolerate it no longer. Ice cream, hand packed, finished the feast. Then we headed for the *New York Times*. Mother went to the book section, Dad to the editorials, and I to the music section. There was complete, wonderful silence for a couple of hours.

At three o'clock the New York Philharmonic broadcast its program. Sunday night the Detroit Symphony aired its program. When we got our green Chrysler with the green velvet upholstery, we went, as most car owners did, for a ride or a spin in the country. You can reach the country then and even today in five minutes east or south out of town. The Great Lake Ontario was north. We had a drive along the Oswego River. Virginia Dean, teacher and friend, told me it was more scenic than the Rhine River in Germany. Fruit Valley Bay was to the west, rolling hills to the east. There were many tempting side roads and Dad used to turn down a narrow dirt road and after a while stop and declare we were lost. This upset Mother only once. She learned that the *modus operandi* was to get LOST for excitement.

I, along with many of my children, used to be sorry for "Big Paul," (as Dad was known later to differentiate him from his grandson Paul). Mother would say, "Paul, turn right. Paul, turn left…" Paul, do this; Paul, do that. After Mother died, I said to Dad, "Didn't it bother you with Mother nagging you all the time in the car?" He turned to me with a surprised look. "Why, I was a terrible driver; I depended on her completely." It was then that I remembered the time he told me that right before they married he said to her, "You are my balance wheel."

Mother was very, very shy and she always talked about how she was going to entertain, but this actually occurred but once a year. She was busy, however, taking me to dancing lessons and sometimes accompanying the dancers from Professor Smith's dancing classes. She was completely absorbed with her daughter, and her husband, I think, in some ways resented it.

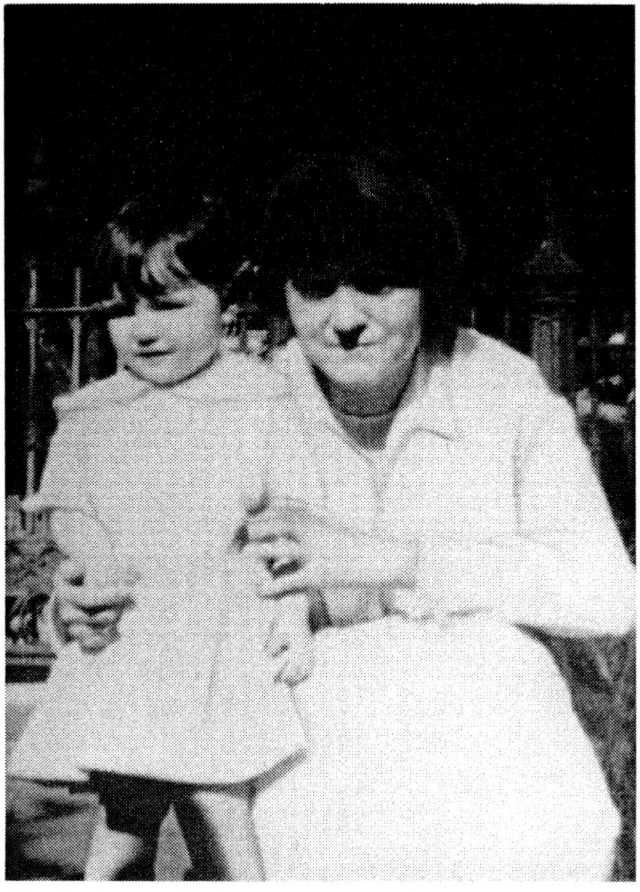

This beautifully-clothed-at-all-times girl was not allowed to do any chores. Nothing. Not set the table, wash or wipe dishes, clean or vacuum. I practiced about two hours a day but never could play the piano like my mother. My fingers were never swift, no matter how long or how hard I tried. I think I had good taste because I couldn't stand my own playing. For example, I remember working on the last movement of the Beethoven "Moonlight Sonata," which is technically challenging. Then I heard it performed on the radio and hardly recognized it.

7

Early Education

School was a real love of mine. I couldn't wait to get there. Walking and talking to my girl friends on the way home was a delight. There was sweet, pure, dear Jane. We would walk in the spring, dragging our feet, snug under her father's big black umbrella. She would walk me part of the way, then I would turn and walk her part of the way, hating to end the delightful experience. There was Doris Sommors. To listen to her was a delight. She had great dreams, great imagination and when it came time to go our different ways, we just stood at the corner for a time. As we parted Doris said, "I have to hurry home and do the laundry, get dinner and bathe the kids and you, Mary, go home and practice the piano!" She said it not in envy but as a fact of life. I don't remember her circumstances, but I think her mother had died and she was doing what she could to help. Doris was a ten year old with a heavy burden, bravely hustling home.

The city library was a place of wonder; it was the oldest building I had ever been in. The children's part was in the basement and had its own entrance. The chairs were small and like "Goldilocks," they fit just right. When I was older, around eleven, I ventured into the adult section. The scent of varnish and the choice of so many books thrilled me. I chose books with titles containing LOVE. I would meet a friend there, Helen Mary Gill. We would walk home together. She checked out the books I had chosen. She said, "Mary, you need help. You must learn to choose by author, not by title." Dickens, Twain, O'Neil, Tennessee Williams, Willa Cather, etc., etc. All at once, my world changed. I will forever be grateful to Helen Mary Gill for opening for me the doors to great literature.

Mother loved clothes. When she was young, she used to promenade over at the fort on a Sunday in her purple velvet dress and her plumed hats. The first time I saw a Serrano painting, "Sunday in the Park" I could see, mentally, my mother joining the Victorian ladies in the painting. When I came along, she wanted to sew clothes for me. She studied the styles in the *New York Times*. None of the stores in little Oswego carried the latest fashions. New York carried the latest fashions. She embroidered beautifully, making lovely lace edges for hankies. She bought some material and a pattern. The pattern baffled her and she despaired of figuring it out. My father became interested in her dilemma. He got on his hands and knees, studied the pattern for a while, then showed Mother what to do, and she was on her way.

Dresses with matching cuffed pants, challis, wools, silks, and cotton frocks appeared. One outfit was black cotton with many, many red cherries embroidered all over it. Mother took me in the dress to Lovell, the photographer. I couldn't believe what happened. He told me to take off my dress and he did a head and shoulder portrait of me. I was really down in spirits especially with my two front teeth missing. The story has a happy ending. Mr. Lovell, genius that he was, painted two teeth. Even today when one looks at the picture you really have to scrutinize hard to notice the painted-in teeth.

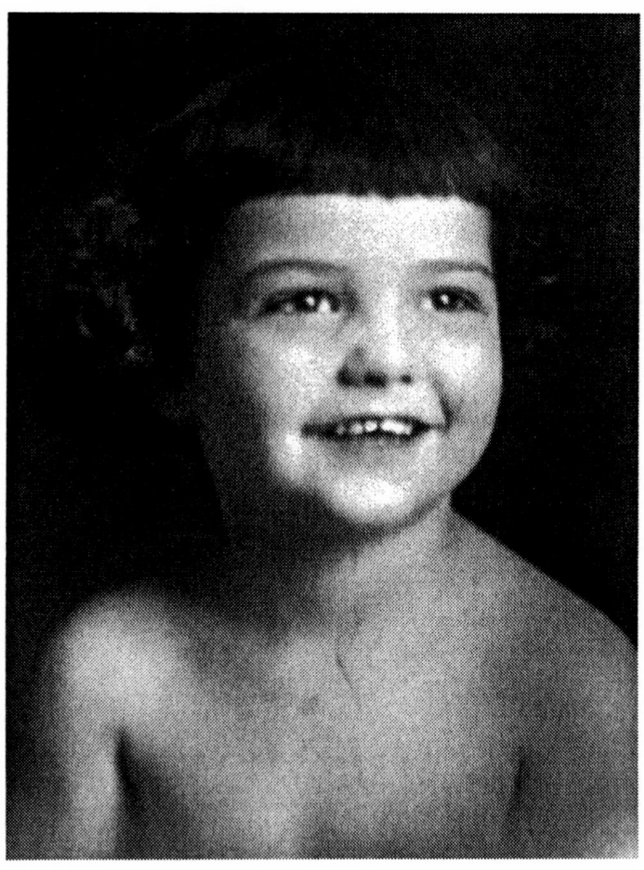

I was taken to furriers. They fashioned a rich wool plaid coat with fox collar and cuffs. It seemed I had to stand for hours for fittings. There were many more outfits among them, including a chinchilla and a raccoon. In my dance recitals, for the jigs and clogs, I wore green satin with sequins and, on my head, was an upside down petal with satin top and sequin petals, held on under my chin by satin covered elastic. The hat was adorable but it kept slipping while I did my gyrations. I was dressed like no one else. I wondered why some of the kids said mean things. As I became older, I began to notice the difference. Mother said I came home once with the lament, "Can't I wear black bloomers like everyone else?"

Dancing lessons were with Professor Smith in a big dance hall upstairs on East First Street. Professor Smith was English, homely, with a British accent. His shiny shoes and agile feet are a real memory. He had classes and also taught privately. I studied privately, learning soft-shoe, tap and ballet. The day I went into hard toe ballet slippers was a big thrill for me. I was in a lot of shows until I was ten, when suddenly I became awkward and self-conscious and my dancing career ended.

Beneath the dance hall was the Nancy Tracy Shop. The treasures in the store were wonderful and Miss Nancy and Miss Tracy were nice to me and let me snoop around and hold the art objects while Mother made a purchase. I still like the sound of "Nancy Tracy."

Anyway, Oswego was an ideal setting to be reared. I had a mother and father who loved each other and weren't afraid to admit it; aunties and uncles and grandparents to love and visit; a passion for school. What could go wrong?

But something was wrong, but I couldn't tell what it was and I became very uneasy. In retrospect I know now many years later we were something of a *ménage a trois*. Why did Daddy seem aloof? I'd tell him, while he was shaving, about my adventures. He'd stop me—Mother had already told him about them. In spring he had always put violets in the crystal toothpick holder, (I still have it in my own cupboard). But now at my plate every morning was a cartoon of "The Goop," a disgusting idiot who behaved shamefully.

I learned to swim in my sleep. One night I dreamed I was swimming. The next day I went to the beach; I swam. I was so elated I begged Dad to come and watch me. I left him standing on a hill, jumped into the water, swam a few strokes, turned to wave, and he was gone.

So the green-eyed dragon appeared at this time. I'd tell Daddy an event at school and he'd say, "Your mother already told me" and he would walk away. The horrible "Goop" cartoon appeared at the breakfast table where just a year before there had been violets. The feelings at home were very strange—lots of silences and did I see a tear in an eye from time to time? Believe it or not, our insurance man's name was Jimmy Joy. One night he came and when he left, Mother and Dad were both upset. Even I sensed something was terribly wrong. Daddy was a believer in lots of insurance. Business was so bad that to keep up he had, bit by bit, to cash in his policies. Seeing Jimmy Joy sit at our dining room table brought no joy.

8

Summer Delights

After school finished and the summer lay ahead, I would be bored and restless at times; then something wonderful would happen. Posters in store windows announced that the circus was coming to town. Snarling animals glared out at us from the ads. I wasn't the only one who was elated. My dad, on the day the circus arrived at 2:00 AM, would go to the place where the train unloaded circus gear, as well as performers and the animals. He would offer to help unload, to assist the men working feverishly to erect the enormous tent and the smaller ones.

In the morning about 10:00 AM the parade started. They marched down the main street for about six miles; then we waited while they reversed and marched back to headquarters. The band players were generous. The girls smiled astride the beautiful horses. It was over all too soon and, as the calliope strains faded, we were left with an annoying amount of animal droppings.

At 2:00 PM they finally returned and we were hysterical. The barkers were shouting about strange people who were waiting for us in the sideshows. People everywhere were vending balloons, peanuts, popcorn, beverages, etc. One thing I always yearned for was a stick with a string. At the end of the string was a feathered bird. As you waved and swung the bird around, it would give pretty chirps.

The three rings that were erected in the main tent kept us busy and dizzy trying to keep abreast of the action. I know you are supposed to laugh at clowns, but as a child I didn't get the humor. What I *did* love was the tiny car that drove out into the middle of the ring, stopped, and then about twenty-five people emerged. I loved the trapeze artists the best. They were so beautiful in their colorful robes of chiffon. At the end of their performance they swung by their teeth, waving their arms and looking like butterflies. How truly beautiful!

Chataqua was another summer event. They came and stayed in town for two weeks. People bought tickets, didn't use them, but gave them to me. Until I was ten I went to the children's programs in the park and in the school. I remember one afternoon a man came on stage. Boxes containing hundreds of bees surrounded him. After a lecture, he asked for volunteers to come on stage. Good old Mary O'Brien, the queen of volunteers, raised her hand and was selected. I bounced up the steps and happily stood next to the man. All at once I was covered from head to toe with bees.

With Chataqua providing me with lectures, music soloists and with the circus and talkies at the movies, with occasional trips to the beach, frequent trips on the train to Syracuse—life in the summer was wonderful. To have parents who adored each other made me happy and delighted with their loving ways of dealing with each other. Sometimes I would be practicing the piano before dinner and I could hear my dad come in and Mother laughing, "Paul, Paul, put me down! Stop it, you hear?"

9

Back to School

I truly loved school and the nuns were my joy as they swished around, their rosaries jingling at their sides. I loved their sweet aroma as they bent to help with a problem. Sister Evangelista was my 8th grade teacher. She prepared us so well in all subjects, especially English, that when we went to 9th grade at the high school we outshone all the others. I was so tuned into her that I responded to her every mood. When she was happy, so was I; when she was angry, I felt her rage. When she was sad, tears would fill my eyes.

A new boy entered our class when I was in 8th grade. I fell in love with him at first sight. He was tall, lanky, tow-headed, and had a New York City accent. He was fresh from Cornwall on the Hudson, a military school. He stood at attention at all times. He rushed to open doors for all women, nuns, priests, etc. His manners were impeccable. He knew the answers to all the questions. He was a star student and a star in my heart. I thought of nothing but him.

Just before dismissal around 3:00 a ray of sunshine would filter through the window of the classroom and place a halo on his head. Even God seemed to favor him. The other boys in the class turned into ugly oafs. I learned that for a surprise birthday gift his father had purchased a mansion on a hill overlooking the lake. On his wife's birthday he gave her the deed to the house. In my mind his father, Mr. Toomey, was beyond romantic to do such a thing.

As we were dismissed from school, I rushed down the back stairs and arrived breathlessly at the front stairs. It was timed just right because I arrived just as he exited, usually talking to his friends as he did. Gasping, I croaked, "Hi!" He looked at me with utter disdain. I did this every day. From day to day his response varied; one time a glare, then just a haughty look from his 6'2" height. There was a sneer with the upper lip curled (I really liked that one!) One day there was a Mothers' Luncheon and my mother and his seemed to get along pretty well.

As we left for school for Christmas vacation, he waited for me and said, "I hope you choke on your turkey dinner." I came home devastated and told Mother what he had said. I was really crushed. "That means he likes you," she said. How could that be? Life was certainly a puzzle.

He was the best speller in the school and was elected to compete for the city prize. The morning he left school, I went to the pencil sharpener and watched out the window as he walked down the street with long, confident strides. I prayed he would win. Sister's suggestion that I return to my seat brought me out of my reverie. After he won, he went to the State Fair. He came back triumphant and gave me a gold leaf pin with MARY written on it. He went to Washington. He didn't win but held the course for a good amount of time. I loved the way he said May-ry. I can still hear him saying it just as I can hear Mother calling, "Paul!"

Neil was a speaker at 8th grade graduation; the title was "George Washington." I played the piano for Jane McCormack's violin solo; then I sang, "Home Sweet Home." Afterwards a woman came up to me and said that she had cried all the way through it. I thought, *Was it that bad?* Some people suggested I take voice lessons. I thought, *If I sing OK, why would I need lessons?* In the meantime my sweetheart was studying piano and progressing rapidly. After graduation, I brooded, because I wouldn't see him until the fall.

I took a summer course in Civics and had my first male teacher, Ralph Faust. I couldn't wait to attend class. I was always answering and asking questions. One day Mr. Faust said, "Miss O'Brien, why don't you take over the class?" I was only too glad to do so. I rushed up, turned to face the class and went BLANK! After a long time, he told me to return to my seat. I continued as before, not getting his point. He was a wonderful teacher and later became principal and was respected by the community. I was so lucky to have such an auspicious start.

10

1932

1932 was a happy one indeed. That fabulous summer found us, Fran and me, going to Sheldon daily in storm, in heat, in rain. Our lifeguard, Goofer Chetney, made us feel secure. The only upset was when Neil, my sweet boy, and his friend, Donald, went on the high hill to change into their swim trunks and came into contact with poison ivy. Neil had to take shots and was absent for two weeks, the longest two weeks, at that time, of my life. Then one day he was there, swimming his Australian crawl, out so far I became frightened.

One late afternoon the sky suddenly became angry. We rushed up the steep hill looking for shelter. Some one yelled, "Hey, guys, there's a tent over here you can use!" Fran, Vena, Donald, Neil and I entered gasping. Then all hell broke loose, the rain turning vicious, the thunder roaring and ranting. We stood in our dripping bathing suits fully aware of Mother Nature. I was so overcome by the emotion of the display that my heart started to pound. I wondered, *Can he hear the drum beat of my heart?*

Our summer also involved attending movies. That summer I stayed for weeks in Syracuse with the Schumanns for piano lessons. Mama Schumann loved the movies. She went to every new film. The theater she attended was just five minutes away by streetcar. They had double features, "Pathe News," and comedies such as Laurel and Hardy movies. Not only that, on Wednesday night they gave away free dishes! Professor Schumann for some reason never went. One morning at breakfast, however, he said, "I've been reading about a movie showing at the Lowe's Theater called 'Mother's Millions.' It features Flora Mae Robson and we are going to see it." We boarded the streetcar. The trip to downtown Syracuse was fun because I had never been anywhere with him before.

When he approached the box office, he declared, "One adult, one child."

The girl said, "Oh no, two adults."

Professor said, "She's only twelve." That was true, but I did look and dress older. "Two adults," the girl kept saying over and over. Professor turned an odd shade of purple and said, "She's fat, she's overgrown."

"Two adults."

"I won't, I can't do it!" he shrieked.

We stepped aside to let the growing line go through. Then he pulled himself together, approached the box office, and grudgingly said, "Two adults."

Despite my humiliation of being called fat and overgrown, we had a great time. Robson was a wonderful actress and we were two happy people coming home on the streetcar. For breakfast, lunch, and dinner Professor discussed "Mother's Millions": the cinematography, the sets, costumes, etc. He analyzed each character thoroughly. One night at dinner his son Benno whispered, "I don't think Father is ever going to stop talking about 'Mother's Millions.' Years later when we met, one of us uttered "Mother's Millions" and we laughed.

Mamma Schumann was a good cook and proud of "mine own inventions." When she was in awe of something, she would say, "I can't get it over." She was short, dark, and attractive—and I was very fond of her. She was very sweet and considerate of me.

Professor put in long days teaching. He would sometimes burst through the French doors, slap his forehead with the palm of his hand in desperation and gasp, "No talent, no talent!" Then he would reopen the door and return to his student. After the student left, I would practice and it drove him mad because I guess I was doing everything wrong. The results were every day lessons.

Teaching and being a cantor at the Synagogue were Professor's only income. Some days Professor would come racing from the studio, demanding we search for his glasses. They were usually on top of his head. He said I would learn Russian in a short time and I did learn about 25 words total. At dinner he would look at me, strike his head and discuss in Russian or Hebrew about me. Sometimes he was smiling and indulgent. Other times he would shake his finger, frown, and shrug his shoulders. Based on such gestures, I would have an idea of whether my stock was up or down.

Benno hated himself and thought he was ugly with scrawny muscles. He sent for Charles Atlas weights and faithfully worked out after dinner every night. But his conquering English was a hard won achievement for him and that made him very proud.

Meal times at Professors was lacking in English. Some agitated remarks were made and unpleasant glares and unfriendly glances came my way. (Um, I wonder what I've done now.) Professor would call me, out of the blue, "Puskugnaught" which I thought was a term of endearment. I later learned it meant "lowest of the witches."

When I returned to Oswego from Syracuse, my gang at Sheldon's Beach acted aloof and avoided me. They'd be chatting but when I appeared they would stop talking. I was so hurt, especially about my tow headed sweetheart's distance. It was a sad time and I kept wondering what I had done to offend them.

My birthday, August 19, dawned and I went to the beach, my happy place. The gang did not show up. Then Fran Brown appeared and said there was something going on down the beach and we should check it out. They were all there with a party laid out and presents and everything. "Soaring Spirits" came to mind. One of the happiest days of my life. O yes, boy-love gave me a cherry box with a polo player embossed in silver on the cover. *He* loved that box!

11
Trouble

Fran was a senior in high school and I was a freshman. She guided me through my first year. She shared her locker with me on the third floor. Most freshmen used the basement lockers. She advised me what teachers I should choose, suggesting I sign up for orchestra, glee club, chorus and courses I wasn't even aware existed.

I couldn't wait to get to classes, come home for lunch with Mother, and regale her with all the news of school. I put in a half hour of practicing the piano and back to school I went. Neil picked me up every morning and, when he dropped me off at home and returned to his house, he called me and we would talk after dinner; and then another call from him later that night and so to bed.

I loved my teachers and singing in the choirs. It was the frosting on the cake. Neil was in all my classes. After only one month into Latin, I received a note from him: "*Ego amo Te.*" My Latin teacher said "*Amo Te*" would be enough—the "*Ego*" was egocentric! Neil aced all his subjects. While I worked on my homework, he had already grasped the subject.

Something was not right at home. Daddy was not his usual buoyant self. Something was wrong and I was baffled. Mother had lost interest in her favorite sport: the World Series. It was quiet—too quiet. One morning when I went to the bathroom, I smelled something strange, like a smell from a drink they took for colds called a "Sling"—only no one had a cold. Oh, oh, my father had been drinking. This odor persisted for weeks and weeks and weeks. He didn't go to Mass, and Mother moved to another bedroom. The meals were grim events, seeming to last forever. The insurance man, Jimmy Joy, no longer came because there was no more insurance.

Daddy was a happy-go-lucky, smart man. He was hard working. He was forty years old at the time and the family had advised him to help out his older brother Frank at a bar and eating-place. Frank was an easy-going guy. As a 13-year-old, I wondered why Dad would work there. It was just another bar. One had to descend three or four steps in order to enter. There was a Chinese cook (he looked like Charlie Chan), who cooked and lived over the bar. I suspect he was on opium. He was seldom seen before or after mealtime. Mother never went there.

Then Frank wasn't doing well at his bar and lunch place. The family thought the two brothers would do better together than apart. Frank was laid back and Dad was a go-getter. They did fairly well for a while but the Depression was hurting everyone. Dad was sick of Frank not coming to work on time, which gave Dad no break. He'd come home too late for the movies, too late for a ride around town, too late to go shopping. Then the drinking started and this strange person was living with us. What happened to the punster, the poet, the "*Saturday Evening Post*" and cigar-smoking guy? Mother was mystified. She didn't know about menopause in men. As for me, I didn't know anything except I felt my heart shriveling.

This went on for two years. Finally at the end of her patience, Mother took matters into her own hands, and called Dad's younger brother Bill. Bill was very successful, as an auditor for the Neal Lumber Company. Mr. Neal had one daughter but no sons. He could see Bill's worth and advanced him until Bill became a partner in the company, later known as Neal-O'Brien Lumber Company. Bill was a great guy with four children and a peach of a wife, Louise.

Bill came to the house and Mother, weeping and shaking, told him the story. A month later, Dad was working for the lumber company, the one in Lacona, NY. Another month and he was showing signs of improvement. He stopped drinking entirely. He wasn't an alcoholic. He was never a drinker. He was just one unhappy guy depressed about going nowhere. He literally bounced back and life as we knew it returned, and we cherished him more than ever. Without Uncle Bill I shudder to think what could have happened. God bless Uncle Bill O'Brien.

Dad really loved the lumber business: the yard with huge piles of different woods, the hardware department with all kinds of tools and equipment, but most of all he loved the customers. He was one happy fellow. The year was 1932, the year the Lindberg baby was kidnapped, and we went to church daily to pray for his life, to pray that they found him safe and alive. That August was the surprise birthday party on the beach for my 13th birthday.

12

Ninth Grade

Ninth grade was very exciting. The music teacher, Beryl Lewis, was putting on the Flora Dora Sextette in one of the shows. Six couples were involved. There was a fun dance routine. My partner was "Bunny" Patch, brother of Miss Patch, the English teacher. She had a party after the show. They lived in a huge apartment. We sat around with a fire in the fireplace, the lights out, playing word games and roasting apples. The costumes were turn-of-the-century. I was the only freshman; what fun it was!

That's me on the far right; Fran is 4th from the left.

I was the maid in one of the plays and then, glory of glories, I discovered Sock Hops on Fridays once a month. I danced every dance. The McGann five-piece orchestra accompanied all the dances. I feel so sorry today for the kids with their DJ's and "canned" music. They don't know what "live" music really is.

There was a Halloween dance at the high school gym. Fran and I were invited that night to Neil's house for dinner. I was looking forward to seeing the inside of the mansion. Neil's parents worked in New York City. His dad specialized in fabrics. His wife acted as his secretary. Every weekend they came home to Oswego by train. One weekend Neil said, "I want you to meet my mother and father when they come in Friday night." I wasn't too happy about meeting them; besides, I had a cold and one of my monthly cold sores.

Whenever the sores appeared, I said, "No kissing" but he said he wanted to experiment and see if they were contagious. They weren't. It was one of those invigorating evenings. The sun had just dropped as the train chugged into the station. Out came Neil's mother and father. In the twilight she seemed very pretty. He was huge in stature and not handsome at all. We shook hands and talked about nothing while they waited for a cab to take them home. We went for a long walk. The next day Neil called and said that when he asked his mother what she thought about his girl, she said, "Too bad she has a hare lip." Then I remembered my cold sore—we had a good laugh; then he said, "My mother said, 'Everyone to his own taste said the woman when she kissed the cow.'" Okay! Okay! That's her opinion!

Fran Brown was a good friend of Neil's sister, Jane. Fran was also invited to dinner at the Toomey home. I had been reading *Forsythe Saga* by James Galsworthy. I vicariously lived an elegant life in England: we dined at 8:00, went to art galleries, etc. I suggested to Mother that we lunch at noon and dine at night. Mother changed the heavy meals at noon to a light repast. Dinner was not at 8:00 but at 6:00. After the invitation came, I said to Fran, "You don't think we should dress for dinner, do you?"

"Don't be silly," she said.

I don't remember what Fran wore, but I had on a plaid wool dress with a pique collar and cuffs. Our hostess greeted us in a full-length gown. Oh, well, win some, lose some…

It was a truly beautiful house. A huge Checkering Piano that was also a player piano. When I arrived, it was playing a Grieg concerto. The keys were dancing up and down—how odd! I had never seen a player piano before. The huge library was filled floor to ceiling with books. The breakfast room was circular with pale green tiles and a huge bay window that gave a panoramic view of the lake. Lovely sight! The elegant dining room was all linen and crystals. The dishes were Spode "Buttercup" pattern. Elizabeth, Jane's sister, had taken maple leaves that had fallen and washed them, and then placed them up and down on the table—very lovely! I admit I spent most of the evening with Grieg. I couldn't resist sitting on the piano bench, listening, and watching the keys go up and down.

While I was reading Galsworthy, Neil was reading Raphael Sabatini so, as we walked, he would dart behind trees, trip over lawns, jump over fences, slaying many enemies, and fencing with an imaginary sword. If a stranger came by, I am sure they were baffled. But I knew exactly what he was doing because he was relating his adventures to me. That summer we were back to my happy place, Sheldon. The same cast of characters: Fran, Verna, Donald, Neil and I. This time we experimented kissing under water. Mother wondered why my eyes were so bloodshot when I came home.

13

Another Idyllic Summer

That summer, in August, Mother had me give a party for Fran Brown as she went off to Syracuse University. Mother called the Pontiac Hotel, made reservations for 20 people, chose the menu and sent the invitations. The day of the luncheon arrived; Mother was not attending. At 14, I was in charge of the luncheon; what a rotten trick. Armed with candies, Benson Hedges cigarettes, playing cards and prizes I, the hostess, arrived. Luncheon was at 1:00; I arrived at 11:30. The hotel was a very nice place then. I set upon the rotunda and greeted the guests as they arrived. When we were seated for lunch, the waitress brought a dish to me. I said, "No. Guests first." She whispered, "You are supposed to taste the food, approve it, and then I'll serve it to your guests." It was a very nerve-wrenching day!

The only other nerve-wrenching day I had ever had was in 8th grade when Mother Evangelista ordered me to take over a kindergarten class because the teacher, Sister Anne Joseph, was ill. I knew no children, none in the neighborhood or family. I had never babysat a child. Thirty wonderfully assorted faces greeted me. I told a story; they didn't listen. I sang a song; they threw pencils. I got cross; they mimicked me. "Dear God, will that bell ever ring?" When it finally rang, they nearly knocked me down. One kid threw his hat and it landed on the edge of a picture of the Sacred Heart. I took a long stick that they used to open the windows and retrieved it. I walked out of the classroom to home, in the front door and into bed and I didn't appear until the next morning.

I really missed my big boss, my mentor. Fran entertained in the summer on her porch with many glasses of grape juice mixed with ginger ale, cookies, etc. Mrs. Brown was a superb cook; her blueberry muffins were a treat. She ordered in bulk and one time she ordered a five-pound box of huge gumdrops. Boxes of Whitman Samplers, chests holding gold coins (chocolate covered in gold foil) abounded. Fran's dresser was covered with many bottles of perfume. My favorite was *Toujour Moi.* I finally broke down and bought my own bottle. I wore it exclusively. Her closet was full, her jewelry ample. She always had money. I never had any money and when I did, I spent it immediately. I was in a play and I had three lines. I was the maid. Fran sent me a telegram with the words, "There are no small parts, just small players."

Fran was majoring in speech and drama. Mrs. Brown was feisty, elegant, fun. She would start to sing her conversations in a recitative manner, and we would respond with a few invented arias, about the beauty of the day, about what was new, or about a recent movie—most enjoyable! Mrs. Brown read constantly, I mean two or three books a day. Fran followed in her mother's footsteps, but sometimes I was suspicious when she was too vague about the content of a book. Rose Brown cared not about her appearance. I met her once in a meat market and she was wearing a large white apron!

Rose Brown was convent educated in Montreal and spoke French fluently. She was really hard on Fran. When Fran received only a C in class, her mother berated her in front of me. I never felt warm toward her again. The Brown house, to put it mildly, was a disaster area, almost as bad as Miss Haversham's in *Great Expectations*. It remained in that condition and never, ever changed.

I was studying Schubert's "Serenade" with Professor. One lesson he told me he wanted to have a few of his pupils to play a program on the station WSYR in Syracuse. He told me that the Schubert that I knew was a good selection. I don't remember the drive to Syracuse. Mother must have driven me. I was beyond scared: rattled and discombobulated for sure. I do remember I did an awful job and was full of shame. Professor just couldn't understand me. I guess he wasn't acquainted with my "case of nerves." The program aired on a Sunday night at 7:00 PM. Monday morning Neil was full of *joie de vivre*, fresh, showered as he picked me up for school. The first thing he said was, "I tried to get the station, but I couldn't."

"It was ok," I said but I thought, *Thank God!*

Visiting Professor Schumann every summer was a cherished memory. Benno and I experimented in mental telepathy. At 6:00 PM on a Friday on the back porch, I would send him messages. At the same time he would send me messages. It never worked. Things were so grim at home that I informed Professor I was not going to study any more. He couldn't believe it and in an unbelievable gesture offered to teach me for free! But it was ended.

The romance was thriving that summer. We went to the prom. His parents let him drive. The car was a foreign make with a right wheel drive. Neil's sister had a deformed arm and this type of car allowed her to drive. Fran and her boy friend George double-dated with us. I was startled when we entered the gym that night. It was totally transformed. Rose entwined trellises abounded. There were gazebos. A ten piece, live band was playing. Except for a slight scent of gym shoes, it was total enchantment.

14

Transition to High School

I joined the drama club and started to work toward a membership in "Owls Head"; the requirements were two years in succession of honors. One English marking I was just below a 90. I asked Jesse Ward to raise the mark and she did. I am forever grateful to this woman for her excellent teaching. Every morning when we entered the class, she had an inspiring motto on the board. In English we studied *As You Like It,* and I didn't. I thought it too foolish. A bad introduction to Shakespeare. The next year, when we studied *MacBeth,* I became enamored of the bard.

Miss Lewis assigned me a solo in "Cabaret" that spring. I had the sweetest light pink organdy evening gown. The night of the performance as I was entering the auditorium holding my gown on a hanger very high to keep it from hitting the floor, I could see the auditorium was empty but for one person in the front row. It was Neil. How did he get in? He had asked the janitor. I was impressed. As I entered the cabaret scene to do my number, I was overcome by a scent—what was it? The stage was filled with the smell of beer. Carl McGann and his orchestra were feeling no pain and they were great.

In the 8th grade I had had the opportunity to hear the Syracuse Symphony play at the college. There was no Hi Fi, stereo or mikes in those days. The conductor looked and acted like a monkey as he waved his arms back and forth. They played Cesar Franck's "Symphony in D Minor" and today it still remains one of my favorites. But better than the symphony to me was Carl McGann's orchestra. They gave me a great beat to start and all fear or nervousness disappeared and I was with it. "A boy and girl were dancing tonight…" was the beginning lyrics—what fun to sing, to connect with an audience! "In a Garden" was the big orchestra selection at school. I was assigned the triangle. Loved it! By my senior year I played the bass viol, so I was promoted. I heard Miss Lewis tell someone that I was chosen to play this instrument because I was strong enough to carry it. I thought I had been chosen because of my talent! I can still see her expression at one competition, the look of one who had been struck. I had put my finger in the wrong place and I can tell you right now the sound was not lovely!

The piano player for all these events was big (man-boy) John Hanley. He played mostly by ear, but he was better than good—he was great. One day he handed me a piece of music. "You must learn this for our next program." It was "Street of Dreams"—"Gold, Silver and Gold, all you can hold is in the moonlight/Poor, no one is poor as long as love is sure on the street of dreams."

The orchestra was on the floor and I was on the stage. After I sang it, everyone went wild. They loved it. John yelled, "Repeat!" so I started to sing but something was wrong; he was in a different key entirely. I followed along and suddenly I couldn't reach the notes and I started to squeak—I fled off the stage. The principal was in the wings waiting to go on for an announcement. I flung myself into his arms sobbing, "Oh, my God, wasn't that awful?" He hastily unwrapped my arms, which were tightly entwined around his neck, and he said, "Miss O'Brien, let me alone this minute." I released him and, humiliated, I knew my life as I knew it was over.

A few of the faculty protested when I sang "Shuffle Off to Buffalo." "You go home to get your panties,/I go home to get my scanties/And away we'll go/...Off we're going to shuffle, shuffle off to Buffalo..."

Miss Cullen, the Latin teacher, had me take the student papers home and correct them. I had such a good foundation, thanks to Sister Evangelista, that I was acing Latin. In English we read *Ivanhoe*. One of the girls in class was Marian Corrigan. We became good friends. Geometry was a true mystery. I received a 50 at midterm. Miss Mary Jane Glann was the teacher. She remained after school every day to help those who needed it. She was very volatile in class. I was very tuned into her; when she laughed, I laughed. One day she was upset and I wept. Every afternoon I was in her room and she helped me. At home I would sit at a card table, determined to conquer the angles and triangles. This subject helped me so much through life. When a problem arose, I would consider all angles and try to solve the many problems that would confront me. On the other hand, being in the Glee Club and chorus was a joy. Our teachers' selections were varied and lovely. I hated those periods to end.

For the musical that year, Miss Lewis told me she wanted me to sing "Smoke Gets In Your Eyes." I said I'd like to sing "Night and Day." No, she had already assigned it to someone else. "Smoke" was nice and I thought about its meaning. "When your heart's on fire,/You must realize/Smoke gets in your eyes." Mother bought me an outfit at Flahs in Syracuse, a tangerine net gown with a train. It had a tight fitting bodice and layered skirt. There were three performances. When my turn came and I sang the song, the audience went wild. I had three encores. This happened all three nights.

Every audience was different. As soon as you would step out on stage, you could feel the vibes; good, bad or indifferent. The biggest thrill one can have is to connect with an audience thoroughly. When I walked through the halls in school, everyone stopped me and said, "Nice going," the ultimate peer tribute. I would come out of homeroom and four or five boys were lined up to talk to me, and Miss Schulte had to shoo them away. Pretty heady stuff!

In the meantime Neil's family was in big financial crisis and they moved to New York City—talk about bereft! I felt as if my arm had been amputated. Lonesome was a word I never considered but felt deeply now. We wrote daily. He was going to Peter Stuyvesant High School in New York City. He'd write about seeing people scrounging garbage cans for any kind of food on his way to school. His father was in textiles and he was going to night school to study fabrics because fabrics fascinated him. He continued to receive high honors, managed to play the piano and was working on "*Bar carolle*" by Hoffman on his own.

At first I went nowhere, did nothing, and moaned and groaned without him. This lasted about two months. I didn't date but became friends with Charles Walsh, a nice baritone in the chorale. I went to stag dances and when they played "Good Night Sweetheart" Charles appeared out of nowhere and walked me home. He was a true and loyal friend and we talked about our dreams, schemes and futures. He also helped me out of a number of predicaments and always seemed to be there when I needed him.

My favorite place on Friday nights was to go to the Dante Alighieri Hall two blocks away to hear the magnificent Carl McGann's orchestra. There were sock hops at school with the same band and I didn't miss one performance. I had no curfew. Life was sweet. After school a group of us would go to Savas' Restaurant and order Cokes for a nickel, which I usually borrowed. We would crowd into a booth until the manager would beg us to go home so they could get ready for the dinner crowd.

A guest trumpet player played for the school. One number was "My Buddy" a favorite in World War I. "I miss your voice, the touch of your hand./My buddy, my buddy,/Your buddy misses you." I was missing my buddy.

I went frequently to Doris the hairdressers. I wore my hair short and Neil always said, "Shorn, Shorn" and shook his head in disapproval. One day, after he left for New York City, I was sitting under the dryer at the hairdressers. I sensed someone in front of me. I looked down from the dryer and saw a man's size thirteen shoes. I couldn't believe he would come to a salon but there he was in all his glory. He had found a ride to Oswego. I canceled all appointments and we had a short but wonderful weekend together.

His letters started to reprimand me for socializing so much. A sophomore in high school can't give up these events. I wrote that I would be forever faithful, that he was the only one, but that I was going to date. We were in crisis in our relationship. Things were not going well. I was no longer "lost Queen of Ireland" but a mercenary, outrageous flirt (true enough). He rued the day he met me. He accused me of bothering his friend Donald—ridiculous! He then stalked me and that was it. We exchanged pictures and he said, "If I can't have you, then no one can and I will kill you." The end, finis, over, kaput!

One day I was summoned to the Principal's office. The vice principal, Florence Robinson, wanted to talk to me. "Why didn't you say hello to me last week when we met?" I vaguely remembered meeting her the previous week. I couldn't recall who said hello first. If I didn't say hello, I must have thought the older woman should greet a mere student first. Apparently not. She was really irked with me. I didn't apologize. She said she hoped just because I was so popular, I wouldn't get a big head or forget my place. I said I would try not to and that was that—dismissed. I thought about the encounter. Maybe I *was* getting a big head.

I have to admit that I was a poor sport. The kids fought over me because some wanted me on their team. I couldn't pitch or bat. I took tennis lessons and had a weak wobbly wrist. Neil had always been patient. I made about two baskets in my entire life but I was a true spectator at the football games. Maybe some year we will win just one game. The basketball team was doing well. I went to the school boxing matches. One of my classmates always won. One night I went to the fight and he got a severe bloody nose. I never went to another bout.

There were two high school sororities in town: Delta Gamma and Kappa Epsilon, aka, "Dirty Girls" and "Kiss Easys." I rightfully joined, at their request, the K.E.'s. The initiation was held at the County Jail. We were blindfolded and fed Limburger cheese. I also had to stand on Bridge Street and sell pencils. The girls were the nicest people, but I wasn't about to limit my friendships to just KE's. We held dances but the big one was New Year's Eve at the Yacht Club. We always had a live band. The club was full of twinkling candles and lights. I garnered many happy memories there.

I joined the Drama Club. Miss Steinberg had a tiny closet of a room. She directed the two plays; one in the fall, one in the spring. We had great talent. Doris Shores was the top star. She was small, pretty, and a real actress. Later, my cousin Ellen took Doris' place; she was extremely gifted. Robert Schuler was the best leading man. I still remember the wonderful performances they gave; Miss Steinberg was always lazing around and shooting the breeze. I always had the feeling the actors were superior to the director. I was often the maid or some other minor part. It was a fun experience. I was not much of an actress; it was hard not to be anything but ME. But it was fun to be with such talent.

Fran Brown had me become involved in my freshman year; then she went off to Syracuse University to major in Speech and Drama. Later my cousin Ellen followed in Fran's footsteps. A special friend of Fran's was Leslie Davis. He was small, slight, whimsical, delightful and mad about theater. He knew every play on Broadway and all the names in the casts. In 1933 Broadway was glowing in drama and musicals. It was a banner year. Leslie would go to New York City and attend shows, regaling us on his return with tales of the many performances. He later became our life-long friend.

Life was a thrill with Easter Balls and Christmas dances at the hotel. There were only three minutes between classes. Most of the girls repaired to the Ladies Room but I seized the opportunity to pass and receive notes. My purse was full of notes. One day Mother mentioned something she could only know by reading my notes. I wrote a note and put it in my purse. It said, "Whoever reads this is a nosy witch." She laughed months later when she said she got the message. Lunch with Mother is one of my favorite memories. I'd tell her blow by blow everything that went on—the faculty, the romances, etc. Sometimes she would recall her youth and romances. We always ended lunch with éclairs, cream puffs, or chocolate sundaes. I loved her deeply.

The shrinking violet, the timid one, the one who was afraid to answer the door bell, the one who never said hello to my many dates, my mother took me and Grandpa to the fair. She went on every ride. Grandpa and I tried to be good sports. On one ride Grandpa turned a gray green shade. When Mother saw his situation, she demanded that the ride be stopped immediately. Of course, no one listened to her. After the ride while Grandpa and I weaved around for a while, Mother spotted the roller coaster. She assured us we would love it. She explained the first dip was harmless and the last dip was the worst but by that time we would be prepared for the Big One. It so happened that the first one was the deepest. Slowly we chugged up the steep climb. Grandpa and I were trying to smile and wild Margaret was in ecstasy. I can't believe we lived through it. As Grandpa and I staggered out clinging to each other, Mother wanted to know if we wanted to go again. "It's better the second time," she said. We deferred to another time!

The New York State Fair was wonderful. Visiting real Indians from the Onondaga tribe was most fascinating. They wore beautiful garments. They occupied an acre of land at the State Fair. Their tepees were amazing. The next year Mother asked Grandpa, who was in his mid-eighties, if he would like to go to the fair; he declined. He was no dummy.

Koberg Pond was a mile and a half out West Fifth Street. It was a joy to ice skate there. Inside a hut there was a pot-bellied stove. My ankles were so weak they swelled and hurt. I bought ankle supports that helped a little. The pain was worth it. Huge fir trees surrounded the pond. It was a charming, fairyland ice palace. The snow made the sun shine in a myriad of colors. The best part was when the boys guided me around with our arms crossed over each other. Pure bliss!

One Saturday as we were walking home, three boys (I remember only Pete Osmon) with our skates over our shoulders went by St. John's Church, I said, "It's Saturday. Let's go to Confession." We clumped in making a terrible racket clanging our skates against the wooden pews. The line in front of the confessional was small. I think I was number five. When my turn came, I entered, knelt, and the slide door opened. "Bless me, Father, for I have sinned…" The menu was usually the same. "I sassed my parents 100 times; I lied 50 times." Some times I would make up sins…

"Well, now," said Father McLaughlin on the other side of the grill, "tell me, girlie, so you like the boys?"

"Definitely," I replied.

"Do you like to be with them?"

He was beginning to sound sinister.

"Yes, Father."

"Do you like them to feel you and touch your breasts?"

I jumped up, left the confessional, grabbed my skates, and ran out of church. The three boys followed me.

"What's the matter?" they quizzed.

"I got sick in there. Let's hurry home."

You can believe I never returned to that creep again. My gosh, just because I was with three boys doesn't mean I was that kind of girl! Besides, my boobs were just bumps.

15

Freshman/Sophomore Year, 1932

Life was better. The three of us were healing and gradually Daddy became the wonderful, happy-go-lucky, optimistic guy he always was. He loved his job. He sang in the morning, quoting Shakespeare and Confucius. "God's in his heaven/ All's right with the world."

Summer would find me at the beach, especially Sheldon's. The most serious talks were about what shape the clouds had formed. If there was a dance I was there; the sock hops at school, or Friday night at Dante Alighieri Hall. I danced every dance, was never without a partner. "Hold That Tiger" was played at least once every dance. "Moon River," "Stars Fell On Alabama," "Star Dust" were usually used to warn us that the last dance was coming up. Then "Goodnight, Sweetheart" and THEN you go home with the boy you were dancing with. I would hear the song; I'd panic. Who would take me home? This worry came in the middle of "Star Dust." I could see Jimmy Monaghan smiling at me, also Ferdinand Tremiti. Just as "Good Night, Sweetheart" started, Chuck Walsh appeared out of nowhere. He had no money for the dance but right at 11:00 they let him in and there he was, my pal, my friend, ready to walk me home. He was the best dancer I ever experienced. His appearance always moved me. And when he was able to come to the dances, he was always so musical, so blithe, so smooth.

The street cars disappeared, the high touring cars with their celluloid flaps to snap on in rain and storms disappeared; they were replaced by cars that didn't need to be cranked up in front to get them started. Radio was more audible. The static was more subdued. The rage in hats that fall was a derby like hat called Empress Eugenia. It was a small bowler hat with a feather about a half-yard long perched jauntily on the left side. There were no "teen" clothes in 1932. One went from children's clothes to the adult's clothing section. So on any given day in school it would be hard to differentiate between the faculty and the students.

Clark Gable and Joan Crawford were the big movie stars. We were beginning to be sated with Al Jolson. "David Copperfield" was released. Mother and Dad loved it and Daddy was forever saying, "Barkus is willing" to Mother. "Vagabond King" was also released that year and I saw it four times. There was a new product on the market: Mum Deodorant. But an anti-perspirant also appeared called ODORONO. It was a red liquid and we loved to scream, "Odor! Oh, No!" On the radio at about 11:00 PM line dance music was broadcast, LIVE! It was Eddie Duchin along with Ozzie Nelson with a new singer named Harriet. The Dorsey Brothers with Frank Sinatra and Bing Crosby made guest appearances. What a treat and what an ideal time to dance in the living room after a treat movie!

Vinyl records were improving and we no longer cranked our record machines. Every year, the week before Thanksgiving, Mother traded the old radio in for a new one. She had some deal with Mr. Fenske that she'd turn the old into new. "Hi-Fi" or "Stereo" were not in our vocabulary those days.

In school I was having real trouble with Geometry. Mary Jane Glann who looked like an identical twin to Edna Mae Oliver (i. e. not pretty—but very interesting), remained every day after school to help the helpless one: me. One day I was standing behind a boy who was troubled by trigonometry. He was about 5'7" with green eyes, a perfect nose along with a wide smile. He was very, very handsome. I asked someone his name. It was Jack Flanigan. Every time I was at Fran Brown's house, her cousin Larry was there and he would say to me, "Jack Flanigan wants to date you." I'd always say, "You know I'm in the phone book." That was that. One night a few months later I was in Savas' Restaurant enjoying a Black and White (vanilla scoop, chocolate syrup, marshmallow syrup, cherry and nuts—15 cents) and a boy gave me a note. It said, "If you'll let me, I'll drive you home." It was Jack Flanigan. I wrote back, "OK." He was parked in front of the restaurant. I got in the car an off we went for a ride around the "Loop" which was a drive around the lake and around again. Great place to park. We talked for a while. He was nice, a senior, track enthusiast, interested in going to Georgetown University. He said he wanted to be a doctor. A few days later he called me and we started dating. And then: Damn, if we weren't considered "going steady." He lived with an aunt because he had lost his mother and father as an infant to the flu epidemic.

I have to admit that he was spoiled and, of course, so was I, which meant that our relationship was volatile. One night in February he invited me to the May prom. At dances we were always cheek-to-cheek but one time when I tried to lead him he twisted my arm so hard I never led him again! One night he was late for our date. I admit I never kept a date waiting. The date was for 7:30; he showed up at 9:00. He was very excited. His uncle, Dr. Marsden had called him. He was doing a Caesarian section that evening and invited Jack to observe the procedure.

Jack was overcome by the experience. The incision of the skin, then the cutting into the uterus, and then his uncle reached in and took the baby out. To Jack, who was in a sterile gown so he could get a closer look, it was an enthralling experience. The incident made him more than ever determined to become a doctor.

In March the College at Oswego held a dance in Fulton at a big ballroom with a 10-piece band. I was all dollied up but Jack was late! He forgot. He was playing pinochle. I could feel the romance start to cool. He showed up at 9:00; we arrived at 9:30; that meant we only had two hours to dance. The crowd was festive and the slightest hint of spring was in the air. In front of the bandstand were about fifty jars of daffodils. As we danced around we'd stop and sniff the golden blossoms. All at once it was 11:30 and "Star Dust" was playing. Jack knew I was still simmering so he kept dancing. The orchestra members by now were packing their instruments. Everyone was heading home. We still danced. Finally he stopped and started to pick up armfuls of daffodils, handing some to me and taking some for himself. We staggered out to his black car that had a rumble seat and loaded it with flowers and the pungent earthy smell pervaded the air. It was snowing gently and we were under a spell of enchantment. What started out on a low note ended on a celestial high: such a happy memory!

My swain was getting bossy. "Why don't you wear the red outfit? That white pique looks smashing so wear it." I thought, *Like fun I will! I'll wear what I feel like!* He was the handsomest one at the prom; even the girls couldn't vie with him. He wore black slacks and a cream jacket. I was so impressed I can't even remember what I wore that night! He belonged to Pleasant Point Country Club and we danced the summer away. The dances were held in an open pavilion overlooking Lake Ontario. The bands came down from Syracuse. We'd dance a few dances and then walk on the shore within earshot of the music. He had never heard of Sheldon's Beach and he was not going to stoop so low as to find out where it was. Yet one day I looked up and there on the hill was Jack, condescending to join me. Another day I was standing in front of my house. It was a perfect summer evening. The poem Jack Flanigan had made up was going through my mind:

> Mary O'Brien is a girl divine
> With teeth that shine and lips like wine.

One of my friends was running toward me. She was breathless but told me she saw Flanagan in his car with another girl. He had called out to my friend, "Don't tell Mary." Of course she couldn't wait to tell me. In one moment the romance was icy with icicles plus! That same night there was a dance at the college. It was a mile walk to the college, but I went. Mostly college kids were there. Towards the end of the dance I decided to leave. One guy followed me out and started to harass me. I started to run but heard a groan. I turned to look back. The guy was on the ground and who was standing over him with a menacing look but Chuck Walsh. I can't describe how relieved I was. He was mad for music and had a beautiful baritone voice. That is why he attended all the dances. He walked me home, my defender, by hero.

Chuck Walsh had a job in Minetto for the summer; he thumbed his way up and back. One night he stopped by and asked me out on a date for the next Thursday. His shift ended early and he would call me and confirm it. The next Thursday I waited for his call. It got to be 6:00 and no call. At 7:00 the phone rang and it was Jack Flanagan who wanted to know if I wanted to go to a movie. I wanted to go and I said, "OK." At 7:30 I was standing on the porch and a terrible thing happened. Jack and Chuck came up the steps together! I was dumbstruck. Each one said, "You take her." I should have said, "You both go home" but to get even with you-know-who, I said, "Well, I think I'll go with you, Chuck, because you asked me first and not on a whim 30 minutes ago." The romance with Flanigan was over. Finis, Amen.

16

Junior Year, 1935

Beryl Lewis and Anna Favori were big influences my junior year. I loved to go to the basketball games at the Armory. The team was extraordinary, unlike the football team, which was an embarrassment. I sat in the bleachers at the beginning of the game. Mr. Bennet shot off a cap gun to commence the game. Some wit invariably tossed a dead bird on the court. It was hurriedly disposed of and then I eased myself up to the VIP section. The boys, Diddle Tully, Cookie Wise, Max Robinson, Banana Head Schaffer, Dudley Leonard, etc. were so in tune to each other that they couldn't lose. Their choreography was superb. When I see games today, I note the winning teams are so synchronized that I recognize the teamwork. They were so good they were in the Eastern State Tournament. We hung around the Western Union waiting for their score to be sent in. They won the entire tournament and they will always remain true heroes in my heart.

I had some great girl friends: Marion Corrigan lived nearby. Her parents worked and after class about six of us hung out at her house while she made cookies and pin-curled her hair. She used a minimum of forty pins. It wasn't until years later that I found out that her hair was naturally curly! We had many girl talks. We wondered about a lot of things. Marion was very competitive with me. But not I with her. Another friend Betty Diment lived in Minetto. She had a green car, which always stalled at First Street and Bridge. Betty had big brown eyes and blonde hair, lovely figure, was shy but fun. I was so impressed with her parents. Mrs. Diment was a Vassar graduate and an active golfer, bowler, gardener, and Country Club member. Mr. Diment had a big job at the shade mills in Minetto. The house belonged to the company and was a treasure on three acres, a large frame house containing spacious rooms. Mister and Missus D were obviously so in love that one felt good in their presence. At dinner when Mrs. Diment rang a bell under the table with her foot, a pretty young girl appeared and served us. I really thought that was super keen.

Beryl Lewis, our music teacher, gave us mini selections of various operas. She assigned me most of the soprano solos except "Carmen" which I coveted. Mrs. Lewis sang the "Carmen" parts with beauty and style. I looked forward to these sessions. She had two degrees, one in music, one in art. She was very moody. One had to be wary and test the waters, so to speak, to discover the mood she was in. That fall she produced "Minstrels"; these consisted of a front line of seated performers. In the middle was Mr. Interlocutor, a white man (the principal, Mr. Riley); on either side were six boys in black face. (Yes, this is true. Can you believe it?) Each black-faced boy would ask a question of Mr. Interlocutor and he would reply with a punch line. Since he was blonde bordering on gold it was a scary sight to behold. As a part of the show, I sang a Jerome Kern number, which I forget right now, but it was a lovely tune.

Miss Murdoch was my English teacher. She was elderly and no one loved her more than she. "He don't, she don't, it don't," were her favorite expressions and frankly this irked me. After school one day she told me she had taught my father and that he was a wonderful student. She then sniffed a little and said, "Of *course*, I know nothing about your mother." I thought, *You and a lot of other people don't know my mother*. I started to do a lot of writing. One of my papers was on the Station of the Cross: "Jesus Is Stripped Of His Garments." The day before I wrote the paper I stopped at St. Joseph's church to say the Stations and the inspiration for the paper came to me. She accused me of not writing it. She did the same thing with a book review, a biography of Sibelius, which was really interesting. I was furious. Then I made one the biggest, dumbest mistakes of my life. She requested that we write about our favorite teacher. I wrote not about Minnie Murdoch but about Virginia Dean. After that it was outright war.

Virginia Dean taught Cicero in third year Latin. Julius Caesar the year before had been a pain: he was always breaking up camp, but Cicero was a great orator and reading about him was fascinating. Fourth year Latin was Virgil, supposedly a favorite of many, but Cicero was my favorite. One day in English class Miss Murdoch gave a review of a program for students, something we called "Auditorium." It was held once a week on Fridays. I really think I participated in all of them. One day a girl stopped me and asked, "Aren't you ever going to graduate?" I said, "Sorry, honey, I have another year ahead of me." She was so anxious to get her chance to perform. Miss Murdoch for some reason was on the muscle; she said the program was inferior, no comparison to the one she produced. Then she said, "Of course, Miss O'Brien is lacking in all the phases of the skits, as usual." She said it as if I weren't there. Then a wonderful thing happened. Robert O'Brien who sat behind me started to hum. Some one else picked up the sound and suddenly there were thirty hums going from *piano* to *forte* and back to *piano* again. Miss Murdoch turned red and changed the subject. I'll never, never forget their loyalty to me and the message they delivered to her.

Once our history class teacher was absent. The substitute teacher was only with us a week but I learned a lot from her. I think she must have been a psych major. She talked about women and moods and how women would have highs and lows, sometimes feel weepy, sometimes excessively euphoric.

I always had a crush on Alfred Lunt and Lynne Fontaine. They were the idols of the theater then. I had never seen them perform. They did make one movie, "The Guardsman." I read in the paper that Wednesday was the final performance. I had to see it so I trotted over the bridge to the Capitol Theater. To think I was not aware that it had been shown for a week. Today was the last day so I had to skip school. There were about fifteen people in the theater. It was as wonderful as I thought it would be; great dialogue, wonderful flair, two fascinating people. I trotted happily home. Who do you think was parked in the driveway as I came merrily up the street? It was the truant officer, Dickie Dietz. I told him where I was. He took copious notes, shook his head in disapproval, and drove off. I waited to get the call that I was expelled but "Thank you, Lord" it never came.

17

"HMS Pinafore" and Jack Callaghan

Miss Lewis decided to produce Gilbert and Sullivan's "HMS Pinafore" with try-outs in the auditorium. Some of the faculty acted as judges. There was a senior soloist who was due to get the lead. Chuck Walsh tried out and so did Katherine Mattot, a girl with a lovely mezzo quality. About fifty of us lined up. The cast names would be posted on the music room door. I was one thrilled person to see the lead role of Josephine assigned to me. Next I looked for the name of the male lead to play Ralph Rackstraw, hoping to see chuck Walsh but instead it was Jack Callaghan. Oh well, Chuck got the part of Joseph Porter. I knew John Callaghan slightly; he had a nice tenor voice. He was rather aloof and had already graduated. He was on a post grad program at the school. Rehearsals started the end of February at Miss Lewis' house. Just the leads attended. Learning our parts and tuning into the Gilbert and Sullivan style was hard work but great fun. I had an aria in the second act that ended in a B flat; it was a real challenge to me. All the voices were lovely and well chosen and blended well.

We didn't get on stage until mid-April and the rehearsals were so frequent that I was beginning to wonder if we'd ever really perform. Chuck Walsh and I were an item. Jack Callaghan has the first song to start the operetta, a very sweet song and I looked forward to hearing him sing it. He had a mass of curly hair and lovely slightly hooded blue eyes. One day he came back to where I was sitting, waiting my turn. I was surprised because he was rather remote. He had a book in his hand and he said he thought I might like to read it. It was the story of Florence Nightingale. I said my thanks but I knew this biography would not appeal to me. At home I belonged to a book club. The book that month was *Lanny, Troubled Teen*. Next rehearsal I presented him with my selection.

On Holy Thursday the Catholics did a pilgrimage to the churches. The Blessed Sacrament was exposed in each of the seven churches. The altars were resplendent with flowers, candles, statues, everything a sight to behold. St. Mary's was chaste, dignified. St. John's was minimal. The Polish church was medium garish. St. Joseph, the Italian church, my all time favorite church in the world, was something grand to behold. The sanctuary was a maze of lilies; vigil lights spelled out JESUS. Near the ceiling on a platform was placed a large version of the "*Pieta.*" I could really sense the presence of the Lord in the garlic scented little church! John Baptista was hovering over the entire display, fixing, praying and genuflecting constantly. As he bobbed up and down, he made crosses on his forehead, his lips and heart. If there were a competition, St. Joseph Church would win hands down.

St. Paul Church was next. Miss Riddle, the pastor's cousin, contrived huge lame drapes and had fans blowing on each hanging drape in such a way as to make the fabric glisten and shimmer. Then there was a little church, St. Peter, where the display was modest but lovely. That year 1935 as I was leaving St. Peter Church, who was leaving also but Jack Callaghan. After a brief hello he told me he was organist at that church. He said, "Why don't you come to Mass on Christmas?"

I said, "Christmas? You mean Easter, don't you?"

"Of course," he said.

"Oh no," I replied. "I go to my own church with my mother and dad."

At that time I was studying voice with a woman who took a bus from Albany to Oswego once a week. Her name was Anna Favori. I could hardly wait between lessons. She sang and accompanied beautifully. She rented a room from the Catholic Daughters of America. It was upstairs over a drug store. She started me on a real varied repertoire: Italian, German, French, etc. She taught me how to stand, how to pronounce those beautiful, singable Italian words. She opened quite a few doors for me. Not only that, I was fond of her. I still don't know why a young lady (about 25 years old) with so much talent would come to Oswego to teach.

At one rehearsal Jack asked me if I would like to sing in his choir at St. Peter Church. It was quite a trek from my house on West Third Street to the church on East Seventh Street. I considered it for a couple of weeks. Chuck Walsh also sang in the choir so I thought I'd give it a try.

Virginia Dean, my Latin teacher, to my surprise, invited me to tea on that Easter Tuesday at 3:00 PM at her home, which was two blocks from where I lived. I was all dressed up in my Easter finery, a plaid coat and a double brimmed red shiny straw hat. This was my very first tea. She had a lovely home and we sat at a small table, which had the makings of tea and a super yummy plate of cookies. The cookies were balls surrounded with white frosting. I think they were called bon-bons. I hate to tell that I ate all but one, which I left for her. Oh well, it was my first tea party! We got along well. Virginia lived to travel and she traveled often and alone. Because she was an outstanding bridge player, she was most welcome on cruises and tours.

That morning Jack Callaghan had called me and said he wanted to show me his church organ. I said I'd be there late afternoon, so after the tea, my stomach contented, I trotted over the bridge to the east side and his church. The organ was playing as I entered and climbed the stairs. I sat down to listen. The piece was definitely a Caesar Franck Prelude but I didn't know which one. It went on for some time and it was nice. Then he looked at me in surprise and said he didn't know I had been sitting there. Oh, yeah? Like fun…

St. Peter's choir rehearsals were on a Friday and I liked singing in a choir. It wasn't too bad considering the parish was so small. Chuck Walsh would walk me home or we'd go to the DA hall to dance. One night Jack asked me if I wanted to go to a benefit dance because he had bought a ticket. I said no because I was going with Chuck Walsh. I thought if he had purchased a ticket he should have asked me earlier.

One night after rehearsal, Jack took me to a late showing of "Naughty Marietta" with Jeanette MacDonald and Nelson Eddy. Then he invited me to a play. I told Mother, "I have a date with Jack Callaghan."

"What Callaghan is he?"

"Gosh, I don't know. He is just a guy in the cast." Mother liked Chuck Walsh because she had taught his mother and she liked Flannigan because he had a beautiful mother and dad who died when he was one year old. The 1918 Flu Epidemic had taken them and an aunt was rearing him.

"Well," she said, "if it's the Callaghan I know, his mother is a saint and I really dislike the father."

The play we attended was great and done by local actors. When we came home and he saw my music he went right to the piano and one by one he studied my repertoire, which was extensive. What an odd date! How about a little attention to the girl he dated? I really was amused. This was a new experience…

Another new experience: Fran brown and her boyfriend George Budd loved to go horse back riding. Kingsford Woods had bridle paths like none other. They would take me with them. Axle was my mount. He was gray and old and harmless. George loved his mount, Colonel. This horse was stunning. They think at one time a woman had abused him because anytime he was with a woman he shied away and refused to let them get on him. Those trails in early spring were pine-scented and full of patches of violets and trillium. Fran bought me jodhpurs and I felt like a true equestrian.

18

The Performance

Life was full and I was giddy and happy. Finally, finally, the show was ready to go. The costumes were ordered from a prestigious place in New York City. Chuck Walsh started to write me notes signed, "Your worried suitor," or "Your anxious suitor," etc. In the second act of "Pinafore," Ralph Rackstraw played by Jack Callaghan, is so depressed about hopelessly loving Josephine (me), the Captain's daughter who is of a higher rank, that he is contemplating suicide. In front stage he has a gun and after a sad aria he puts the gun to his head. Josephine who is up high on the ship spies him and sings, "Ah, stay your hand. I love you."

"Loves me?"

"Yes, Yes, I love you."

Then she rushes down the stage, steps to Ralph stage center, who is about to do away with himself. They embrace and KISS! Miss Lewis wanted us to practice early so when the performance came, we wouldn't look too awkward. (Not bad, not bad at all!) Some unkind person after one of the performances remarked how Josephine gained so much momentum running down the stairs with her enthusiasm that she almost knocked him down! The costumes were lovely. I had two beautiful full skirted outfits; one velvet, one cotton. They had off the shoulder bodices. The sailors looked almost real. Ralph Rackstraw looked adorable. Wearing the costumes put us in a great mood and it was easy to stay in character.

Mother and Dad came to every performance. Dad took a place at the exit and greeted everyone as they left. What an empty feeling when it was over! If anyone took pictures, I didn't see any. Just a memory, just a memory. John Cullinan took the part of Dick Dead Eye, the villain. John's father was a funeral director. John invited me and Jack to go to Rochester, NY to attend a performance of "*Tannenhausen*" by Wagner given by the Metropolitan Opera Company that toured every spring and Rochester was one of the chosen places. Miss Lewis, the music teacher, and Ethel Watts, who accompanied for us on the piano, were also invited. A limo picked Jack and me up and Miss Lewis, Ethel, John Cullinan and his sister, Miriam. Jack and I were chauffeured to the opera. The seats were second row center. We were all totally transported to another world. Remember, there was no stereo or Hi-Fi (they hadn't even been invented). So when the orchestra began, the sound that come forth was beyond thrilling. Lawrence Melchior, Kirstin Flagstaff, Lawrence Tibbet, the greatest singers in the world at that time, were in it. It was an utterly fantastic experience. I had a total loving regard for John Cullinan's father for arranging this occasion. The only previous thing I had known about him was that every Christmas my grandpa who was in his eighties at the time, received a dozen roses from him. This so infuriated Grandpa that he wanted the competition (Dain Funeral Home) to take care of him when his time came.

Chuck Walsh was busy being president of his class. Jack's choir was coming along nicely. Memorial Day approached and Jack asked me if I would like to go to Rochester with his sister Margaret to visit relatives. Yes, I would. On the way there, he kept making funny faces. I wondered what these grimaces meant. I found out later he had terrible allergies. We went to the movie "*Les Miserable*" with Frederic March as Jean Valjean. Super good movie! The lilacs are at their peak at the end of May and Rochester was known for its spectacular display. The relatives we visited were very nice. They had a two-year old child. When I went upstairs to go to the bathroom, I turned half way up the stairs and Jack was holding the child in mid air and playing with him. Just a flash came into my mind: he would make a nice father.

Now that "Pinafore" was over, I didn't know if our relationship was over. He called and the next time he came over he brought me a *St. Gregory Hymnal* and suggested I learn to play some of the hymns. I really liked this assignment and having abandoned the piano for a while I got back to the keyboard. Jack was practicing many hours a day. His goal was to get a scholarship to Syracuse University in organ studies. The competition was in July. Around the house I began declaring, "Jackums" which replaced "Chuckums." Another date and the *Kryiale* had been placed in my hands. I started to work on the Requiem Mass, Masses to the Blessed Mother, etc. The chant Masses were stunning with their lack of bar restraints. The flow of the music up and down was a perfect way to sing to the Lord.

Jack came back triumphant from the competition. The award was half tuition for four years. "Jackums" started to teach me to play the organ. The organ at St. Peter Church was not complicated but it had a nice foot pedal and a few sweet stops. The pedaling was hard for me. I called the pastor of the Baptist church on the east side and asked if I could practice there. He was very gracious and two days a week I'd concentrate on pedal with manual. There were three staffs to read and I found it most difficult. One afternoon I was determined to conquer the pedal work. I must have worked three hours. When Jack picked me up to go for a walk my legs gave out. I had to turn and go back home. I never, never could play the organ well—just enough to get by. But it wasn't that I didn't try!

"Jackums" had played the organ at a church in Minetto when he was fourteen years old. He was deeply engrossed in the organ and church music. And for what motive I know not, but for a while he was engrossed with me, especially in my learning Masses. Jack had very little money, but none of us had money. His family was no help at all. His brother Jim was in the seminary, his sister Margaret was a nurse at the hospital in town, Teddy and Chuddy were twins in high school, Bobby, who was the youngest was also at the high school.

"Fishy" Edward Callaghan, the father, was a plumber. He was short, stocky and some of his clothes came from the Boy's Department in the store. He made up for his size with vocal observations. He loved to play cards, drink, and be with the guys. Mrs. Callaghan was strict and a little severe in manner. They had differences between them. When I met them, I thought, *How sad! They don't seem to like each other.* How naïve I was. I found out as the years went by that they loved each other dearly but would be darned if they would admit it. They certainly weren't huggy-bear, kissy-face and in times of dissent quiet reigned.

Chuck Walsh and I were still dating. I just couldn't tell him that I loved him. As we said goodbye after one date, I shook his hand. He was one of my dearest friends, ever! Jack was getting ready to go to the university. He signed me up to take his weekday Masses and any funerals that came along. He would come home on weekends, rehearse the choir, and take the bus back to Syracuse. The bus was the smelliest vehicle in the world. After an hour on this thing, one would reek until one showered. Even the clothes stank. Before he left I gave him an 8 by 10 picture of *moi!*

19

The End of Senior Year

My father drove me in the lumber truck at 6:30 AM so I could play the Masses; then I walked to school. Well, here I was, a senior. I took Virgil with Virginia Dean and that is interesting. I signed up for French III but the teacher, Miss LeRoy, behaved in a very bizarre manner: one student sat on her desk; she was unkempt; so I cancelled out of that class. I really disliked the American History teacher who wore spats, didn't follow the syllabus, and made fun of me so I bided my time and switched to Miss Schulte's class in the second semester. She was very soft spoken. I chose a seat up front by her desk which always held a vase with a single rose. What a wonderful teacher! I was so glad I left Mr. Spats. You can't guess who I had for English? Egads, Help, Help! It was Minnie Murdock. She no longer demeaned me in class and we tolerated each other—barely.

Jack came home on weekends to teach the choir and take the weddings that showed up on the calendar along with Sunday services. He lived in an attic of a boarding house. Financially he was just getting by. I did like playing the weekday Masses. I needed an assignment and there it was. My first funeral was for a man who had no one to grieve for him. The pallbearers were a few kind men who had volunteered. It was very sad. Imagine having no one to mourn you. I wept through the entire Mass. At least he had one mourner.

Daddy was a happy man. His skip was back, his poems returned and he was back kissing Mother in the kitchen. "Thank you, Lord, for giving my father back to us." Mother was acquiring all kinds of gadgets in preparation of some day entertaining—whenever that would be. She studied herself in the mirrors which were in most of the rooms; not in a vain way, but searching, searching to find out who she really was. She was having trouble with her teeth. She needed one extraction. I was worried to pieces and so anxious for her. I certainly didn't want anything to happen to the face I loved above all others. The extraction turned out OK; then two days later I arrived home from school and she was in a panic. She said she was dying. What could I do? I was terrorized. I rushed to the phone and called Aunt Louise O'Brien who came right over and took her to the doctor.

As she left, Mother said, "The money is in your father's top drawer." What in God's name did she mean by that? I fell to my knees and beseeched the Lord to help. The house was as quiet as a tomb. I heard the front door open an hour later. She looked sheepish and said that on her own she had applied hot packs to her face and had reactivated the Novocain. The entire side of her face had become numb and when that happened she just knew she was dying.

In early fall Jack and I would walk down by the lake and sit on the bank. We watched the boats and talked about our dreams. One time we noticed the sun was about to set. It was later than we thought. He walked me home and then continued to walk over the bridge to his home. As I come in the door, the phone rang. It was Jack's mother. Did I know anything about Jack? I said that he had just left me. She said, "I can't understand this. He's never missed a meal in his life."

20

In Love

Senior year—and I was very busy which made me happy. By now I was completely and totally in love. I couldn't wait for him to get home weekends and on Sunday night when he boarded the bus at West First and Mohawk, I wept. But life went on. One distraction was going to the show featuring movies, comedy skits on film, and Pathe News. One night we all laughed audibly at a clip showing a little man screaming into a microphone. He looked like Charlie Chaplin with a funny little mustache. His name was Adolph Hitler. I thought, *The poor Germans! Imagine having a clown like that for a leader.* Of course, I was aware of only one president, Franklin Delano Roosevelt. He was my hero: helping the banks out, forming camps (CCC) for high school boys to work and get paid when there were no paying jobs for many young men.

One glistening day in May a group of us approached the doors of the school. All at once the five of us stopped. "I absolutely cannot go in," I lamented. "Nor I," each repeated. We turned and headed for Betty Diment's car. Off we went to Syracuse on a lark. We found a pond, enjoying the sun and the smell of things coming through the soil. We felt so evil having skipped school which made the day perfect, even more enjoyable. No one missed us except you-know-who, Miss Murdoch. She reported us. The next day five of us: Dick Coe, Dudley Leonard, Betty, Betty's brother Buddy, and I were summoned to the principal's office. Mr. Riley looked grim. We told him exactly what happened. He grinned a little, then dismissed us. I have a feeling he envied us our perfect day in May.

One day Virginia Dean and I went to Syracuse for a symphony concert. Andre Polah, a little man, was difficult to watch conducting because of his awkward monkey-like gestures. They meandered through the Brahms "Second Symphony." I was distracted thinking about whether Jack was there, hoping so much to see him. After all, it had been five days that we were apart. Aha, there he was with a group of friends. He came over and said, "Hello," then immediately joined his buddies. I don't remember the remaining concert and I was very quiet on the way home. Fran Brown invited me to visit her at her dorm. I went to classes. In one class, Psychology, the teacher fascinated me. His name was Dr. Shepard. He looked like a football player. He talked about how to keep from being in a rut. He said not to take the same route every day. Vary your life, etc. I put that idea to work immediately. Fran was majoring in Speech and Drama. I auditioned, nervy, for a play. Mr. Falk, the head to the drama department wrote, "Ingénue with a tendency for comedy." It was a fun weekend. She gave me a bottle of perfume to take home, *Toujour Moi*. It was my favorite scent.

I was in the school library one day. The French teacher, Miss Ward, asked me to see her outside in the hall. "Do you smell *Toujour Moi* on me?"

"Just a trace," I said.

"This scent is tricky because after you put it on you can't tell if it's too much or too little."

"It's OK," I said. "And while we're at it how about sniffing me?"

She leaned forward and said, "Just a trace." A real smelly encounter!

Miss Lewis assigned me "Indian Love Call" for the spring show. It was pretty but I tired of it right away. It was a fit for Jeanette MacDonald but not for me. I was so spoiled by the audiences. On stage I felt warm vibes from dancing as a child up to senior in high school. It's an unbelievable experience to be in synch with your listeners.

The senior festivities were going great guns. One dinner was at the Dubois Inn in Minetto. The K.E. Sorority held it. I was having fun with my sorority sisters when a waiter approached me saying, "Some man is in the lobby and he wants to see you immediately." There was a guy waiting for me. He said he was from the movie theater and did I know a competition was in progress. He asked me to leave immediately and sing in the finals at the theater. I said I was not interested and started to return to the party. He said the one who wins goes to a special summer music school in the Catskills.

I came right back to him and fifteen minutes later, dressed in a formal, I was on my way to the theater. The accompanist said he knew "Indian Love Call" and suddenly I was on stage singing. I was the last one and I had no idea who the competition was. I won hands down. I was pleased until I saw Chuck Walsh and Mildred Felshaw sitting on the side. Good Grief, what had I done? My first instinct had been right. I felt totally embarrassed to be part of an obvious setup.

So now I had to go to Watertown and join sixteen others in the finals. We went on a steamy hot ride. The theater was huge. Kathy Mattot was generous enough to accompany me. I wore a soft wool orchid suit, a navy hat with a veil. I started singing and felt a chill go through me. This was my first encounter with an audience I could tell really hated me. "When I'm calling you-ooh-ooh-ooh-ooh-ooh." I didn't drop dead although I felt sure I would. At last, it was over. Standing back stage I couldn't hear the other performers except one, a lovely pianist and she was the one who won. I felt a little blue, but she was the daughter of the mayor; of course, she would win. On the way home I apologized for all the wasted time and the long drive in the rain. I asked how I placed and learned I was number 16, last. Wow, was I that bad? I knew the outfit was wrong and the song stank, but number 16, last?

Anna Favori taught me some lovely songs to sing for graduation and Miss Lewis asked me to perform. I had sung solos at previous graduations but as part of the chorus renditions. Anna gave me a short simple Italian song, a short German song and a fanciful French song. The final selection was the "Cuckoo." The four songs were printed in the program. I was so proud I couldn't wait. The parents and graduates were good sports but as I was singing the final number, "At one o'clock every day, 'Cuckoo, I Love You.' And when the hour has passed away, 'Cuckoo, I Love You! Ah, Ah, Cuckoo!'" As I was singing this I was casing my fellow graduates. Some of their expressions read, *How could you; how could you do this to us?* The number was short and the graduates of 1936 were damn good sports.

Mr. Leighton (sour puss), the superintendent of schools, was the main speaker. He warned of disaster, coming war, the evil of Hitler. *He must be wrong,* I thought. But recently I had seen in the Pathe News at the theater a German Bundt meeting in Madison Square Garden of all places. It showed a funny looking symbol on these people's shirts. They made weird salutes. I thought they were a bizarre, off-center group and kind of funny. The musings left a pall on the celebration afterwards. The aunties were waiting when I got home. I gave them a brief greeting and went on to all the parties. What a brat I was!

21

Post-Graduation

Jack's brother James was ordained a priest in June of 1936. I went to his ordination. I think there were about ten ordained in the Cathedral in Syracuse. Mrs. Callaghan couldn't attend because she had phlebitis. She was enthroned in a tiny bed in the tiny living room. How awful, not to see your son ordained but the doctor absolutely refused to let her go. She did enjoy the festivities the next day when her son said his first Mass. Red hair, devout, too scrupulous maybe, and with a lovely singing voice, he celebrated. All our hearts were beyond proud. Jack had left St. Peter's in Oswego and now was organist at St. Vincent DePaul's in Syracuse. He started at $100 a year. Anything to help him continue in school. A couple of times he almost had to quit. The College Club came across with $100 to tide him over. His wardrobe consisted of a relative's (Dr. Burden) collection of suits. They fit him perfectly and he looked better than Dr. Burden in them. No one worked harder than Jack at his studies, learning all the facets of the liturgy of the Catholic Church.

Jack's pastor at St. Vincent DePaul's was originally from Oswego. His name was Fr. Daugherty. His church was an old, almost-nice-Gothic structure, on top of a steep hill in Syracuse. He fancied himself. He was a handsome, white-haired Irishman with a gift for oratory. "R-R-Render unto Caesar the things that are Caesar's (tripping the tongue). Unto God the things that are God's" was one of his favorite deliveries. He loved good music, then when Jack's brother Jim was ordained he with many other pastors in Syracuse bid for Jim as an assistant priest. Fr. Daugherty won and Jim and Jack were both at St. Vincent's. Jim was a fine singer and he enhanced both the liturgy and homilies and his other duties with his many talents. Jack had a fine choir and an adequate organ.

I was going to try out for music scholarships in voice at Syracuse University. But I was really despondent after the Watertown fiasco. With fear and trepidation, I arrived at the Music School. There were 200 students in total vying for positions. The vocal line up when I arrived was about 10. A girl ahead of me went into the studio. I could hear her performance. This lovely sound of a coloratura wafted into the hall. Oh, oh, goodbye scholarship. Her name was Beatrice Cotly. With a plea to the Lord, I entered the studio. The voice faculty was present. Jack accompanied me. My listeners looked foreboding but one man caught my eye and actually smiled. He sang silently, mouthing the words as I sang. I concentrated on him and sang directly to him. I learned later he was dean of the School of Music and Arts. There was an hour wait after we all performed. Finally, they come out with a list of finalists for that night. I placed! It was noon so we went to lunch, then to a Tarzan movie which Jack unabashedly reveled in. I was amused by his involvement with Tarzan. I kept thinking of the coming night. Jack took me to the house where he roomed. The woman who lived there let me change clothes. She followed me into the room and stood and watched me disrobe. I was embarrassed and furious. I had only known her about ten minutes.

We treated ourselves to a taxi which took no time at all to deliver us "up on the hill." No place to vocalize. The temperature was beyond 90 degrees. The place where I was to sing was airless, humid, suffocating. I heard the competition and they were all very good. When, oh, when will they call my name? Finally they called my name; at last, my turn. I went on stage and felt good vibes. Then Jack came out to accompany. There was a quiet ripple of laughter and to this day I'm not quite sure, but I thought, *What is so funny?* I mentally checked myself out: my graduation dress of soft green voile, floor length with a three quarter length lined multi-colored pastel coat. OK? So I embarked on my pieces which were my graduation numbers. I was totally familiar with them and enjoyed singing them.

After another endless wait, the announcement came: Ten scholarships were awarded; 2 violin, 3 piano, 3 school of music, then Beatrice Colby. My heart sank. Then I heard, "Mary O'Brien!" I couldn't believe it. I think it is one of my happiest memories. We gathered in the foyer at the back of the auditorium. Someone told me that Florence Girton Hartman would be my teacher. I dashed up to her and said, "Isn't it wonderful? You are going to be by teacher!" She looked startled and I couldn't believe that she wasn't as thrilled as I. Jack and I walked over to Professor's house. I was overjoyed.

Professor said he knew I would get the scholarship because he personally talked to Dean Butler about me and I should be grateful to him for getting me the award. It was so good to sit on the porch where I had spent so much time years before. Professor and Mrs. Schumann made a suggestion that I live with them off campus. They would charge $7.50 a week room and board. Wait until Mother and Dad hear this! We walked to the bus station and came home full of fumes from the bus but I was the happiest girl in the world.

I had dated Jack Callaghan over a year and I was deeply in love with him. I kept complaining to my parents, "He's perfect, perfect, perfect!" My parents' eyes would roll in their heads.

"Oh, really. In what way?"

I didn't answer but reflected on my reasons why. I liked his brains, his ambitions, his faith, his dreams, his work plans for me. He was a handsome boy also, but that was never my criteria. I always looked for a sense of character. He wasn't as serious or gloomy as Chuck Walsh. He wasn't as light weighted as Flanigan. The best part of all: he was not jealous. After the jealous rages and stalking of Neil, Jack was a blessed relief. Physically our relationship was bordering on dangerous.

22

Syracuse

When I arrived that fall at Professors, I was fired up to begin my studies. Professor and Mrs. Schumann gave me the best bedroom: large with a huge bay window, a lovely desk. I was so happy to be with them. The first day of school was hectic. I went to register for English. There were about one hundred students packed into a small classroom. The teacher was a sissy with red hair and a strident voice. "This will not do!" he screamed. "Volunteers to leave, please." My hand went up so fast and a few of us were assigned to a teacher down the hall. When I walked into the classroom, I couldn't believe it. There in all his glory was Dr. Shepard. I had audited his Psych Class the year before when I visited Fran. Was I lucky or what? He turned out to be a real English teacher. Speech was a huge winner. Excellent sight singing, ear training, then Italian, great! Then joy of joys, two lessons a week with Mrs. Hartman. I was so delighted I couldn't wait to begin lessons.

The walk from Schumann's to the hall (campus) was a bit of a hike but lovely scenes accompanied me. The multitude of trees started to turn into their colored leaves. The air was pungent and exhilarating. The music school was a castle-like building. There were lots of stairs to conquer before I reached Florence Hartman's studio. I told her how I had recently studied an aria from "Aida." I also mentioned that in high school I performed frequently and I was anxious to continue in that vein. She smiled and started me on vocalizes and then gave me a piece to learn, Mozart's "Lullaby." I said nothing but a dinky tune of Mozart's was not my idea of a challenge. I soon learned that to sing a simple song simply is an art in itself.

Her studio was about 30 feet long, painted blue, and bright from its many windows. To gaze out the windows from that height gave a panoramic view of the campus and of the city below. There was a large grand piano and a full-length mirror where Mrs. Hartman stood often, preening. It was bothersome for me to look in the mirror and watch my movements while singing. But I did enjoy watching her watching herself.

A musical snob is a detestable person. I thought Mozart was boring, unsophisticated drivel. Can you imagine that? Wagner, on the other hand, was profound, mystical—his orchestrations, the operas, were beyond criticism. I did have the sense to know that there was no one like Bach, especially to listen to, but also to study, but mostly to perform. His compositions are always endlessly pleasing to perform. Never a boring moment with JSB! That fall Florence Hartman soloed with the Syracuse Symphony. She sang "*Aria De Lia*" by Debussy, absolutely stunning. She also sang and trained a woman's chorale for a part of Debussy's "*La Mer.*" My lessons went very well. I was studying Schubert, Brahms, Hugo Wolf Lieder in German. I also studied some exciting songs in English by American composers; more and more doors were opening. Once a month Mrs. Hartman's students met and sang for each other. There were quite a few talented and untalented students.

Mr. Cleasby was the Monday, Wednesday, Friday 8:00 AM Italian teacher. We were semi-comatose after the weekend. He always, always wore the same ornate flowered, hideous tie and looked so unhappy it was almost contagious. Since I had four years of Latin, Italian was a cinch and I aced the class. In high school I studied my Latin every day. I never spent under an hour a day studying and translating. Virginia Dean was my teacher and I wanted to please her. To tell the truth, I liked the discipline. I was completely exhausted after the Virgil regents. I went home, had dinner and went to a movie. When I came home, Mother said Virginia called and I had scored a 98, the highest score ever. It was a real victory for me and I craved victories.

My English classes on campus were the best. Dr. Shepard had been a fullback on the Northwestern football team and he looked it. He looked fierce. We had creative writing and I wrote reams and at first when my papers were returned I was appalled to see how much criticism appeared. Then I studied the corrections. It was obvious he devoted time to his students' writings. He was always interesting, telling about the authors he knew and their *modus operandi.* He read aloud Carl Sandburg with its stunning onomatopoeia. His voice was gentle but firm. He told us that his daughter was seven years old and studying the violin and so was he and that so far only strange noises were emanating from the instrument. One day he invited me to his home for dinner. He said he would talk it over with his wife and he would let me know the date. About two months later he stopped me and said there would be no dinner party. His wife was sick and had been diagnosed with rheumatoid arthritis.

Professor knocked on my bedroom door one evening. I was writing a note to my parents which I did every evening. I knew he and Mama were entertaining guests that evening. He asked me if I would sing for his friends. Ask me? Would I? He said to sing some of my lieder. I grabbed my Schubert and all but knocked him down in my haste to perform. There were about eight people in the living room/studio. I launched into three German songs. I remember "*Die Forelle*" was one number. They smiled and clapped and I returned to my room. As I was studying, I could hear them go into gales of laughter. I wondered what that was all about. The next morning, as we all sat around the big dining room table for breakfast and Professor was drinking his huge glass of hot tea with raspberry jam in it and his usual can of sardines, he said, "Mary, you were a riot last night. Do you know you sing German with a Jewish accent? An Irish girl singing German with a Jewish accent is very, very funny!"

We didn't use the living room/studio except for state occasions such as the time Joshua Heifitz's accompanist came to visit while he was in town for a concert. Out of nowhere came the most beautiful samovar and Mama was busy for days preparing goodies for the occasion. I was NOT invited to this party. Most evenings we sat around the table, reading, writing, etc. Quietly at 9:45 Professor went to the bathroom across the hall; noisily scrubbed his teeth, then did a remarkable lengthy gargle. At the end of this performance lights were turned off and we went to bed.

Their daughter Henrietta was scheduled to play a Rachmaninoff concerto. Her picture was in all the newspapers which announced that she would play and also conduct. One morning I awoke and Henrietta was in residence. She was eating breakfast and graciously acknowledged my presence. She was about 5'7" with a Slavic look. She was eighteen years old and had been playing since she was three years old. Her arms were muscular and she had no trace of an accent. She complained of her father's thick accent. "You know," she told me, "Father and I came to this country together and one can hardly understand a word he says." She shook her finger at him and he lowered his head sheepishly. "It is those Hebrew papers and periodicals he reads that hinders him," she said. She excused herself and went into the studio and played for an hour. She played Czerny and every technique written. She did this all from memory. It was a musical work out. "I must be at rehearsal at 10:00," she said. Mama said, "Gita, darling, let me call you a taxi."

"Oh, no," she replied. "I'll hitch hike." To our horror she left the apartment and stood on the corner. She nearly caused an accident and, three men later, she was off in someone's car to rehearse. When she returned later in the day, Professor said, "Well?"

"A sensation. I was positively a sensation," she replied. I was completely enthralled. That night she had a standing ovation. We had box seats. Professor, Mama, Dr. Berwald, who taught piano at the university, me and, I don't remember how they got there, but Jack and his brother Jim. Mama had a weakness for red hair and was depressed about Fr. James Callaghan being a priest.

"So good looking," she said and shook her head sadly.

Henrietta was very assured and wore a slinky black dress with a white satin bodice. Jack thought she was "fair." What a musical snob! The truth was she was phenomenal. What put the frosting on the cake was she conducted the "*Caprice Espanole.*" For conducting, she wore a black jacket with coattails just like a male conductor. Believe me, she was stunning. The next day she departed for New York City to perform for a month at Roxy's. She was to perform a Tchaikovsky piano concerto. She confessed to us that she was sick and tired of playing the concerto and after a month of playing it every night, she would surely hate it. At one of the meals Henrietta announced she could not stand to hear anyone whistle. It annoyed her. I went to my room and suddenly she opened the door. She stared at me quizzically. "Mary, whatever are you doing?" I had been whistling for ten minutes and I had never whistled before. Strange!

Early one evening I began to draw water in the tub before taking a bath. I went back to my room to get a robe and towels, all the time the water was running. Professor startled me by standing in front of the bathroom door. "You going to commit suicide" he demanded.

Puzzled, I said, "Whatever are you talking about?"

"I know you want to drown yourself, don't you?" he accused.

"Just what are you talking about?" I demanded. "All I want is a bath."

"You don't look dirty to me," he said. "Not so dirty that you have to use a full tub of expensive water."

"OK. OK. I'll be careful in the future." I pushed him aside and slammed the door.

Later that evening Mama said, "You must excuse him. You know, Mary, he is not stingy but frugal. You don't know but we are marked people. When we left Riga, we traveled in boxcars. We were herded so tight we couldn't breathe. We didn't even have shoes. We had to wear pillow cases around our feet but it didn't keep our feet warm."

I got my first hint on how hard their past had been.

Benno had finally graduated from high school. His marks weren't that good. What could he do? What job could he get? One evening he came home triumphant; he carried a huge box. He went to his room and emerged resplendent in a powder blue uniform with gold-fringed epaulets and dazzling gold buttons. He had been hired, excuse me, as head usher at Lowe's Theater. We were all thrilled for him. Once he started making money, he would bring little things: candy, cologne, kitchen gadgets to his mother. Everything was a struggle for him, and we rejoiced in his success.

Professor asked Jack to play at the Synagogue. Mama suggested that for a small fee she would serve Jack a Sunday night supper. Jack at this time was playing Masses, directing a choir, attending classes and practicing for hours. He really had a full plate. As for me, I wanted a little of his time too. Professor's daughter Ella had returned from a Fulbright in Germany. She returned with a handsome German husband whom she had met in Germany. His name was Paul Hugent. Ella had a soft mustache. Paul loved this feature of his wife, always praising it and gently touching it. They had an adorable little girl named Hedda. Professor worshipped her. Gary, the other son, was seldom seen but I heard that he was head of ROTC and a big man on campus. He was, in contrast to Benno, a very handsome man. How the genes bounce! Benno looked like his father.

23

Rehearsing

In the depths of the Fine Arts building were the practice rooms. There was a fee involved with their use. Sometimes the rooms were empty. As you descended into the lower level, the cacophony was amazing. Voices, organs, pianos, violins were all performing at once. I used to wait for an empty room. The rooms contained an upright piano and good lighting. Some of us would get together and one of the students, a great improviser, would make up music on the piano and about six of us would invent songs, operas, etc. We had a hilarious time. Sometimes I'd stop in to see Jack as he was practicing and we'd have a few love pats. One of the students had a full-length raccoon coat, which he wore from September to March.

Eleanor Farley was in all my classes. She was from Chicago. Her father was with Deere Tractor and had just recently located in Syracuse. She was a voice major with a bubbly air about her. I called her "Twinkle." She advised me one day to change my appearance, that I was overdressed. She was right and I calmed down my "look." I liked spending time with her. One day I found a practice room and started vocalizing. I seemed to have competition in the room next door. I paused and listened. The voice was really poor in tone quality, pitch, etc. After a while "Twinkle" came in. I said, "Listen to the singer next door; she's awful." We were quiet for a moment. No sound. Twinkle said, "I just left that room." I am still chagrined at that terrible *faux pas*. I wouldn't have hurt her for the world. She was good enough to forgive me. We exchanged weekends and her family took me to my first hockey game.

Jack was as busy as could be with playing Masses, school, practice, choir rehearsals, etc. Our romance was on fire and I tell you I wasn't going to confession but I know definitely I was going to hell. Lotte Lehman was my idol. Whenever she was in town, I attended her recitals. Her accompanist, Ernest Balow, was completely devoted to her. They had a delightful rapport. I heard somewhere she had a studio in California. She also had novels published. Her stage presence, her interpretations, were all perfect.

One night when I come back to Professor's, I was so enthralled with her that I couldn't sleep. I wanted to find out where she was staying, throw myself at her feet, and beg her to take me with her as a servant. I could wash her lingerie, be her wardrobe mistress, whatever it would take for me to be with her and have her teach me. When the dawn came, reality hit and I knew it was pure fantasy.

Virginia Dean called me and wanted me to meet her at the Hotel Syracuse for lunch. We had a nice lunch and chat. Then she said that since I was graduated from Oswego High, she wanted to share some events with me. She graduated at 17 from college and immediately began teaching Latin in the high school. Each period was 45 minutes long. Also on the faculty was Minnie Murdoch. Minnie's classes in English preceded Virginia's Latin classes. Minnie would teach overtime; first five minutes, then ten, etc. Virginia asked her to please give her the full 45 minutes she needed to teach her Latin class properly. Murdoch said OK, but didn't keep her promise. Finally, after beseeching her a few more times, Virginia went to the principal who disciplined Minnie. Minnie, a senior teacher, was furious. From then on, she had it in for Virginia.

When I wrote a paper that my favorite teacher was Miss Dean, Mrs. Murdoch used it for revenge. At a faculty meeting she got up and demeaned Virginia, saying how unseemly it was to have faculty consorting with a student. Miss Murdoch announced to the faculty that she was appalled by Virginia's behavior, and she should in some way be censored. Mr. Riley, the principal, refused to consider the suggestion, lauding Virginia Dean as a person and as a teacher. I was completely unaware of this at the time I was in school, but I'm glad she told me the story. Poor Miss Murdoch, poor petty, spiteful, Miss Murdoch…

When Jack and I went window-shopping, I kept leading him to jewelry stores and had him gaze with me at diamond rings. No comment, no interest. Of course, the previous Christmas after midnight Mass on the corner of East Seventh and Utica, in the presence of Virginia Dean, he had presented me with a ring, my birthstone, peridot, in a lovely setting. He then trotted off to get some shuteye for the festivities the following morning. Do you know what I wanted? I wanted to get married. I wanted a place where we could be together and study together and get our degrees and then have a big family. Mama Schumann had four children. I always dreamed of having four children; two boys and two girls; Margaret and Kathleen the girls, Paul and John the boys. Of course, this would not interfere with my fabulous career in opera and touring all over the world like Lotte Lehman, my idol.

Every once in a while, I would vocalize at Professor's, maybe once or twice a week at the most. I was surprised one day when he told me the people in the apartment below complained about my singing; I was mortified. One day as I was coming in the house, I accidentally ran into some of the downstairs tenants. I stopped them and briefly apologized for bothering them. They were puzzled and said they didn't know what I was talking about. Oh, Oh, right then and there, I knew who was being annoyed. I was in a purple fit when I accosted Professor. He just kept backing away from my onslaught. I cried, "You didn't have the guts to tell me how you felt; how could you do this?" It was our first and only spat.

Professor and I went to a concert one night; the symphony played Sibelius' "First Symphony." I was overcome by the first movement and quietly wept at the beauty of it. Afterward, Professor said, "I saw you weep and I know why. You are crying because you wanted to go up and direct and you can't." At intermission we gathered to visit with people, most of whom I didn't know. One woman came up to us. "Aha," Professor said, "Mary, I want to introduce you to so and so." I just smiled and turned away. Afterwards Professor was furious with me for not being friendlier since the woman was the *critic* of music in Syracuse.

I came down with one of my frequent bouts of bronchitis. It didn't seem to clear up. Dr. Levine who took care of me as a child for tonsillitis, diphtheria, etc. had moved to Syracuse. I called for an appointment. I was glad to see him when I entered the office, someone from home. He asked me to change into a smock, which I did, and then he tried to rape me. I was absolutely devastated, disillusioned. It was a terrible thing and I had such trust in the doctor of my childhood.

Jack was always on my mind; he was so perfect and we had so much in common: our faith, our love of music, our physical compatibility. I was wild and he was reserved and that was good. Finally in November of 1936 I was in a student recital. I hadn't performed since high school graduation. One number chosen for me was "*Sebben Crudele*," which I almost hated; "The Piper" by Michael Head and "I Know Where I'm Goin'." That little recital changed my life. Mrs. Hartman really became interested in me. She started calling me her "colleen." I would wear a small bow in my hair. In the middle of one lesson she said, "Promise me, Mary, you will always wear a little bow in your hair." I was learning more about her. She went once a week to New York City to study with a Maude Douglas Tweedy. Her great joy was to rise at dawn on a Saturday and go to market. I stopped in her studio one day and she was about to rehearse for a series of concerts featuring voice and harp. I stayed as quiet as could be while they performed songs, all by Grieg. I was completely enthralled. What a beautiful composer he was, especially his songs. The solo harp and solo voice were a delightful combo. I was like a sponge at my two lessons a week, absorbing all I could.

24

Marriage

One January night Jack stopped by. Fr. Howard, pastor of St. Paul's in Oswego, the church that had a great organ, called and was coming to Syracuse to interview Jack for the position of organist and choir director. The organ at St. Paul's was special: four manuals, built in Detroit by Farrand and Votey. Its history included Wiegard and Courboin, great organists of the past. Just to have this instrument at his disposal was a joy to contemplate.

The interview went well and Jack had to insist on a decent wage. He was to earn $1500 a year. His current salary was $700. "Wow," I said, "Now we can be married and both be worthy of heaven." He was to begin the job Easter break week. We went to Oswego, told our parents who thought we were crazy and wondered, why the rush? We asked Jim, Jack's brother, to marry us at St. Vincent's in Syracuse. The wedding would be Easter Sunday. Jack's sister Margaret would be bridesmaid, my dad the best man.

I was thrilled, of course. I would probably be like Mother and have to wait five years to have a baby; but by then I would be graduated and well on my way to a great career. Let me see; I would travel the country giving recitals; open a studio and teach voice. Of course, I would have a lovely studio like Mrs. Hartman. Maybe Jack and I could give joint recitals. My goodness, Madame Schuman-Heink had a huge family of ten children and it didn't interfere with her career!

Rudolf's Jewelry store was on Salina Street in Syracuse. There was a front entrance and a side entrance. We went to Rudolf's to study wedding rings. A white gold band encrusted with ten diamonds was selected. Then they took Jack into an office to arrange for a lifetime of payments. I waited; and waited, and waited some more. Where the hell was he? Finally a young, skinny man with his curls awry and a look of panic emerged. Thank God he hadn't gone out the side door!

It was embarrassing to me that Jack, since he was only twenty years old, had to get his parent's permission to marry. I at eighteen years of age was at a legal age to marry! Next we had to get permission from the chancellor and dean of women, respectively, to get married. In 1936 there were not many (if any) married students on campus. So far, everyone, reluctantly, gave permission. Finally, Easter Sunday was the date set. Jim would marry us at St. Vincent DePaul's Church. We would have Easter week to ourselves. In the meantime, we were both busy with school.

On Friday when I finished classes early, I headed home to Professor's. It was about 11:30 A.M. when I reached the upstairs apartment. I scaled the steps to the top and beheld a strange sight. Mama was standing in the hall nude. I started to laugh but then I could see she was in deep distress. Professor was pacing up and down, saying, "I'll sue, I'll sue." A great help he was! Mama told me her steam cooker had exploded. Her upper body was burned. I nearly fainted. She was in great pain. I bolted down the steps and ran as fast as I could to a drugstore, about a half-mile away. I yelled at the man in the store, "For God's sake, give me something for burns." He gave me a tube of Unguentine. I raced home with it and covered Mama's chest and breasts. She seemed to be worse! What could I do? The doctor, of course. I called the operator but she said all doctors were at lunch. It was about 12:30. I'll call that bastard, Dr. Levine, I thought, anybody to help. He came immediately; I'll say that much for him. Mama had serious 3rd degree burns and Unguentine was the absolute worst thing for such a serious condition. Oh, God, I had doubled that lovely woman's suffering! I weep now as I write this.

She was in bed for weeks and Gita, her daughter, came home from New York and stayed two weeks with her. She nursed her and helped to keep her spirits up. As Gita sat by her mother's bed, she knitted. The suit in progress was a maroon knit. She taught me to knit and allowed me to do a row, which didn't match any of the rest, but it didn't seem to bother her at all. Every time I saw Dr. Levine was coming, I made myself scarce. It was a horrible experience.

I started to shop for a dress for the wedding. I found a navy blue voile over a taffeta slip, which had two appliqués of silk on the slip; one red and one green. I know this sounds ugly, but it was lovely. In the hat department there was a navy wide brim straw with an appliqué of one red and one green silk flower on the brim. Perfect match. I bought blue shoes. They were expensive at $9.95 and I was made to return them. I was a free spender with my parents' money. It never occurred to me that I should have a job and be helping out and how about Mother stepping to the bat. But at that time women were homemakers and an only daughter was spoiled.

Jack was teaching the choir a Palestrina *Credo*, which was beyond difficult, but we struggled with it. I think only Jack knew how it should sound. It was a priority of Easter Sunday Mass. I don't think it went that well and after ten o'clock Mass when everyone had left, I walked up the aisle resplendent in my Easter/bride outfit. I wore a corsage of red roses that dropped their petals. Jack's sister Margaret processed in front of me. I think I was my own flower girl, with rose petals dropping in front of me.

Daddy and Jack were waiting at the altar as were Jim and the pastor, Fr. Dougherty. A few Latin phrases and Jim, who was officiating at his first wedding, asked me if I would take Jack as my wife. I said, "You mean, 'husband?'" Father Dougherty was also officiating—sort of. He was supposedly helping Jim. I looked at Jack out of the corner of my eye. "Who was this kid?" Good grief: richer, poorer, sickness, health, until DEATH! Poor Jack. I don't know what he felt or if he felt at all.

The bride and the groom.

Suddenly we were MARRIED and all I could think of was, Is this folly? Everyone was happy except Fishy who wept. Jim had made reservations at a nice restaurant. Mrs. C had dental problems and she had trouble eating.

25

The Months That Follow

Jack couldn't wait to get his hands on the organ at St. Paul's. I think more eager than to get his hands on me but that was OK. We returned to school the next week after Easter week. I had my unpaid Rudolf ring on a chain around my neck. We told Professor about our marriage and he was red with fury. He kept saying every time he looked at my new husband, "Poor Chack, Poor Chack." Which really wasn't nice at all.

Now I started to plan what we would do when school ended in late June. Guess what? I got pregnant immediately. I really was surprised. Aha, I'm not like my mother at all! In May I was nauseous and in June when I gave a speech in Speech class the teacher, Mrs. Parsons, was pleased at how reflective and introverted I seemed; reflective, baloney! I was as sick as a dog. At the chorus concert I absented myself at intermission to be sick on the hill behind the Fine Arts Building, bending way over so as not to ruin my gown. I'd walk into Woolworth's and walk out immediately. The smells of popcorn, and caramel corn did me in. The week before our last week I told Mrs. Hartman I was married. She couldn't believe it and she couldn't forgive me for giving up my career for a "mess of pottage" which I believe is a Bible expression.

Jack got out of school before me and he and Mother went apartment hunting. They found a place on West Fourth; four rooms in a house owned by Mr. Lochery. There were three apartments tucked here and there in the white house in the middle of the block. School was over and I rushed for the reeking, smelly bus. As soon as I boarded, I took my wedding ring off the chain and put it on my finger. The apartment was darling, lacking just one thing: the kitchen had no sink! In fact, when you entered the apartment, you entered the kitchen. So I had to do dishes in the bathroom. Beyond the kitchen was a living room with a big sunny window, a pull out couch and chairs. To the left of the kitchen was a nice sized bedroom. Heaven on earth, our first nest for $35 a month, was furnished.

Jack had a six o'clock Mass on weekdays. When he finished, he hastened to his Mother's. In the meantime, when I arose, I hotfooted it down the street, hopped a fence and was in my Mother's kitchen. The aunties gave a surprise kitchen shower. They made quite a racket and the landlord, Mr. Lochery, complained. It was a lot of fun!

One thing I NEVER did was take a nap; but Jack did every day. One day he enticed me to join him; I always found him irresistible. The door was being knocked on loudly during one of our afternoon "naps." It was about 10 of our friends from Syracuse. I was surprised when I opened the door and said, "Oh, we were just having a fiesta." I meant *siesta*. It was a baby shower. It was exciting opening all the lovely gifts. In those days baby dresses came from the Philippines and they were very fine embroidered cottons.

One afternoon I came into the apartment and I had a strange feeling someone had been in it. My imagination, of course. But having this sensation a couple of more times, I was convinced our landlord was snooping around. One evening we retired early and I thought I heard someone in the kitchen. I got out of bed and who was there in the dark but Mr. Lochery. "What's going on?" I asked.

"Oh, there's a leak somewhere and I'm checking it," he replied. He spent about five minutes in the bathroom and he left. However, he knew that I knew what a creep he was.

The fourth of July came and I was going to celebrate. We had a geranium in the sunny window, the day was lonely and the fireworks were being displayed at Otis Field, which wasn't far, and we could walk there. Lo and behold, Jack said he definitely wasn't going and he really didn't care a bit for fireworks. How strange! The year previous was an entirely different scenario. We had celebrated the Fourth by going out to dinner, which in those days was rare; and then, hand in hand, we walked to the fireworks and hand in hand enjoyed the spectacle. Well, I tell you, I was miffed. I pulled out the sofa bed and slept there. I don't think I made my point because the apartment was so small I wasn't that far from him and he seemed not to care at all.

Jack was so happy to play the wonderful organ. The acoustics of the church were perfect. He inherited a fine men's choir and he was starting to teach private piano lessons. Our priority was for him to earn his degree and for me to have our baby.

When we were first married and went to Dr. Mowry, he gave us a book on the ways to celebrate a marriage. I read it and all it seemed to say was to use a lot of pillows, which we did but it didn't seem to enhance the ritual so we eliminated them completely. Of course I could cook not at all and at that time the word "fast food" was not even invented. But I would be a fabulous cook; I just knew I would be the BEST. From 2:00 to 3:00 PM every day a classical music program was aired from the CBC. It emanated from Toronto. The theme was from Handel's "Water Music." We cherished those programs sitting by the window with the single geranium: a happy memory.

Our wedding announcement was in the paper the week after school ended. So we received cards and greetings and congratulations. One note I received was from Professor Snyder, my theory teacher, who said he was impressed that a married woman had been in his class. Mrs. Hartman was livid. I told her I was desperately in love and it would not interfere with my career at all. "Remember," I said, "Schuman Heink was married and even had ten kids. Why couldn't I?" I consoled her and said, "I'd like at least four children." Secretly I thought I could never have as many as my mother-in-law: six! Of course, we would have separate studios and give joint recitals. Our children would be perfect, talented and musical also. Two boys, John and Paul, and two girls, Margaret and Kathleen. "We will raise a family: two boys for you; two girls for me. Oh, cant' you see how happy we will be." "Tea For Two"—just like a movie I saw. At the end, a couple is sitting on a hill overlooking a pastoral scene (Raymond Navarro is sitting close to Dorothy Chapman); he is wearing a cape. Their backs are to us and as the movie ends he takes part of the enormous cape that he is wearing and gently puts it on her shoulder in a loving protective fashion. Fade out. *Finis*: that's the way it will be. So back to reality.

People met me on the street and oohed and aahed about how lucky Jack was to be organist at St. Paul's. I disagreed and said, "*Au contraire*. St. Paul's was lucky to have him." In retrospect, though, I realize it was fortunate for Jack to continue the tradition of St. Paul's having outstanding musicians and then too Jack was only twenty at the time. The acoustics at St. Paul's were superb and the organ very lively with lovely stops. Four manuals: Solo, Swell, Great and Choir each with wonderful stops. Jack loved it and the choir consisted of old timers who had sung under Courboin. I have a picture of my mother in the choir many years ago. Jack also had a boy's choir.

In the meantime, all sorts of changes were happening to my body. I started to have nice breasts, which leaked occasionally. My legs hurt a little and I started to blossom. My doctor was very thorough and meticulous. I felt very secure. One day I was sailing down Main Street and caught sight of my reflection in the mirror. Wow! Impressive! The fall came and Jack was back at school, working hard. I spent a lot of time going to Mother's and we would go for long walks. It was a very special, loving time. When the leaves turned color, the West Park became a magic place. One afternoon early in October Mother and I decided to take in a movie with a new actress who we heard was interesting. I checked her out and her name was Joan Blondell. We were discussing this new breezy actress as we left the theater. Suddenly my legs felt weird. I started to walk with difficulty. When we reached home, Mother was making our usual afternoon chocolate sundaes when my head felt odd.

I went to the bathroom and expelled blood clots. How odd since our baby was not expected until much later. I thought maybe I should call Jack's sister who was a nurse. I called her. She didn't say anything except to be quiet. Thirty minutes later Margaret and Dr. Mowry appeared. Mother was startled because I had not confided to her about my problem. We talked awhile and then the doctor suggested I go to the hospital. I protested: I didn't have any pain except in my legs. Margaret went to the hospital with me. Then a terrible thing happened. Margaret got into her uniform and shaved me. I was totally unprepared for this being done by my sister-in-law: Good grief!

About seven o'clock Jack returned from school. He asked Mother where I was. She said, "Hospital." He started to look behind couches and chairs when he realized this was true. He scurried up to the hospital. The hospital is small (but not to me that day!) Private rooms were $6.00 a day. Signs were all over the place declaring "*Silentio*!"—these signs were meant for the Italians who were famous for loud emoting.

The next day Dr. Mowry stood at the door to my room and said, "You look like a brave sort. We are going to do a Caesarian section because you have *placenta previa*. This is very dangerous for the mother and the child." The first thought that came to mind was Jack Flanigan's vivid description of a C-section when we were dating. Damn him, anyway! Believe me, some times ignorance can be bliss. Jack has an uncle who was a beloved doctor to all. Jack asked Dr. Burden to do the surgery but he was hesitant because of my age of 19. Dr. Mowry wanted Dr. Burns, THE surgeon in town at the time. Finally Dr. Grover was chosen and his nephew Dr. Elder was to be the anesthesiologist. It was discovered that Jack had the same blood type; so they took him off to give blood. Now they shaved my stomach. Is there no modesty left? They gave me a shot and I don't know what was in it but I made many jokes and funny (to me) observations as they wheeled me into the OR. I thought, "Thy will be done…Thy will be done."

In the meantime, Bertha Glynn, a friend of the family, was visiting a patient in the hospital. Bertha related how there was a wave of excitement going through the rooms. Someone poked their head in the room and asked, "Do you want to come see it? They are doing a C-section on Mary O'Brien." Bertha said, "Absolutely not!" Margaret said later that the observation place was crowded. Dr. Elder entered and said, "Sorry, this is not Dr. Burns, just good old Dr. Elder." Dr. Mowry and Dr. Burden were also present. Our first child, Margaret Virginia, was born at 5:00 PM, October 20, 1937.

There was panic because when she was born there was no cry, just awful silence. Burden called for Margaret to get two tubs of water; one warm, one cold, and he took the baby and dunked her alternately. Then the great sound came, a loud, healthy cry. I was so full of anesthesia, it had affected her. When I came to, Jack was alongside of me with a dozen red roses. I smelled them and they immediately drooped and died. It seemed an eternity before they brought in the baby. The corners of her mouth were drooping as if to say, "How stressful and what happened?" I couldn't hold her because they had IV's in both my legs. The hospital stay was two weeks. It seemed an eternity. Jack spent time in the rocker with Margaret because Margaret, my sister-in-law, would sneak her in from the nursery. Mother and Dad visited and Dad was funny, saying, "Friend or enema?" and I begged him not to be funny because my stitches hurt so much. Dr. Mowry said I should nurse and I agreed. I didn't know what a painful fight it was to achieve this goal but things finally went great.

When Margaret and I came home after my two-week stay in the hospital, we were very excited. The baby was dressed in a white organdy puffed sleeve dress and bundled in a white lacy shawl. As we exited the ambulance in the side drive of my parent's home, Margaret gave a long audible sigh, then a long audible groan. We had to laugh. "Oh, dear," Mother said, "I hope she likes us."

Jack had to get a loan to pay the bills and we had to give up the apartment and move to my parents' home at 162 West Third. This really hurt, but what could we do? Later I found out that Mother and Dad were also very unhappy with the set up. I had been reading about motherhood and, let me tell you, I was going to be the best mother in the world. The only thing, books differed; one said to feed on demand; the other book said to feed no more than every four hours. I realized that Margaret and I were unique and between the two of us we would work it out. She put on weight fast and turned into a real cherub. I kept a day-to-day diary about her activities: her burps, her eliminations, her smiles, etc. I never did see Dr. Mowry smile. (He was a moody Methodist and preached often at his church in Minetto, a small village near Oswego).

26

Winter, 1937

The winter of '37 was quite cold. Dr. Mowry suggested it would be healthful for the baby if I put her for an hour outside in her carriage. I piled blankets on her and did as directed. I kept peeking out the window and all that was exposed were her blue eyes and a pink nose. I did this for a few weeks but cancelled her visits outside. Somehow it seemed a horrible idea. She flourished in spite of her family. In the spring Jack and I would take her around town in her carriage. When people stopped us, Jack raised one of her chubby legs and said, "Look at her legs; aren't they amazing?"

Professor had surgery and someone brought me to Syracuse to see him. I was so anxious and upset that as I entered the hospital I had a nervous spell, then a nosebleed. After finally pulling myself together, I approached the hospital room with great trepidation. There was the impossible Professor looking great and in a fury. "Sue…I am going to sue. The schlemiels not only took my appendix but also my gall bladder without my permission." I was so relieved to see him acting 'normal,' I started to laugh uncontrollably which made him madder.

For Christmas that year Mother took me to Flah's for a fur coat. We chose a black lapin. When we got home from Syracuse, I put on the coat to show Daddy and Mother looked up *lapin* in the dictionary. The word *lapin* means a hare or rabbit. A RABBIT! The next day the coat went back to Syracuse. We went and emerged with a nubby wool coat with eastern mink collar and cuffs. No coat has ever equaled it.

I was back at Schumann's for spring break. I wore my new gorgeous coat. Mama Schumann had me model it this way and that way.

"Turn around, turn around…Not right in the back," she declared. "Tomorrow we go to Flahs and have it corrected."

"Oh, no," I protested. "I'll take it back myself…soon."

She shook her head. "Oh, darlink, we go tomorrow."

When we entered the store she exclaimed loudly, "Paul Flah, please. Emergency." Gosh, I didn't know the owner's name was Flah. The store was exclusive and grandiose. We were quickly on an elevator and personally ushered into an office and there behind a huge desk was Paul Flah. He was very small and seemed unworthy of the enormous desk. After enthusiastic greetings Mama Schumann got right down to business. She had me twirl and twirl and then asked, "Paul, darlink, one thing I ask you: is this girl a creeple? In fact, I demand to know is this girl a creeple?" I was mortified. Darlink Paul had to admit I was not a cripple. "Then, alterations, please; of course, no charge." Mr. Flah agreed heartily and ushered us quickly out and into alterations.

One Saturday morning as we were sitting after lunch, Professor said to Mama, "What a pity. What a pity." Mama nodded enthusiastically. "Such food," Professor continued, "especially the cake. I never ate such a wonderful cake—never." Mama's expression darkened. "That cake was a bought cake."

"Oh, no. Such a cake was paradise."

Mama, infuriated by now, said, "We'll soon find out, sunny boy!" She went to the phone in the hall. Professor started tapping his fingers nervously on the table. He now realized he was in hot water and he was enjoying it immensely.

"Rebecca, sweetheart. Such a grand time we had last night. Such a party! One thing, sweetheart, the cake was so great I must, you hear me, I must have the recipe." Pause. "Oh, you bought it!" she screamed. Professor at the table hung his head to his chest.

The Christmas of 1937 and Margaret was two months old and thriving. We exclaimed over every smile and worried over every tear. When New Year's Eve approached and the K of C dance was to be given, I was truly elated; back on the floor again, the room filled with music, the decorations, the trees with lights and all my friends would be there. My husband was standing with his back to a tall ivory colored chest of drawers, which was in the front bedroom. He said absolutely NO. I couldn't believe it. I coaxed, I cajoled, I begged. "NO," was the answer. I raised my arms and beat him once on the chest. At that moment I realized that there would be no more dances. I also realized the Fourth of July and New Year's ushered in a new phase into my life. Shall we call it A.M.? (After Marriage).

We met a couple, the Laningans. Mary, the wife, was a sweet pure naïve girl. Her husband, Harold, sang in the choir. We went to a few movies together (Harold's idea). One movie was "San Francisco" about the earthquake. Great movie. Harold worked for the electric company and when Jack wanted to buy a mixer for his mother, Harold got him one at discount. He demonstrated it to us in the living room. He thought he had unplugged it after the demo, but it wasn't and he nipped two of his fingers badly.

27

Daughter-In-Law

I naturally was going to be the best daughter-in-law and I chose (not Mrs. C) to visit her every Wednesday whether she liked it or not. Mrs. C was a hard worker. She was always cleaning, cooking, ironing and washing clothes as all women in the late thirties did. She still had Teddy, Margaret and Bobby at home. Jim, the priest, would come home weekends exhausted and spend most of his time in bed. The house on East Eighth Street stood at the bottom of a very steep hill. At that time most of the gentry sat on the front porch and so Mr. And Mrs. C did too. The steep hill ended on the main drag, Bridge Street. Because of the location of the house one could view the citizens descend the hill to reach Bridge Street. The parade was very interesting. Mrs. C would comment that so and so looked peaked or that girl is gaining a pound or two or Mrs. So and So had a new expensive hat and her husband couldn't afford it because he drank all his wages. They labeled some of the children who frolicked up and down the street: sassy, bold, snippy, snotty, dumb, smart, etc. "There goes so and so staggering up the hill with a snout full!"

Mrs. C was a great cook. Jack has fine memories of her weekend offerings of cakes and pies, rolls, bread and coffee cakes, and the ultimate...great donuts. Jack's father was short and stocky. He was a plumber. He would come home tired and would immediately approach the kitchen sink and proceed to do a long hand scrubbing with a lye smelling soap. He would remove his shirt, a vision to behold, in long-sleeved, tight fitting flannel underwear that revealed his ample tummy. There was a rocker in the kitchen, which was his exclusively. The old coal stove heated the room; it contained a huge oven, also. The ceiling in the kitchen, the hub of the house, was shiny tin with a lovely pattern.

Fishy and Mrs. C made quite a contrast. She wasn't tall but had the appearance of being tall, especially in contrast to her short husband and average sized sons. Fishy was brash: a party boy and a drinker. She was the exact opposite. She loved to play cards and bingo. She would often, during a card game, tap her fingers with impatience. Their attitude to each other was not very friendly and I thought they didn't like each other. So sad! My parents were always huggy-bear, kissy-face. I didn't know that beneath the barbs they truly loved each other.

When Mrs. C was the young Margaret Hogan, she had very long blonde pigtails. She would play in the East Park with her friends. Along came Fishy Callaghan from the west side of town. He chased the girls away and kept pulling Margaret Hogan's pigtails. The famous pastor of St. Paul's Church, Dean Barry, hired Margaret right out of high school and had her teach the boys who attended the parochial school. My mother remembered her as an almost grim young woman who put up with no nonsense. The pastor would humiliate her by paying with pennies. Can you imagine? PENNIES! This humble salary was handed over immediately to her mother. With her background of handling so many little boys, she was more than capable of rearing boys when she had her own.

When Margaret Hogan decided to get married, the Dean was not pleased. In fact, as she walked the long aisle to the front of the church, she marched without music. She had forgotten to hire an organist. So she was deprived of the musical support of one of the greatest church organists I ever heard! To make matters worse, as she and Fishy stood, hand in hand, nervously waiting to exchange vows, Dean Barry decided to say a few words. "Maggie," he said, "This is your last chance to say NO! And I think you should say NO." The couple couldn't believe what they were hearing. They ignored his suggestion and after a long pause the priest conducted the ceremony.

Their first-born was James; then Margaret, a miscarriage, then Jack, who was born before the doctor arrived and then, surprise, twin boys, Edward and Charles. When Aunt Minnie hustled up to 77 East Eighth to inquire of her sister's condition, Fishy said, "We have twins." She cursed him, pushed him aside and ran up the stairs to discover that it was true: TWINS! It was said that the night before the twins were born, Jack had inexplicably left his own bed and slept along side his older brother Jim. A son, Robert, was born five years later.

The Callaghan family (*circa* 1925): Nana and Fishy are seated with Bobby on their laps, the twins on either side (Chud on the left, Ted on the right). Top row are (left to right) Margaret, Jim and Jack.

Margaret Hogan Callaghan was severe in appearance, probably from having dealt with all those boys in school. She seldom smiled and was hard to please. Corporal punishment was no stranger to her. There was a teacher, Minnie Doran, who traipsed up and down the famous hill, frequently. One day Jack, as a child, hid behind a tree and called out, "Minnie Ha-Ha. Minnie Ha-Ha!" Miss Doran reported the offense immediately to the culprit's mother. She proceeded to inflict pain on Jack and he recalls it even to this day. Jack loved to hear his mother read to the family. "Sleeping Beauty" was his favorite story. Nana enhanced it by narrating the story in episodes. He looked forward each night in great anticipation for the next section of the story. One night Jack decided to play a trick on Teddy. He preceded Teddy to bed, crawled under the bed and waited for Teddy to come. As Teddy sat on the edge of the bed a hand came out and grabbed his leg. Teddy was in terror and one can only imagine the punishment that followed.

When Jack was in 8th grade, he had an enormous crush on Nancy Lynch, a lovely blond, brown eyed girl with impressive developing breasts. He would occasionally leave a candy bar on her desk. The nuns who taught seventh, eighth and ninth grade at St. Paul's were wonderful. Jack loved and appreciated Sister Alexis and Sister Armanda. Mrs. C, like my mother, loved to play the piano. Her big number was "The Black Hawk Waltz." There was a tiny room off the dining room, which had just enough room to embrace an upright piano where Jack spent many hours.

His mother never tired of hearing him play. I can't say that about Jack's wife. He became serious about music as an early teen. He was an altar server and a member of the boy's choir, which was beneficial to him musically. He loved the liturgies and the singing exposed him to good music. All the Callaghan boys served. Fr. Howard was pastor when the family was young. Jack's brother Chuddy was a devout child and served for years. When he was in eighth grade, he appeared suddenly at most funerals. He sat in the front seat opposite the mourners. Fr. Howard observed the strange behavior and became concerned enough to call him in for a talk.

"Charles, what on earth is your problem? Why are you attending all these funerals?"

"Well," Chuddy replied, "Mr. Cullinan, the undertaker, pays me a quarter every time I come. You see, he wants me to sit, stand and kneel at the right times so everyone will follow me."

Fr. Howard turned an ugly red, which was his wont anyway, but this time his shade was more like purple.

"Why, that lazy son of a gun. The gall of him to be standing outside of church on the steps, chewing his tobacco and spitting it on the steps. I want never to see you again at a funeral that Cullinan has."

Thus ended the quarters.

28

Pregnant Again

The spring semester of 1938 I studied with Mrs. Hartman. I got rides to Syracuse with different people. One couple, Jack and Shirley Rosenbaum, had a daughter about 8 years old who was studying harp at the university. They were a young, fun-filled couple who were very, very nice to me. Since I was nursing Margaret, I brought along a breast pump in my music case. After my lesson I would go to the ladies' room and take care of my excess milk. One day I came early and Mrs. Hartman was rehearsing with the head harpist at the university, Betty Love. They were planning to take this recital to various cities in New York. I heard Mrs. Hartman sing four Grieg songs, one called "*Eine Traum.*" It was so painfully beautiful I wept. Mrs. Hartman kept telling me I was her Colleen and I should always wear a bow in my hair. The bow disappeared forever shortly after that.

Jack was getting his degree in June. His teacher was a young, handsome man with unbelievably fierce blue eyes, accented by dark skin. Professor Verees, like so many organists, came from Belgium. He taught cello as well as organ and he was just the ticket after elderly Dr. Parker. Jack had a full plate of work to ready himself for his graduate recital. What a remarkable achievement: to graduate in three years! It was very thrilling. Jack's brother babysat while we went to the recital. When I arrived, I saw Jack and Verees in a strange position. Jack was dressed formally. Behind him, on a stool, stood Verees with his hands over Jack's shoulder hand-tying his black tie. It was very amusing and broke the tension a little. Verees said to me, "I vant you to see that he improvises more. Promise?" I nodded "Yes." He did a beautiful job and we were proud beyond proud. Right after the concert Jack learned he was chosen over all other music students to receive a full scholarship for his Masters. Glory Halleluiah!

That December just before the holidays Margaret took her first steps to cheers from her parents and grandparents. In January of 1939 I became pregnant and that summer we moved to a duplex on East Sixth Street. It would be putting it mildly to say I was overcome with joy. To finally have my own nest! My own space, my own things, my own smells. How absolutely marvelous.

The house was a duplex with bright shiny windows. There was a stone porch with the entrance on the right. As one entered a vestibule, there were two entrances. Our entrance was on the left. I put criss-cross organdy curtains everywhere. The living room had an oriental rug with blue tones; a real leather club chair, a wing chair, which today is covered in its 15th change of material and is sitting in our living room. Taking up most of the room was a huge upright piano with a full pedal board attached to it. I remember the tuner coming often; his name was Mr. Clark. He said he liked to come because he loved my blueberry muffins. The dining room had three large windows side by side. We put a Duncan Fife table and shield-backed chairs in the room. They were mahogany.

Fishy bought us a brand new stove. We bought a kitchen table and chairs. There was a glassed in porch shared by both families. A nice stairway with a landing was off the dining room. Three bedrooms were off the hall and at the end was a bathroom. The back porch was enclosed and a nice yard followed. When no one was around, I danced all over the place. I came up with all sorts of meals. I perfected my ironing and starched Jack's shirts perfectly. I was proud of the ironed shirt that I could do in sixteen minutes. We also bought a bed and dresser. On the bed was the thickest, highest Ostermoor mattress. We paid so much a month on these articles.

When we moved into the duplex, a family by the name of Lasher lived on the other side. They had a little girl about six months older than Margaret. Her name was Mary Louise. We were in my castle a few days when one evening a wonderful aroma wafted its way into our side of the house. It was the smell of popped corn. The very next morning Jack hustled to the store two blocks away and the next evening both houses were popcorn scented.

After a few months the Lashers moved out and in came a family by the name of Foote; Ken Foote worked at the paper mills: his wife Sarah and year-old son Dudley made up the family. Mrs. Kinney, who was tiny, bleach-haired and elderly, lived directly next door. Her driveway separated the houses. It seemed that Mrs. Kinney was always calling (which she wasn't) and talking about her arthritis. I admit I cut her off and was not patient or even Christian. I think of her at times and since I have arthritis myself I feel, alas, too late, that now I have a great compassion for her. All she needed was someone to talk to, someone to listen for just a few minutes.

I started to find Sarah very interesting. She was a few years older than I was. Her maiden name was Folsom. Her father taught law and coached football at the

University of Colorado. They later named a stadium after him, Folsom Stadium. After graduating from U of C, Sarah went to the Merrill Palmer School in Detroit where she studied courses on early childhood. When she came to Oswego to supervise the pre-schools set up in different colleges in the surrounding parts of New York State, she met and married Ken and they had Dudley.

Now wouldn't you think with her background in early childcare, she would have a perfect child? *Au contraire.* Dudley was a monster. He cried, he kicked, he pouted. He was a real pain in the neck. When Margaret played with Dudley and there was a tiff, I let Sarah handle the problem. I learned many things from Sarah. I loved being with her. She had the best ideas and was expert at many things. I liked living so close to her. She enhanced my life in many ways. Ken was handsome, easy-going, affable and tolerant, so tolerant that, when the toilet overflowed and the water leaked through the ceiling into his kitchen, he poked a hole in the ceiling and placed a bucket under it. What a guy! Sarah had hand-made pottery, madras cloth and artifacts which I enjoyed seeing her use.

Our second child was due in September. I had a great hunger for Clark bars and I ate many. For this baby I went full term and when I weighed in that early September, I was 180 lbs., a gain of 50 pounds. Sarah and I would go for walks in the evening and we became closer as each day passed. "Margaret, Margaret, step up on the stool, dear, and see your baby brother," declared my sister-in-law who was in her nurse's uniform. I had only a half hour earlier come out of the ether and threw up in front of Jack's relatives. Then I held this 9 pound, 12 ounce boy with a bruised eye. He looked male, tough, and he was mine. Jack and I were more than impressed with our son. Margaret on the stool that had been placed besides the bed smiled at her brother. She smiled because she knew she was supposed to smile at her brother, John Foster Callaghan, Jr.

Dr. Mowry, bless his heart, let me deliver naturally defying the saying: "Once a caesarian, always a caesarian." I kept asking the Doctor when I was in labor to hold my hand. He did but after awhile he told me if I wanted the baby he had other things to do. I remember hearing an ungodly scream and thinking, "My Lord, that's me!" Dr. Mowry suggested Jack attend the birth—unheard of in those days. So, standing in a white coat, he witnessed John's birth. John nursed for three months. When he was ill at three months, the doctor felt the top of his head and exclaimed on the fact that the opening on the top of John's scalp was completely closed. The doctor also said you have a very poor crutch to lean on. I said, "This cigarette is my friend, but I can drop my friend anytime I want." I exhaled a puff of smoke as if to say "So there." How foolish I was.

Margaret was having tummy aches and when I took her to the doctor's he said, after a thorough exam, "These aches of Margaret's are Johnny aches." She was jealous. Johnny was all boy and full of pranks, laughable tricks which amused Jack and me no end; but apparently not Margaret.

All at once I was pregnant again. Every morning, the first thing I did was call Mother. I could call my mother-in-law just at certain times because she could become irritable if I called her in the midst of her soap operas on the radio. "Amanda of Honeymoon Hills" was a favorite. Sometimes when I called Mrs. C, she would say, "I'm pushing myself around." This statement mystified me. Now, years later, I know exactly what she meant.

My meals were turning out in an acceptable manner. On most afternoons I would dress my two darlings and take them walking. Mother took either child one day a week. She loved to bubble bathe John and put sissy blue shirts on him and see the frown on his face from all the attention he was receiving. She confided to me that it was easier to baby-sit her grandchildren when they had a slight fever, not real high, but up a notch or two. It made watching them easier.

I am ashamed to tell this, but I did have diaper service. No disposable diapers were available at that time. My father would come over in his lumber truck, pick up the stinkers and then return them sweet, fresh and IRONED! Sarah said she thought it was really excessive. Some days Jack would practice hour after hour after hour. Although I knew it was the most important thing, my nerves became shattered.

Fran was teaching speech and drama at Kingsford Park Elementary School. After school she would pop over and regale me with stories of the events at school and her adventures of teaching. After dinner we would put the little ones to bed and Sarah would come over and we'd visit until Jack returned from school or from one of his evening Church services. Some theater buffs started a club called "The Players." Jack and I were the first to join. The original group met at the YMCA. I had never entered the place because it was taboo to Catholics. On entering the building we met many nice, pleasant people. And as a Catholic I wasn't supposed to go? How strange! Gladys Steinberg, the drama teacher from Oswego High School; Jesse Wood, English teacher; Leslie Davis, a real devotee of the theater; Doris Sharer, actress; Robert Schuler, actor; Larry Clancy and a few others made up the nucleus.

Fran Brown was the brains and the pioneer behind the project. Right away we chose a play, put it into production, and showed it in the auditorium at the high school. Jesse Wood starred in the first production and it was a great success. "Outward," with Jack as leading man; "The Man Who Came to Dinner" with cousin Ellen O'Brien doing a fabulous job; "You Can't Take It With You" with me in a minute role; "Little Women" with Ellen as Jo was a great success. We were involved in many ways with props, scenery, prompting, etc. I prompted one man who came close to the wings to get his cues and received a big spray of spit in return. You never know what hazards accompany the most menial of tasks. It was fun and I looked forward to going to the meetings. It was even better when Ken and Sarah joined.

When I was on the play committee, I was suggesting "Death Takes a Holiday." I was told it would never be a choice. I thought it was a fascinating play at the time. It was great fun to put on skits for the orphans. I dressed as a doll and with wooden doll movements sang "You Better Watch Out." We had the kids write us letters and tell us what they wanted for Christmas.

Jack and Fran Brown at the time of the "Players" phase around 1941.

In January Doris Shores called me to try out for a play she was doing, "Glamour in the Pocono's." Three teachers take a vacation in the Pocono's, only one gets a man—ME! The rehearsals were enjoyable and a distraction from baby detail. March 15 was the date set for the showing. There were a few delays. Every time there was a delay, I became nervous because I was pregnant with Paul who was due in October. It was produced in May and the ingénue wore the tightest girdle she could find. Jack was busy practicing, studying, teaching the choir, etc.

He started a music club. The meetings were monthly at the Catholic Daughters rooms on West First Street. The recitals were excellent. We had a good turnout and the local artists had a chance to show their talents.

While I was in labor with Paul, I looked at Jack who was placidly reading his prayer book. I thought if I lived through this experience—I probably would not—I would either leave him or kill him. Paul was a lovely baby and Mrs. C couldn't say as she did about John that he looked like a little rat, so that was good. Poor Paul though had colic. There just was no consoling him. Josie Riley, a real Irish looking, witty woman, stayed with me when I came home from the hospital. In those days a woman remained in bed in the hospital for ten days after delivering a baby.

Having Josie with me was great but she left after three days because she couldn't take the crying. She was a wonderful help and even a better storyteller. When I had visitors, she sat right in on the conversations and brutally criticized all who visited.

As usual, I was gung-ho for Christmas. I posted gold stars on all the mirrors and doors. I made gingerbread men that didn't look right. I resigned myself to a limited budget. Sarah and Ken had a baby girl, Anna, and we were overjoyed at their happiness. The baby was eight pounds and a dear. She was only home a week when she got sick, then sicker, then hospitalized. The diagnosis was spinal meningitis. Sarah drove back and forth to nurse her. A few days before the holiday, the baby died. Our hearts were broken. The Christmas stars on the doors seemed a mockery. We truly mourned.

29
After Oswego

Jack was having fun learning the instruments of the orchestra. Some of the clarinet notes he played set him laughing. The toot of the trumpet and the squeak of the strings were challenging but he had a goal in mind: to become accredited to teach music in the schools. With the music certificate in his hands, Jack asked the superintendent of schools if he could teach music in the schools in Oswego. The superintendent, Mr. Riley, was dismayed over the idea. "People will talk," he said. "Having two jobs is not a good idea." Right then and there Jack asked Leslie Davis to help him send resumes out to different churches. We were leaving Oswego. Incidentally, six months after we left Oswego, one of the church organists took a position teaching music at one of the schools.

At this time Jack traveled by bus to Mexico, NY to teach piano. He went every Wednesday. He liked the town, the students. What he really liked best was a raisin pie he ordered at a local restaurant. Life was busy. Our three children were work, but a joy. My nerves were not that good and at times it seemed as if a piece of chalk was constantly being scratched on a chalkboard. When we lived on East Sixth we spent time with both the Callaghans and O'Briens. It really annoyed me when I visited Jack's family. Fishy constantly offered Margaret beer to drink from his glass. My, how cute and funny he thought it was! I was seriously concerned that she might like it and become addicted. Mother O'Brien took on each child one at a time each week. Johnny was very active. Paul was less of a challenge and very serious. Margaret, of course, was everyone's joy.

Jack earned his master's degree in 1939. That summer he gave a recital at St. Paul's in Oswego. He included in the selections a number his piano teacher wrote for the organ. Dr. Berwald came up to Oswego for the event. He stayed with us for lunch. It was an honor to have this elderly, elegant man in our home. Around the same time, St. Paul's had a fashion show and the committee asked me to sing. One of the numbers requested was, "Welcome, Sweet Springtime" which was an old chestnut even then. When I started to sing, the microphone went awry, making an intermittent but loud raspberry hiss. "Welcome, Sweet Springtime," shriek, hiss…"Sweet Springtime, we greet thee"…shriek, hiss. I was furious and insulted. At the end I walked off in a huff. The pastor, Fr. Howard, approached me with tears in his eyes, tears of laughter. "Mary," he said, "What is your problem? Where is your sense of humor?" I just glared and departed. It took me a few months of reflection to realize it *was* funny.

Fr. LaBelle, one of the assistants at St. Paul's, was transferred to another parish. He was a fragile, serious, talented man. I sang at his farewell reception "My Heart at Thy Sweet Voice" from *Samson and Delilah*. In the text Delilah tries to seduce Samson. The music is sultry and passionate. I was just learning this aria and most anxious to perform it. "All my soul for thee is yearning. Samson, Samson, I love thee." Fr. LaBelle looked amazed when I finished and not until that moment did I realize how inappropriate the selection had been. He was a good sport about it.

I went once a week for a lesson. Jack and Shirley Rosenbaum had a daughter taking lessons and they kindly drove me as well. I was working on a selection called "When I Have Sung My Songs." I tried it out on them and when I came to the lyrics where I sing, "I will sing no more," Jack would joke, "Thank God." They asked me to give a recital at the synagogue which was a nice experience for me.

On one of these trips, I had lunch with Mrs. Hartmann. She was very dear to me and I cherished her as an artist and teacher. But then Dean Butler summoned me to his office. He was a big man. I liked him very much and at exam time I directed the song's message directly to him. He told me my voice wasn't progressing as it should. I was straining and trying too hard. This was true enough. Then he said it was time for Jack and I to decide who would have the career. We must talk it over soon because only one of us could be successful, not both. At first I was determined that no one was going to stop me, but in my heart of hearts I knew this was not true.

I was on a committee for the Players spring dinner. Marian Corrigan, who was still going to Syracuse and majoring in art, was in charge of the decorations. I was in charge of the program. The 369th black regiment was stationed at Fort Ontario. I thought it would be keen, since most of the men were from New York City, if one of them would talk about the blacks' contributions to the theater in 1939. The man who answered the phone when I called and made the request referred me to the chaplain who said he would be delighted to speak. "Porgy and Bess" was new on Broadway. Cab Calloway was 'Sportin' Life" and I was right. The chaplain gave a great talk. About forty people were at the dinner. I had kept our speaker a secret. They were surprised and I was secretly thrilled to give a little jolt in Lily White Oswego. The food was great but the best part of all was Marion Corrigan's decorations. She had exquisite hand painted eggs and placed one at each setting. Absolutely beautiful. Wonderful parties, wonderful memories.

The summer before Anna Foote was born was full of anticipation for Sarah and Ken. Twice they took me, Jack, Margaret, John and Paul on a picnic by our dear old lake. It was like two kisses from God. I was really surprised when I discovered I was pregnant again. Hey, Lord, I do want a big family, at least four, but so soon? Sarah came to my rescue. She suggested I send (no charge) Margaret and John to nursery school. Margaret was smart and sweet. John was super active and was hard on me especially when I had no knowledge of how to take care of children. I did know how to wash them, feed them, hug them, but how to discipline them was beyond me. I had never been around children even to observe them.

Paul was less adventurous than John. He was steady, serious from the start, and he did recover from the colic but it took four months to settle his tummy. The bus came daily. A lovely young woman who lived across the street was a teacher at the school. Sarah was the supervisor of the nursery school at Oswego State. John took his "bot" (bottle) and traveled in the luggage rack. Margaret sat, of course, in the bus seat. Miss H reported that they gave Johnny tepid baths to soothe and calm him. The baths had absolutely no effect on him. The teacher was surprised; I wasn't. When they came home at 3:00 PM, I scooped them into a buggy and while Jack practiced I would trudge up one hill and down another. One day I met Fran. She asked me if I knew Margaret had on no underwear and that John's shoes were on the wrong feet and that Paul's sweater was inside out. All I could tell her was that *I* was OUT!

Holidays were super. We'd walk to Jack's house, then to our house, then to Grandpa O'Brien's. We would have these great turkey dinners and ate everything. When we were at the University, Jack was always complaining about being hungry, being starved, etc. He was so thin at that time he couldn't have weighed much more than 100 pounds. There was a restaurant on campus that served $1.00 fish dinners. Jack was filled up rapidly but it took more for me to be sated. Here I was 23 years old and waiting for a gift. One evening I received a call; it was my old pal, friend, and lover, Chuck Walsh. He was in town and he wanted to visit and could he come visit tomorrow at 9 AM? Great, I said. The thought of seeing him again thrilled me, but Oh, Oh, how must I look? I ran to the mirror. Not bad, not bad. I turned sideways and there was a revelation. No denying the magnificent bump or bulge was obvious. The next morning Jack went early to play the three of four Masses he did every day. I put on a black dress, not too slimming, but a little help. I was very happy to see him when I answered the door. He looked his same old self.

He was totally impressed with my chicks. We started to try to get back to the way we were when Margaret slammed the door on her hand. I know how painful that is and treated it. As we were consoling Margaret, Johnny tumbled down the stairs and got an egg on his head which we treated with ice. As we had an iced cloth on Johnny's head, Paul cut himself on a sharp tin top to a can of soup. We washed and put a bandage on it. Suddenly C.W. said, "Mary, I can't stand this. I really can't. This place is a menagerie," and he went to the door and left. He didn't even say goodbye. I thought we were buddies forever! This action all took place in about 30 minutes. Jack came home around 10:30 AM. When he came in, we were all crying. "Where's Chuck? Didn't he come?"

On my many walks I visited with a few people; one of them was Grace Riddle. She lived in the rectory at St. Paul's. She was from Detroit, the only person I knew from Detroit. She was Fr. Howard's cousin. She would invite me to cocktails. I would bring Margaret. There were 3 priests, Grace, Margaret and I. Margaret went to each Manhattan and retrieved a cherry from the glass. Grace had a black skinned doll. One day she let Margaret play with it. After studying the doll for a time, she went to the bathroom, took a washcloth, and began to wash the doll. It shouldn't have been but it was hilarious to watch.

The Catholic Daughters had a Mother's Day luncheon and asked me to sing. I sang "O Holy Night" at Christmas, I sang a program at the synagogue; I sang a passionate aria at a farewell party for a priest. I wondered now what would be appropriate? The spring fashion show that I sang at didn't please me at all. For the Mother's Day event at the hotel I brought Margaret. They had a high chair for her. One of the numbers I sang was "Songs My Mother Taught Me" by Dvorzak. It's a sweet, lovely work. The next song was memorable because Margaret moaned and groaned bringing gales of laughter from the audience.

Concetta Castogiavanni was the lovely young organist at St. Joseph's Church. St. Joseph's always had the best Holy Thursday display and the best Nativity set which included all of Bethlehem. Well, Concetta had an emergency appendectomy and I was called to sub for two months. On the staff was a little priest right from Italy. He loved the movies with a passion and was seen first in line at each change of film. Fr. Joe smiled all the time and when you asked him how he was, he said, "High press of the blood." The diocese directory came out one year listing Fr. Joe as deceased. Copies were hidden everywhere so he wouldn't see the error.

The girl's choir that came under my guidance for a while had about thirty members ages twelve to eighteen. They were very attentive and well coached by Concetta. The rehearsals were most interesting. They performed at the 10 O'clock Mass. One Sunday Fr. Joe was the celebrant. The sermon was in Italian and of course in those days before Vatican II, all else was in Latin. I was intrigued with the homily. Fr. Joe stomped up and down. He waved wildly with his left hand and then with his right. He pounded the podium with his fist. Then he did a complete turn to the right and a turn to the left, ending with both arms in the air and a fierce glare on his face.

How impressive, what a performer! I stopped one of the girls when Mass had ended.

"What was Father's sermon about?" I queried.

"Well," she said, "he said if you are good you will go to heaven and if you are bad you will go to hell." I have heard many sermons but Fr. Joe's remains one of the most memorable.

I sang quite a bit when we were on East Sixth Street, vocalizing and studying with my music taped to the cupboard. My very favorite pastime was playing Charades. Fran Brown would have parties and we'd divide into two teams. We took every time span to play. Sometimes there were six of us, sometimes sixteen.

30

Another Baby

On February 1, James Patrick Callaghan literally bounced into this world. He was very fair in coloring, 8 1/2 pounds and feisty. It was a pretty snowy Sunday and everything had a Currier and Ives look to it. We arrived at the hospital around four o'clock. At six the doctor said he would be doing his prayers in the front office. Margaret, my sister-in-law, went home for supper with Jack. All of a sudden Miss Dunning the nurse came in the room. She looked at me and I was in such pain I couldn't cry out but, great nurse that she was, she got the doctor; the only delivery room was occupied so James Patrick bounced into the world on the hospital bed; great delivery. Fran came and tried to roll up the back of the bed. In those days there was a crank handle at the foot of the bed. She accidentally banged her shins. It really hurt her. Later when we spoke of Jim's birth, we recalled the big bruise she carried on her leg for a long time. Margaret was the best nurse; when she cared for me, she was very thorough. She scrubbed me until I shone. She made up an impeccable bed. After the big tussle I came out a finished, glowing woman.

Let's face it. I knew nothing about cooking. In our little apartment on West Fourth Street my meals consisted mostly of lettuce/tomato sandwiches and iced tea. No cake mixes then, no frozen foods. Everything was prepared from scratch and I would scratch my head and hustle home. Now that I was in my new home, I began to read recipes. I did a credible job of scalloped potatoes. My cakes were lopsided. Mrs. C didn't bake from recipes. She put in a little of this and a little of that. Mrs. C helped me make my first cake for my mother's September birthday. It was memorable. The temperature was 93, without a breeze anywhere. She had me beat egg whites over boiling water in order to make a seven-minute frosting. I don't know what happened but nothing worked until a fifteen-minute beating. My hair was wet, my arms ached, and my breathing turned into gasps. Of course, I found out a year later that a simple confection as frosting would have sufficed. She really got me on that one.

Now it was time to conquer pies. I chose a lemon meringue pie. Don't ask me why. The crust wouldn't roll out so I called Mother who tried to take me through the steps. Well, the crust was made, now the filling. It turned out soupy looking but the recipe said it would thicken slowly (like never). Now the meringue and the egg whites refused to fluff up—what a disaster! What perverse part of me chose lemon meringue pie? When Jack came home, I pointed to the pie and went to bed and didn't get up until the next day. I shed a few tears of frustration that night.

We had the prettiest dining room with a large bay window. It was a bright sunny window. We ate by candle light every night. One Friday the puzzled paperboy, who came to collect, mused that we seemed to have a birthday party every night. I loved to iron and sway back and forth to live music on the radio. I loved looking at the beautiful ironed shirts hanging in a row in the closet. Happy wife, happy housekeeper, delighted mother. A few years later one of the shirts was less than lovely. Jack threw the thing down and kicked it. Something snapped in me and my enthusiasm for preparing my husband's shirts disappeared forever.

Dr. Mowry stopped by one day when Johnny was sick. Yes, my friends, doctors made house calls then. I had just finished an awesome-to-behold cake. Two layers, cut sideways to make a torte, lay on the counter thickly frosted. Dr. Mowry was really impressed when he saw it. He lifted it from the counter and cried out in amazement at its heft.

One fall morning I was thoroughly enjoying being a housewife and mother. I probably felt so well because my husband had been paying better attention to me. Charles Courboin, the great organist with whom my mother had studied, was in town to give an organ recital at his first assignment in America, St. Paul's. I was working with a dust mop, seriously searching for dust balls. My ear was listening for Johnny to cry from his crib and wondering how Jack was getting along with his meeting with Courboin. The phone rang and it was Jack. Courboin wanted to take Jack and his wife to lunch. I was to be ready in thirty minutes. After getting a babysitter, bathing, dressing and donning a tall black hat, which would look ridiculous today, I was ready. You know the type of hat: the type Roz Russell wore in the movie with Cary Grant.

At lunch Courboin ordered cocktails and I said no that I was nursing. "Oh," he replied, "your little baby will take a lovely nap when you go home." He ordered steaks for us with a lot of butter. I told him about Mother studying with him. He said he recalled but I don't think he did. He told the story about the young Irishman who came to New York City. A man befriended him and took him to a posh restaurant. During the meal some beautiful women came and went.

The man said to Paddy, "Do they have prostitutes in Ireland?"

"Oh, yes," Paddy said, "but we call them Protestants." We thought it was hilarious.

The concert that evening was superb. It was such a lovely organ. It had lively tone and beautiful stops. He played with great ease and expression, all from memory. Marcel Dupre, another famous organist, also gave a recital at St. Paul's. Dupre played some of his compositions but nothing, nothing could compare to Courboin. He had one son Robert who spent a summer in Oswego and he attended Oswego High School just for a lark. Neil Toomey and he became close friends and, when Neil moved to New York City, he spent weekends with the Courboins.

Things seemed to be going rather well, no teeth were being cut, no flu, no tiffs; almost serene. Maybe it would be a good time to invite Virginia Dean, our friend, to dinner. When she arrived, she seemed to be suspicious of my cooking. One afternoon when I was in high school, she invited me to make brownies with her. She was convinced that anyone who thoroughly followed directions would end up successful. We double-checked every measurement: eggs, flour, etc. and ended up with our brownie batter. We baked it as directed. They were horrible and my critique is mild! I told her steaks were on the menu. She went on at great length that her steak must be rare and in her clear, teacher's voice she admonished me that medium would not do and well done was not acceptable. In her high pitched voice she declared, "Rare, Mary. Remember rare." This rattled me no end so when it came time to cook the steaks I stuck them in the broiler, counted to sixty and withdrew them. She did eat her meat around the edges. I don't remember the rest of the meal. She did bring me a pair of hose, not silk, but a new fiber called nylon. They would last longer and not run as silk does. My nerves were not that good and I never invited her to dinner again. I think if I had she would not have come.

My sister-in-law, Margaret, was due to have an appendectomy. She stopped by to visit on her way to the hospital. The surgery was scheduled for the next day. I fried hamburgers. My, they looked good and seemed to cook up quickly and appeared a lovely color. I served them but on cutting them Margaret discovered they were red inside. She handed it back to me. Gosh, I couldn't win. She said if she had known about my cooking she wouldn't have stopped by on the night before surgery.

One day Margaret and I went shopping or rather window-shopping in the little department stores in Oswego. I spied a pearl necklace. I had never had one and the fact that it was $1.98, I bought it. When we came in the house, Jack had just finished practicing. I couldn't wait to show him the pearls. I was really surprised when he became furious. I pulled down on the necklace and the pearls spilled all over, rolling here and there and everywhere. Poor guy. He was trying to make ends meet I guess and didn't realize my folly. Dinner that night was silent.

Fran Brown came many times after school and she was hungry. I can honestly say she loved my sweet potato apple casserole and she liked my pineapple tapioca pudding topped with meringue so much she claimed it was better than her mother's. Now that is the highest praise I ever received because Mrs. Brown was the best cook ever.

At Christmas when the dear ones were tucked away, I would work on Christmas cookies and Gingerbread men, the kind you roll out. One night the dough was ornery and not responding properly. Around midnight I called Mrs. Brown. She was not too happy with the timing but she was very nice, listened to my problem, and solved it. The process was so exhausting that I rolled cookies on the back burner of my mind. Fran and I always had Pfefernouse cookies, ribbon candy, and French creams on our Christmas list. Fran and I always put up mistletoe until thirty years ago because no one ever caught us and covered us with kisses. Only in our dreams; only in our dreams.

I was in Syracuse one day and took the old streetcar up Genesee to the apartment. The sight of the big gray house with the huge porch evoked many memories. Someone answered the bell and told me the Schumanns lived directly across the street. The house was a twin to the other but painted in white. When I went upstairs I could hear someone playing the piano. Mama Schumann looked a little frail. She called Professor, he invited me in, and we embraced. He turned to me with tears in his eyes and sighed, "You are a woman. You are a woman" and turned his back on me and I was dismissed.

A few months later we heard the tragic news that Gita (Henrietta) had died at age twenty-four of an aneurysm leaving a husband, an 18 month-old baby, and a brilliant career. I can't imagine how devastated Professor and Mama were at losing their jewel. I don't know whom Henrietta married but Mrs. Schumann told me they had a home in Connecticut; with not a few trees, but excuse me, a forest. I know the men loved her but she was very fussy. I remember she played every week on the radio. The sponsor was Ex Lax.

PART II
DETROIT

31

New Job, New City

Jack got a letter (one of only a few) in response to his quest for a new job. He heard from a Fr. William O'Rourke who had written to St. Meinrods Abbey for a music director of Gregorian chant. The Abbey somehow knew of Jack and recommended him. Fr. O'Rourke was the pastor at St. Bernard's in Detroit. He wanted to interview Jack and would meet him half way between Oswego and Detroit in Buffalo, New York.

Jack took the train to Buffalo and met Fr. O'Rourke and Fr. Kirby, a friend of O'Rourke's. They met at the cathedral, visited briefly, and Jack played the "D Minor Fugue" by Bach. O'Rourke said it was over his head and could Jack play something less complicated. So Jack played Bach's "Jesu, Joy of Man's Desiring." This pleased O'Rourke greatly. He had Jack sing and then told him he wanted someone to train the school children and a choral group of young men, a *schola cantorum* to sing Gregorian Chant. They discussed salary and Jack wanted to know if he should have a contract. O'Rourke said if a man is good to his word no contract was necessary. Father warned Jack that housing was hard to find because of the war. He said Jack could live at the rectory until he found a place.

On the preceding December 7, we were relaxing around. It was a quiet Sunday. We had been to my parent's house for a ritual dinner of roast beef, mashed potatoes, and magnificent dishes of ice cream. All at once Ken Foote came and banged on the door. The Japs had bombed Pearl Harbor. We were shocked; everyone was. It was a "day of infamy" for sure: trouble in Europe and now in the Pacific. We were full of fears.

Now it was July and we were going to leave Oswego and go to Detroit where we would have access to the symphony and art galleries and concerts galore. Jack would eventually work himself up the scale and play and teach at the cathedral. He started August 1st, 1942. The plan was that he would take a leave of absence from St. Paul's and, if the Detroit job didn't work out, he could come back to St. Paul's. Since it was summer and the choir was on vacation, Jack recruited me to play the daily and Sunday Masses. I got a babysitter and played and sang the Masses. The organ was a beautiful instrument. Most of the Masses were Requiems and I did love singing the "*Dies Irae.*" This was before congregational singing.

Just before we left Oswego: Dad, Mother and I with the boys (left to right), John, Jim and Paul

The pastor at the time was a very disliked and dislikable priest by the name of Sinnott. He had a miserable, snippy dog. The former pastor, Fr. Howard, had been a dignified and a true Shepard of his flock. This fellow was an uncouth oaf. I met him only when I went for my check. It was on the third month of my stint when he called me in after one of the Masses. I went back to the huge sparse sacristy.

"Now, Mrs. Callaghan, when you asked me for your husband's salary, I thought it was a good idea. But now I've changed my mind." I couldn't believe what I was hearing. "Ask for my husband's salary"—that was a good one. I couldn't believe he would look me straight in the eye and lie like that.

I said, "You know you are lying. I never asked and never discussed finances with you. As of this moment I am finished." For a final flourish I sang an elaborate "*Ite, Missa Est*" and left. I never returned. I walked home in a fury and told Sarah and Ken. Ken wanted to confront Sinnott and have a showdown, but I begged him to let it go. Life was too short. But it made me feel good that Ken was willing to stand up for and defend me.

The store around the corner was unfriendly when I was a week late in paying for our food. I sure didn't like handling finances. The letters from Jack were frequent. Fr. O'Rourke's housekeeper was Rose LaRose. She was from Canada and she had a French accent. She didn't pronounce the letter "h." She had a little suite at the back of the kitchen and after dinner many games of pinochle took place on the table in her living room. Jack was taught the game the first week.

His choirs were shaping up. The school children attended daily Mass and sang daily. The organ was a poor one but at least it was a pipe organ. They were repairing it and placing the console behind a lovely screen off the altar. Jack took the streetcar daily to look at houses. There were few to rent but those said, NO CHILDREN. November came along and finally Fr. Kirby told Jack about a farmhouse that belonged to his family on Kirby Road in Grosse Pointe. The people who rented it were leaving and Father was going to have the rooms painted, etc.

I was excited and thrilled. We took the train with my brave little mother in tow. We had a compartment. We bid adieu to Fran, Sarah, Ken and Dudley who was still a challenge. His mother who had degrees in child psychology admitted when the umbilical cord was involved, it changed things, especially the mother's attitude. Jim wore a fuzzy light blue hat and legging set and I must admit he looked adorable and would sleep all nine hours it took. John and Paul were so used to being active they had a hard time in the confines of the compartment. Margaret was enthralled with the train and the trip.

The train station in Detroit was vast and beautiful. I was ecstatic to see my husband who picked up John right away and John asked me, "Is this the daddy?" Mr. Racitte, the church janitor, drove the car to greet us and proceeded to take us to the house. The enamel paint was just drying as we entered. The house had a huge kitchen, ample dining room, and a bedroom off the dining room, rickety unfinished stairs, and two pathetic bedrooms upstairs. It was half finished with bare floors.

The movers were coming in a few days. The head mover as he was counting our few belongings in Oswego told me someone had shot Fr. Sinnott's dog and everyone said it was Mrs. Callaghan and what did I think? I replied, "I wish I had." The truck he brought our things in could not hold Jack's one hundred books of music, so he had to make a special trip with the books alone.

Our eyes teared up for hours the first two days from the paint fumes. Mother completely lost her voice and could only gesture hopelessly. We went for a little shopping and Mother whispered, "Don't leave me alone. Please. Please." I assured her we would be gone for an hour and after that hour we found her nervously standing at the door watching for us.

The first Mass was at 6:00 AM, which meant Jack had to rise at 4:30 AM, walking a mile to take a bus and then transferring to a streetcar and finally arriving at St. Bernard's. Grosse Pointe is a lovely area on the shores of Lake St. Clair. Most of the homes around this dilapidated farmhouse were mansions. I felt like a hillbilly. In fact, some Southern people lived to the right of us and to the left of the house were two acres of land. We were two blocks from the lake. Jack would leave at 4:30 and return at 6:30 PM. He bought all the groceries and carried them home, arms full. One spring it rained unceasingly. Jack would arrive soaked from his one-mile walk from the bus. Some of the canned goods had fallen through the wet paper bags. (No plastic then). They rolled down the street with Jack in pursuit.

Margaret went to kindergarten. It was a short trip for her. She went mornings and came home for lunch and regaled me with stories of her adventures at school. John and Paul were as good as two little boys could be. Jimmy was spending some time in the playpen until one day he scaled over it and that was that. He was so quick and unpredictable that I had to be aware of his activities at all times. I didn't realize how horribly lonesome I would be. Long distant calls were not on the agenda.

Fr. O'Rourke greeted me at my first visit to the rectory with, "I thought by your picture you had cheekbones, but you don't." A couple of times, as is my wont, I tried to inject an opinion or two but I was immediately cut off. I realized that you listened to O'Rourke orate and in no way would you have a two-way conversation. Rose, the housekeeper, was very witty, very French. She would tell a joke that was rather funny then say, "You know, Madame Callaghan, in French the joke is much funnier."

They tried to teach me Pinochle but it took a while. In fact, Fr. O'Rourke was almost convinced that I would never learn the game. The parish that we lived in was St. Paul's in Grosse Pointe. It was an old brick edifice, but it faced Lake St. Clair and this gave it a touch of beauty. Most of the residents were wealthy. Fr. O'Rourke had a friend, a young woman, whose name was Madge Blaney. She had a large family. She was a typical lively Irish lass. She called her husband, who was a tall, soft-spoken man, "Lover"! He didn't seem like he would be a lover; but they did have six children. Madge was forever reminding Lover that he was ten years older than she was. She brought fun and sunshine into my life. She was very nice to us.

Jack met an organist by the name of August Conen. He was the organist at the Cathedral where Jack should have been. August had a reputation and he was an older man. After all Jack was only twenty-four years old when the job became available. August was married to his second wife; the first one had died. Her name was Fran and August was twelve years older and he had three grown children. Fran and I talked on the phone for hours and we loved discussing the same things. They had a son, James, then a daughter, Jane. Fran taught kindergarten in a school in Highland Park. She had a mixed classroom, mostly black children. She taught them to speak conventional English but after a weekend at home they returned speaking English as it was spoken at home. One time she found herself talking with their lilt, so who was teaching whom? It was interesting hearing her tell her tales and she became my all time favorite friend.

Since I saw little of Jack, these three women enhanced my friend-starved life. Life became bearable in the spring. We started to take walks to the lake. One day we met a woman in a maid's uniform. She had a cute puppy on a leash. When the children saw the puppy, they exclaimed over his cuteness. The maid leaned over, scooped up the puppy into her hands and said, "Come, Precious." She clasped him to her and started to run from us. We were very surprised by her actions.

A woman who lived in the next block was semi-friendly. She had a dear boy who was about four years old. He came to play with John and Paul. The next week John and Paul played at their house. They were home in about an hour, and an hour later the woman rang the bell. She told me some of the parts of their Tinker Toys were missing. Tinker Toys! Do you know how tiny those pieces are? We had a clothes search, a room search, the area around the house, and the path from our house to theirs. Not one Tinker Toy. She was furious and so was I. End of our relationship.

32

Grosse Pointe Christmas

Our first Christmas in Grosse Pointe on Kirby Road was very different. Jack's cheap suit looked pathetic so we decided to go downtown Detroit and find a suit. We wandered around and found a men's store. We were confronted with so many suits to choose from. One suit stood out from all the others. It was a *green* tweed. The more the salesman suggested we avoid it, the more it appealed to me. Actually, it would have looked ugly on anyone. I urged Jack to go for it, which he did. It needed many alterations. This should have been a clue because Jack was always a perfect size 42. They sent the altered suit out to us on Christmas Eve. Jack tried it on and it was so wide on his waist that the trousers fell immediately to the ground. Time was flying and I borrowed 2 of Jimmy's diaper pins and remedied it as best I could. A kiss and he was off to St. Bernard's for his first Christmas service. I prayed real hard that all would go well.

One day a few weeks before Christmas Jack had come in with a Christmas tree he had bought when he got off the bus. He lugged it a mile and entered smiling because he knew I would be happy. It was about three feet and beginning to shed. I was appalled at the sight of the little tree.

"That's a Christmas tree?" I wailed.

Now you must know at my home there was always a big eight or ten foot beauty. Dad would bring home two or three. Mother would sit snugly in the bay window and watch Daddy take each tree out, turning it a few times for Mother to view each side. This ritual would take a while until Daddy's hands turned blue. Then at last, the choice was made. Jack was so furious that he never got, bought or was involved in tree selections afterwards. He did pay for them. I don't remember how I attained another tree, but when Fr. O'Rourke came to visit he remarked about its beauty!

Fr. O'Rourke found a woman to help me once a week. She came twice and told me she would never come again. She said she was a cleaner not a picker upper of toys. She did think Jimmy was poochy and she was right. It was the first time I heard the word, *poochy*.

Rose LaRose treated us to a trip to Detroit. We went to a well-known cafeteria. We attended a movie. It was spirit lifting. Jack babysat Jimmy and we walked to the Jefferson bus to downtown Detroit. It was so good to be out with my three musketeers. We prowled Woolworth's and then went to Hudson's. Hudson's was a remarkable store. It had thirteen floors and two basements. At holiday times the windows were dressed in different themes, everything from "North Pole" to "Nutcracker" with moveable manikins clothed in delightful costumes. The dining room was on the twelfth floor. We checked the children's department first and then to the second basement to observe the children's clothes in that area. The ride to twelfth floor gave a weird jump to one's stomach. We had Maurice salad, their specialty. After lunch Paul asked, "Shouldn't we have had peanut butter?" It was a big thrill for me to share just a little fun with my children. The day in question ended by finding Jack practicing the piano with Jimmy tied to the leg of the piano amusing himself with a pile of toys; a happy little guy. One time when I returned to Grosse Pointe, Jack had had a fire outside and burned some trash including all my papers Dr. Shepard had corrected.

I heard that a Dr. McKenzie was a good doctor. His office was on Jefferson. My legs were bothering me so I made an appointment. When he called me into his office, he asked, "What do you look like with all that makeup off?" He recommended I come once a week for shots of cod liver oil in the veins of my legs. (It upsets me even to write this). There was at least a twenty-minute wait for the bus home and then a two-mile walk from the bus. Painful is a mild term for what I felt. Dr. McKenzie that winter came to the house and lanced the kids' ears. They were continually sick. He said we had better get out of that house. It was old, had no insulation, and the furnace was a coal furnace which Jack would stoke before he went to work and again when he came home.

Mother and Dad and sister-in-law Margaret came to visit. The rats as big as dogs in the basement alarmed Dad. McKenzie said John's tonsils had to come out. I talked to Johnny about the operation and how his throat would hurt for a while. Thank God, for Mother being there. The day of the surgery dawned and Johnny, who was the first to bounce out of bed, was not getting up. He had to be coaxed to rise. We walked, took a bus, and arrived at the appointed time at Cottage Hospital. I remembered how it was when my tonsils were removed and you know a mother wants her children to be spared even a scratch, let alone a throbbing throat. So we talked happily as they prepped him. The nurses put him on a gurney. I said, "See you soon," standing at the foot of the gurney and noticed a tag that said, "Appendectomy." I felt my legs going, grabbed the cart and yelled, "STOP!" After we exchanged words and consulted charts, the toe now bore the name "Tonsillectomy." I was completely undone. I stood by a tall window in the waiting room and dissolved into tears. A woman approached me and put her arms around me.

"My dear, what's your sorrow?"

With my voice quivering I told her my 5 year old was having his tonsils removed. "For goodness sakes," the woman laughed, "there is nothing to having your tonsils out."

I replied, "When it's your boy, then it's serious."

I wanted to buy him a toy sailboat in the shop in the hospital, but I couldn't afford it. I can still see that toy sailboat. Two days later Johnny was home and recovering beautifully.

33

St. Bernard Parish

St. Bernard's Catholic Church was located on Mack Avenue and Lillibridge. The school and convent were also on Lillibridge. The schoolyard had one lonely, large oak tree on the property; along the street were fragile spikes hoping to be trees one day. The oak reminded one of *A Tree Grows in Brooklyn*. The house where we lived was directly across from the schoolyard. All the houses were high off the ground. They all hugged each other as the space between them was at arms length.

Cement stairs with a coping on either side led to the entrance. To the right of the entrance was a large covered porch. A closet was near the front door and to the left was the living room facing the front porch. There was a fireplace and over the mantel a painted scene of three gamboling deer with amazing antlers and chicken legs. It was so bad it was amusing. Beyond the living room were a dark dining room followed by a bright sunroom. The kitchen was also bright and behind that was the brightest, prettiest room with six large windows. A small tiled bathroom was off the breakfast room; a back door led to an adequate yard with a nice elm in place.

On a wagon in front of 3864 Lillibridge: Margaret and Paul (standing) and seated (left to right) Kathy, Brian and Jim.

Fr. O'Rourke let Jack borrow money for the down payment; he charged 2% interest. I was excited, elated, and probably the only one ever who enjoyed leaving Grosse Pointe. We enrolled Margaret at St. Bernard's school. John, very reluctantly, went to kindergarten. Brian cried and cried with teething, and the woman next door implied we might be abusing him. Jim became more independent, and Paul was serious about this new adventure. Down and across the street lived Arnolda Berg and Harriet Elrod; both women were friends of Madge Blaney. Fifty or more young children resided on the block, making their way back and forth in search of fun. One neighbor was very maimed but every day he would force himself to walk the street.

Dr. Dunn's office was upstairs over the dry cleaners on Mack Avenue. Since the war was on, doctors were scarce, the waiting rooms were very crowded, and the waits were long. You could develop all new symptoms by the time they called your name. There was a general store on Mack run by a man whose accent was so heavy that it was not possible to understand him. He was always in a rage; then he would pause, look at me, and say, "Yah?" "Yes, Yes," I would reply and he'd nod and smile. But one day after his usual tirade and I did my usual "Yes, Yes," he became furious and said, "No, No!" I wondered what it was all about.

Little Sam lived on the left side of our house in an upstairs apartment. We called him Sunny Italy because he was so sunny and sweet. We couldn't understand him. He lived with his son and his daughter-in-law, Josephine, who told me her father-in-law's clothes were from the children's department.

In the house on the other side of us were the Montagues (pronounced **MON**-TAG, not related to Romeo or Juliet). They were in their forties when they had a son Leslie, their love and pride. Upstairs lived a younger couple, the Jurkiewicz family, with two children, Ronnie and Diane, who were Margaret and John's ages. Mr. J. was a painter and fixer-upper. He taught me many ways to fix things that I had never known before. His wife seemed sad and remote. I found out in later years that he drank heavily and she wanted to leave but stayed because of the children. Later he stopped the habit and things improved.

The day we moved in and the first time my doorbell rang, I met a very tall young lad who was so Slavic in appearance that he seemed to come directly from Eastern Europe. He declared that his mother sent him and that he was to do my bidding. He said his name was Frank Janeck. Arnolda's daughter rang the bell next and offered to help. I turned both down but they warmed my heart. The convent across the street with the nuns was a sweet scene as we watched them go back and forth, two by two. The head nun was Sr. Phyllis. She was under 5' but knew how to rule. Some big heavy boys attended the high school and when they needed discipline she had them kneel so she could look down on them. All the school children went to Mass every day and sang. Some of the children's pets followed them and went so far as to enter the church. Fr. O'Rourke would become riled and yell at Sister to keep the doggies out of the church.

Fr. O'Rourke loved to bully and scare nuns. He had the reputation of a woman-hater. I do have to admit that he was a handsome man with fierce blue eyes. He would go to the convent, lay down the law, demean and instruct (one time telling them not to put just red peonies in a bowl but to mix them with white peonies). After his big bad wolf routine, he would come to our house and say things like, "You can't scare me, Sister, there are owls in the forest that scare me more." He was proud of that one and repeated it often. He loved to rough house with the boys and they loved it too. One time when they were playing around, Father accidentally hit Brian in the nose and it bled. Father and Brian looked a mess and a chagrined Father O'Rourke went home. He never horse-played with them again. Too bad!

Father O'Rourke had an annoying habit of saying," I am going to tell you the truth." I did not want to hear it. One night after Arnolda and I had painted the living room and dining room aqua and we were standing back to admire our work, Fr. O'Rourke happened to stop by. "I hate blue," he declared.

"It's aqua," I retorted.

"I hate aqua," he replied.

He did not converse; he orated, and Jack was a patient listener and thought Father was the greatest. One evening I was so upset by the U.S. joining with Russia, of all countries, to beat the Nazis that I leaned over closely to him on the couch. All at once he got up and went to a chair nearby. What conceit, what gall he had! I was mortified to think I gave any hint of wanting to be near him. I'm still mad!

Frank Janeck was studying organ and piano with Jack, and Carol Berg, beautiful, sweet and golden, babysat for us. I became pregnant and I was upset, six children! How could I handle six children? I knew I couldn't go home again so I asked Dr. Dunn to recommend a doctor. He recommended a Dr. Henderson whose office had to be reached by streetcar even though it was still on Mack Avenue. The first visit was strange. I had to climb so many stairs I was breathless. Dr. Henderson was not young, not handsome, but tall and thin. He did not write my name down, take my blood pressure or examine me. Dr. Mowry was meticulous, kept a chart, always checked my blood pressure and urine and asked pertinent questions. After two similar visits I called Dr. Dunn, "What kind of doctor did you send me to? He doesn't check me at all and just chats. Give me the name of another doctor."

"Listen, young woman," Dr. Dunn said. "Doctor Henderson can tell by looking at you from the corner of his eye what condition you are in. He has delivered more than a thousand babies." He slammed down the receiver. I continued to see Dr. Henderson.

Carol Berg was musing about Brian one day as she was feeding him baby food. "I wonder how he will turn out. He will be either very handsome or very homely." Brian at a year and a half didn't care at all.

Eastside General Hospital was about an hour away. It was a very small, very good hospital. The nurses were the best. Even the cleaning lady was the best. As she cleaned, she would check out the patients and if they were depressed or wan she would report it to the front desk. Mother came for the event and it was heaven having her there. She said that when Daddy took her to the train station he said he thought he was coming down with a cold and fever. Mother said there was no sign of either and she thought he just didn't want her to leave.

Kathy was born at Eastside General, weighing in at 7 ½ pounds, short, fat, red, dark hair, an adorable bundle. I missed Dr. Mowry, but Dr. Henderson was great in the delivery room. My roommate was sixteen years old from Kentucky. After her delivery she asked for buttermilk. There was none. When they brought her the baby, it was a buttermilk baby! In those days some of the mothers were knocked out cold and didn't see their babies until they were bathed and spruced up. Her baby was beautiful; she confessed to me that during her pregnancy she craved coal. Kathy, named Mary Kathleen, was home for Christmas and then there were six. Jack was delighted and the little people were good sports. I was glad to have a girl after John, Paul, James, and Brian. Kathy was baptized at St. Bernard's and we had a celebration at the house.

On April 12, 1945 when Kathy was 4 months old, they announced on the radio that President Roosevelt had died at Warm Springs, Georgia. He had been president most of my life. The whole nation mourned. Even the music on the radio became classical with Bach, Ravel and Chopin being played for a few days.

34

Drudgery

My job was becoming difficult because of all the drudgery: The washing, the ironing, the diapers, and the three meals a day. One day I fell at my husband's feet and said, "Help!" From that time on, he pitched in helping with diapers and boasting that his diapering was tighter and neater than mine. There were no disposable diapers, no dishwashers, no dryers. My clothes washer had a wringer on it: I would pass the garment through the wringer, rinse them, and do it again.

The basement was my room. I washed every day. It took forever to hang those tiny socks and underwear. John went to kindergarten a few blocks away. Margaret was in second grade at St. Bernard's. She was an angel in the Christmas play that was held on the third floor of the school, a firetrap if ever there was one! Paul was very serious. One day when Mother was visiting, the furnace broke down. When the repairman left, Mother cautioned the children when they returned to play in the basement. "Do not go near the furnace. In fact, don't even look at it." Twenty minutes later Paul came up the steps. "Nana, I can't play down there at all. Everywhere I look I can see the furnace. So I'll stay up here with you."

When Jimmy was in kindergarten, he returned home every day with a new tune. He had such a repertoire that I took him down to the music store, Grinnell's in the city, and had a vinyl record made of his songs. While I was at it, I did a song. The sound engineer said the equipment wasn't adequate to handle my voice! One day when John was in first grade, he said there would be an open house. We hustled over, the room was squeaky clean, and each desk had a representation of one project or another. Oh, but one desk was empty—John's. Puzzled, we asked Sister why there was nothing on John's desk. She was as mystified as we were. She looked in the desk, under it, and around it. She then went to the front of the room and there in the wastebasket was John's work. John didn't have enough confidence in himself.

There was a public school nearby that had after-school crafts. Paul went every day and brought many objects for us to admire. Jim wouldn't be six until January but Sister took him after testing him. I was so grateful to have Mr. Busy occupied. He remembers marching around the classroom with a paper proudly displayed to the tune of "Marche Militaire" by Schubert. Sr. Marie Guadeloupe confided in me that she never met anyone with such confidence in her life. One year he was the star shepherd in the nativity scene at St. Bernard's. Margaret's teacher told me that Margaret was an excellent student but that she was most reluctant to answer out loud in class. She said, "Margaret is afraid to make a mistake." I fought this by making mistakes and pointing them out to her that that is one thing all people have in common: they make mistakes.

Brian, to put it mildly, was a broth of a boy. As soon as he could walk, he trudged along after his brothers, and as the years rolled by he kept asking, "Where are the guys?" One day when John, Paul, and Jim were playing outside and Brian was in the feathers, I decided to have a talk with Margaret, aged 7, about babies and such. We were in the kitchen and at this precious moment when only the two of us were together, I said, "Darling, I want to tell you something."

"Don't bother," she said. "I know there is no Santa Claus."

This was a surprise for me because she never let on that there wasn't a jolly old elf.

"I'm glad you know that, but I want to tell you that no way does a stork bring a baby or is a baby found under a bush. A husband and wife, who love each other very much, make a baby and the baby grows inside the mother. Any questions?"

"No questions."

I started voice lessons again with Cameron MacLean. Jack had been studying with him. I scotch-taped my music over the sink and practiced my songs. MacLean was a wonderful baritone. He was from the Hebrides and he spoke and sang with a delightful brogue. "Porgy and Bess" was popular at that time and was beginning to be appreciated as a truly great work. No matter how hard I thought, tried, vocalized, I couldn't make the sound I longed to hear.

Jack and I, with Cameron MacLean's encouragement, did duets from time to time.

As a boy Cameron did wood carving and sculpted beautiful women and figures, the kind found on boats. I was very much into lieder. He gave me some trite pieces. I thought he used the repertoire to teach different techniques of vocal learning. I bought the duet from "Porgy and Bess." He sang it with me, a great memory. His studio was down in the heart of the city on Wayne State University campus. Cameron's wife was Jessie who always had a nice presentation of flowers on the piano. I remember pansies merrily floating in a bowl.

Mark Wisdom was the best accompanist in the world. He was a tall, thin, gentle, humorous man who was married to a tiny woman called Tee. Mark was an organist at an Episcopalian church. We met them socially at American Guild of Organists meetings. Mark and Tee had no children but they had a cat. Apparently this was no ordinary cat. He was a music critic. When the New York Philharmonic played on the radio, the cat's back would stiffen and he would rush out of the room and hide until the program ended. He did this with the Boston, Detroit and Cleveland symphonies too.

I don't know if it is true but a neighbor told me Josephine next door to us told her, "The kids are a real pain but when she starts to sing, it's the last straw." Carol Berg was our babysitter as well as every day at 3:00 coming by to help me. She was so beautiful; a freckled, golden, sweet, sweet girl. Carol was my lifeline for years and I loved her dearly. Once she came to me and said she could no longer work for me because I swore and she was swearing too. "What did I say?" I asked her.

"You're always saying 'Oh, God!'"

"Good grief, girl, tell your mother I am not swearing. I'm calling on God for His help." So she returned. Arnolda, her mother, was a truly sainted person and I really know where she is now.

When Brian was about a year and a half, on a hot summer day I would put him on the porch in his high chair. He had a great knack of rocking the chair back and forth. This was nerve wracking to watch and, when the sweet little nuns who were sitting on the cement porch across the street saw his performance, they fled one by one into the convent.

Nana, Fishy and Jim visited us one summer and Fr. O'Rourke gave us the use of the convent for Jim and Fishy to sleep because the nuns were at their motherhouse in Kalamazoo. After the first night of sleep the men came across the street for breakfast. I asked, "Did you sleep well?' My naughty father-in-law replied, "It would have been much better if the nuns were there." Jim and Fishy went to a Tiger's game and sought out the "Brass Rail" which boasted of the longest bar in the entire world. Nana and I took a streetcar downtown and I introduced her to Hudson's.

The Montagues who lived on one side of us were very nice. One afternoon I was sitting on the back steps watching John, Paul and Jim scale a tree. I heard her say to another neighbor, "Look at her sitting there. She don't even care." She and I had different ideas. Her husband and son Leslie took John and Paul fishing. They were so proud when they came home with fish and I proudly posed for pictures. The street was busy at all times. Wonderful old and young characters passed up and down Lillibridge. The tree in the schoolyard flourished and the pitiful stalks that peppered the street tried vainly to grow.

Jack joined a choral group. He sang tenor. One of the group singers would drive him home. His name was Dr. Tapert a.k.a. Dody. We also met at that time Ralph and Nova Bransby. Nova was lovely to look at and an excellent organist at the Lutheran church. Jack played a recital there and also a service. I remember how their liturgy was so reverent and satisfying. It was nice to hear in English what we Catholics were doing in Latin. I did love the Gregorian chant and Latin Masses. I never tired of singing or playing them. Our church had no congregational singing in those days and very few congregations even today sing with much gusto. Most of them are anemic. Now the Baptists, especially the black churches, know how to praise the Lord with joy and enthusiasm. I can visualize the Lord rocking back and forth and smiling as the sounds waft to His ears.

It was nice to have another girl in the house. There were seven years difference between Margaret and Kathy. Kathy was a born gypsy and as soon as she walked she had plans to travel. One day I was so tired, so fatigued, so weary, I asked Paul, the only one I could trust, to take Kathy for a walk. I sat in a chair and was quiet. The two were gone about 15 minutes and there was a rapid knock on the front door. There was a very angry man. There was Paul, seven at the time, and Miss Cyanide. "I was backing out of the alley and nearly ran over these two," he yelled. "I hit your little girl a little." There wasn't, fortunately, a mark on her but Paul was beyond upset. "What were you thinking to let this little boy care for a baby girl like this one? You are an unfit mother." He was right, of course. I must have been really desperate to do such a terrible thing.

Kathy talked in the delivery room or so it seemed. She was here, there, and every where. One time as she was recovering from chicken pox, I let her go on the porch after promising me she wouldn't leave. It was a beautiful day. I peeked out on the porch. She was there. The next day the Board of Health appeared and threatened to quarantine the house if I didn't keep my daughter at home. They said a neighbor complained. I asked who it was but they said it was none of my business.

When Kathy was five she kept talking about her friend Nancy. She lived a few houses away. Kathy had a good time and returned home happy. On Kathy's birthday in December it was snowy and miserable and as usual Kathy was out. The doorbell rang. A beautiful young woman in a stewardess airline uniform appeared at the door. "Is Kathy in?" she asked.

"No," I replied, "She is seldom in."

"Well, I'm Nancy."

"Nancy? You mean you are the *real* Nancy?"

She admitted to being Nancy and she knew it was Kathy's birthday and would I accept a gift for her. I told Nancy I thought she was a little girl who lived down the block and we had a good laugh.

The bakery man passed by every day in his truck. One day I was surprised to see the bakery man at the door.

"Hey, lady. You owe me $1.50," he said.

"Oh, no, I don't. I've bought nothing from you."

"Well," he said, "your little girl just ate three of my éclairs."

"How do you know it was my little girl? There are hundreds of little girls on the block."

"Just look at her," he growled. I stepped out on the porch and there was Kathy with her face covered in chocolate.

I read stories to the wee ones every night after their baths. This was most fun for me. "Each one did a dance," said a poem, "sang a song or cavorted." I did want them to have lovely memories. I started to gather them around the table at night for popcorn or candy. I lit candles to make it festive. Then I said, "We are now going to sing." They were a little reluctant but sing they did. I remember thinking, *Darn it all, we are going to have a good time whether they like it or not!*

35

Pregnant Again

I was pregnant again. I threw myself in Fr. Fedewa's arms one day after I played the Masses at St. Bernard's. It seems we never got together and after abstaining, we got together once and I was pregnant. Fr. O'Rourke suggested I was a freak of nature. He had read in a book somewhere (whatever one?) that said every 2 to 3 years was normal for a couple to conceive a child. Fr. Fedewa gave me a chart to follow. In every 28 days of a menstrual cycle there were six days of fertility. These were between the 12th and 18th days. All I had to do was avoid those days like a plague. But I varied from 28 to 32 days. Like Scarlett O'Hara, I'd worry about it tomorrow.

Fr. O'Rourke introduced us to great authors. *Brideshead Revisited* was popular and we read all of Evelyn Waugh's books as they were published. Graham Greene's *The Labyrinth Way* was a great book. We feasted on his great writings. *The Heart of the Matter* had a profound effect on me. Scobie, the protagonist, was a loving, thoughtful man and everything went wrong for him. Goodness did not win out in that book. It bothers me even to this day. *The Woman Who Was Poor* by Bernanos and *The Viper's Tangle* by Francoise Mauriac were masterpieces. Wagner, my early passion, was not played anymore because of the war. I turned to listen to Mozart; at one time, I thought his music was insipid. I discovered pure genius.

Madge Blaney and the girls' club came over one night and this time I had refreshments. It wasn't like the time in Oswego when I had a committee meeting and I served nothing because I had nothing to serve. What a perfect time to try out my voice on the girls. I wanted to test my Brahms's lieder. They were very enthusiastic.

Being pregnant with Eddie didn't cramp my lifestyle too much. I had lots of energy and hundreds of distractions but as every mother-to-be knows I was aware morning, noon, and night of a presence within me. We went to more concerts. Jack performed more. A new organ was built at St. Catherine's Church. Monsignor Vismara, the pastor, had a church envelope made with a slot pocket on the end and urged the parishioners to donate a dime a week. *Casavant* Company who made beautiful organ instruments was located in Quebec. During the war *Casavant* quoted a price and the contract was made. As the war was ending, they raised the price because of the increase in cost of materials. Msgr. Vismara was furious, broke the contract, and hired a company by the name of Moller. It was a beautiful instrument and with the great acoustics of the church it produced thrilling tones. Even with my miserable ability as an organist, I could make the organ sound OK.

We were still alternating services, especially weddings and funerals. Whenever I took the bus to St. Catherine's, I passed the classic gray house on Iroquois Street. There was no garage but the house perched on the left side of a 150' lot. As I approached the property, I would slow down and peek in the yard at the cherry tree. Jack started playing Masses at 6:00 AM; three or more would ensue; then choir rehearsals, home for lunch, a quick nap; back to rehearsals, teach, grocery shop for quite a few items since there were 8 of us to feed; dinner—then a few nights a week return to the church for devotions. He tried to read as much as he could because that was his big delight—and so to bed.

Most women in the 40's did spring and fall cleaning. That meant to spruce up every room in the house for the coming season. One room was at the end of the hall upstairs. I would start there and do walls, windows, curtains, floor. Place a lamp, throw a rug and called it finished. In each room I ended with the lamp table and throw rug; the only problem: it was the same lamp table and rug. We used the living room only on rare occasions because it was so drafty. Mean breezes were forever wafting around the room.

I saw in a catalogue from the Metropolitan Museum in New York some Winslow Home prints advertised. I ordered them and when they arrived I was delighted. There were six scenes from the Bahamas, delicious blue water, white sailing boats and palm trees bending in the wind. I decided to frame them myself. I read directions on how to frame a picture. It suggested a razor blade for cutting. I cut myself and bled on the prints. I ordered a new set and did a better job. They looked great on the wall as we climbed the stairs. Oh my, did I tell you Jack was pleased over the pregnancy?

To save money Jack decided to cut the boys' hair. He did a pitiful job. They looked unloved and uncherished. Our holidays were great but I always panicked about having nice things under the tree for them. Mother and Dad always sent outfits for the children and they fit perfectly. I don't know how she did it. One Christmas I was in a creative mood and I baked gingerbread men and hung them on the tree and was surprised to see the tree horizontal most of the time. We strung popcorn and cranberries. One happy memory I have is of Brian sitting by the tree playing a toy piano and every few minutes pausing to bite a popcorn bit from the tree.

My due date was the end of January. On the 28th I had a few zingers and then experienced the problem I had with Margaret. I panicked but didn't say anything. Jack went over to borrow O'Rourke's car. O'Rourke was in Florida as every respectable priest in January was. The janitor had the car. Fr. Fedewa said Jack could take his but Jack couldn't drive a shift so Fr. Fedewa drove me to the hospital. He was more than edgy and told me later he could see the headlines in the paper: **Baby Born in Clergyman's Car**! But it didn't happen. At his 25th anniversary he did admit it was an unforgettable experience for him.

Eddie arrived at 7:00. My roommate's husband was Larry and I thought it would be nice to name him after my cousin Larry. Jack vetoed that and he was right. We named him Edward after my father-in-law and Dennis after my grandfather. Eddie was jaundiced and reluctant to eat, lost weight, and was a worry for me. After we got him home, he picked up. He was so good I called him my Angel.

Jack started to teach a lovely young girl who led the sodality. Her name was Josephine Schulte. She started to sub for Jack and became our dear friend. Josephine loved Brian and sometimes picked him up with her girlfriend and took him shopping and to carnivals and just out for an ice cream. She was also Eddie's godmother (Frank Janeck was his godfather).

Leonard Bernstein came to Detroit to direct and perform one of the Brandenburg Concertos. "Dynamic," "handsome," "exciting" fail to adequately describe this great talent. There was a reception afterwards at the "Russian Bear," a café for the Bohemians in town. What would I say when I met him? "Maestro, you were magnificent!" That sounded good to me, not too much, not too little. A huge 12' stuffed black bear greeted us as we entered. The taxidermist must have had a challenge stuffing him. He did look a little moth-eaten.

We joined the reception line and there in all his glory in a floor length raccoon coat was Lenny. When it came my turn, I blurted out in a trembling voice, "Agh, Agh, and how do you do?"

Sister Angus who taught music at St. Bernard's suggested that John and Paul take an instrument. She said there was a real need for French horns and oboes. John took the French horn and when he carried the big case, he leaned sideways. Paul took the oboe; later Jim took the cello with Bob Allport, a fine cellist at St.

Catherine's. Still later Brian would join them on trumpet. Margaret and Kathy were the violinists. Kathy also studied piano.

Phone calls to and from Madge Blaney and Fran Conan, August Conan's wife, brightened my days. We could talk for an hour. Our dream was to have Jack go to Tanglewood in Massachusetts, the summer home of the Boston Symphony and study choral conducting with Robert Shaw and Hugh Ross. Shaw was very popular and ended up leading a choral in Atlanta for years and won many Grammy awards.

In the meantime, I had many dental problems. My dentist suggested I go to a Dr. Totte in the same neighborhood because he couldn't help me. He didn't say why he couldn't help. Dr. Totte said my teeth were so bad he would do an immediate denture. He would remove a few teeth and then make a full denture. He would extract eight teeth, put in the fake ones, and that was that. You can imagine how I felt. Was there no way out? Must I do it? Are my teeth that bad? He must be a good dentist, or why would the other dentist send me to him?

It was a hideous time and I ended up with a mouth full of nasty tasting plaster. My life as I knew it was over. The crowning humiliation was in the middle of one night Jack nudged me and I awoke; he silently handed me one of the dentures. My mother's eyes filled with tears when she saw me, and my mother-in-law screamed, "Look at her, look at her, not a tooth in her head!" It didn't bother the kids so that was OK. Jack went off to Tanglewood. He stayed at a dorm, ran out of money, had dysentery, and came home half way through the course.

Fran Brown came every Christmas. One Christmas Eve Fr. Fedewa was at the door with bikes and wagons. He got them on sale at a hardware store. Another evening before Christmas the doorbell rang and I opened the door to a white haired man with a beautiful long snowy beard. The coat he wore was too big and almost covered his shoes. "I have some candy for you," he said and handed me a brown bag and then turned and carefully eased down the steps. I called after him, "Don't go; come back…Thank you!" There were about two pounds of the most delicious fudge in the bag. The nuns at the convent suggested it could have been St. Joseph. You know, it could have been. He was certainly one of my favorites.

"Pillow fight!" The children were having a merry old time when one of the pillows broke and feathers wafted everywhere on their heads, furniture, etc. The doorbell rang just as they tumbled down the stairs into the living room, flinging themselves on the chairs and couch. A severely dressed woman with a severe expression and holding a large piece of paper was at the door. She held up a placard and said in a voice of doom, "Madam, this is your vagina." Well, you could have fooled me. She swept past me and sat on the couch. She looked at the children with contempt and they retreated. She had all these books to sell, and she thought that, of all the people, I was most worthy to purchase some. She went on to explain it was possible to control birth and if I did conceive and didn't want the child there was a way to take care of that, too.

I said I wasn't interested and suggested she leave. She regarded me with pity and with a despairing sigh rose to leave but, lo and behold, she was covered with feathers. She clutched at them but they seemed irremovable. She was red with fury as she walked away and I was red with laughter. It was a banner day for me.

One of my weekly visitors was the egg lady. She also had scripture to share with me and I looked forward to her stops. One morning a lovely young woman came to the door. I don't remember what she was selling. Halfway through her spiel, she broke down and wept. She had lost a little girl who was a year and a half. The child had knocked over a bowl of boiling water and died from the burns. The woman was mad with grief and her doctor suggested she sell something door to door. We wept together and whatever she was selling you know I bought it.

36

Lillibridge and Beyond

Eddie, number 7, was a good baby. When he was just learning to walk, I put a chair upside down at the front of the stairs to prevent him from going up. One day one of the children removed the chair, went to the landing, and urged him to go up. It was early on an Easter Sunday afternoon when he fell. The fall was bad enough but what bruised him the most was his mouth hitting the rungs of the chair. His mouth was unbelievably bruised. The doctors at the hospital said they couldn't stitch him and he would have to heal on his own. It was weeks before he could eat normally.

All the boys were recipients of Jack's haircuts. When Eddie a couple of years later went to the emergency room because of a cut, the nurses were appalled. They took one look at him and said, "Poor little boy...So sad...Who cut his hair?"

The house I loved was up for sale. The Brady girls who lived there had died a few months apart. I called around and learned that the Brady girls had left the house to a niece who lived in Grosse Pointe. Well, my dream was shot; I would never, never get it. Jack said a strange thing: "Let them build a garage and then we'll buy it." It thought, *No way is that going to happen.*

One of my fond hopes was to spend time with Margaret. I mean "fun" time. I saved some Christmas money and planned lunch at Hudson's and a movie. The movie, "The Yearling," was showing at a downtown theater. Perfect. She had an appointment at the dentist. Later, I learned that Dr. Totte had just returned from the service. What a trusting, naïve idiot I was! Margaret had a 9:00 AM appointment for a check up and then we would take the streetcar downtown. She went into the room with the dentist and 30 minutes later came out. I just couldn't believe it. Her face was beginning to swell. But nothing was going to deter me from our day out. We followed the plan and Margaret never said a mumbling word, but she was really hurting.

Margaret had some boys looking her way. John was becoming more confident, Paul less serious, Jimmy had been accepted at the St. Bernard's kindergarten even though he wouldn't be five until February. Brian spent most of his time tracking down his older brothers. "Where are the guys? Where are the guys?" The best thing that would happen: the children would go by train to visit their grandparents in Oswego. One summer Margaret and Paul were hit with the measles. Margaret recovered first but Paul remained with Mother and Dad. When he rejoined us, he was not happy; he longed for Oswego.

Bishop Babcock was to be consecrated at the Cathedral on March 25. Jack was to play the organ selections. The day dawned with a blizzard threatening. After morning Mass Jack skipped home and found me in the basement starting the laundry. The laundry in the chute was taller than 5'6". I gave him the good news that I was starting to labor. It could be a false alarm. What should he do? I told him to go to the Cathedral. After I had rinsed the diapers three times to be sure no blemish would ever appear on their derrieres and after I released Kathy's hand from the wringer, I knew it was real labor.

I called a cab. I called Carol Burg. Because of the storm, no one could promise a taxi for at least two hours. I didn't want to call an ambulance so I called Josephine Schulte who worked nearby for Sealtest. She called her father, "Cap" Schulte, who arrived with shovels and buckets of sand in the back of his car. He eyed me and hoped it would be late afternoon before the baby would come.

I had had a tough year. I had a ligation for varicose veins at 4 months pregnant. I had hepatitis and Jack bought me daffodils, which matched my complexion. I was so lethargic that one day as I was lying on the couch, Eddie pried my eyelids back and peered in. "The supper," he said. "Who is getting the supper?" I must have looked rather poor because the egg lady would have me sit in a chair and pray over me. This had never happened to me before and I felt comfort.

Back to the trip with "Cap" Schulte to the hospital: I walked in and two hours later William Joseph (after Father William O'Rourke) was born. All these beautiful babies coming into our lives. Jack arrived at the scene around noon. People had a few glitches with loss of power and priests not being able to attend the consecration of the bishop. In those days a new mother spent 10 days in bed and didn't get out of bed until the tenth day. So there was time to think. Jack used to come to visit and one day he was so exhausted he said, "I wish you could move over. I am that tired."

Fr. Fedewa was ordained March 29 in Innsbruck, Austria. We were married March 28 so we started to celebrate our anniversaries together. The 29th of that year he appeared with Jack to say hello and then go out to dinner. He bought a box of gardenias. They were so white, so waxy, so heavy scented, that everyone, doctors and nurses, admired them. The nurses brought a bowl of crushed ice for them to lie on. In my reveries I made plans to be a better wife, a better mother, better singer, a person closer to God. I had a lot of energy and a tremendous capacity for love. If a womb could expand from the size of a fist to carry a big baby, my heart could expand to encompass all my children.

Mother came for each baby. It was nice to have near by the one I loved most in the world. William James quickly became William Joseph on the insistence of the Sisters of St. Joseph at St. Bernard's Convent.

Brian had many colds and I think allergies. One time he had a bad cough and we were together in the yard. I was hanging up the clothes. I watched him play around but he seemed to be limping. I didn't say anything but played around with him and, sure enough, he was limping. I rushed down the block to the doctor's office. The doctor was alarmed and carried him home with me, called an ambulance and an hour later we were at Herman Kiefer Hospital where they did a spinal tap for meningitis or polio. The tests were clear but the doctors said he had rheumatoid arthritis and he was to be bedridden for at least 3 weeks. I stormed the heavens on his behalf. When he recovered, he had his tonsils out; but unknown to me when he was home a couple of days later, he got his hands on popcorn. I ice packed him all night and in the morning he was back in the hospital.

Jim also had his tonsils removed. He was the friendliest bon vivant in the hospital. He ignored my warnings of the pain ahead. So when he returned from surgery he said, "You're the best thing my eyes ever saw and my throat hurts too."

So now there were Margaret, John, Paul, Jim, Brian, Kathy, Ed and Bill. I remember saying to my husband one time, "Jack, believe me, I could not possibly have the family your mother had. I could never cope with so many children!" She had six!

Margaret, John, Paul and Jim would walk three blocks away to the Admiral Theater. There were double features and cartoons and continuous showings at the time so Margaret was warned when the feature was over she was to get everyone home. One day they trotted off happily. Their mother was happy to get a little break and concentrate on the remaining tots. I was stunned when 30 minutes later they returned. "Why so soon?" I gasped. "Mother, you said when the show was over to come home." They had walked in on the ending of a feature.

Mrs. Oldani who lived in St. Bernard's parish met me one day. She said, "Mrs. Callaghan, I know your maiden name."

"Really?"

"Yes. It's O'Brien."

She explained that one day as she was walking on Mack Avenue near the Admiral Theater she saw a little boy whom she thought was a Callaghan on the top of a fire escape connected to the theater. She called out, "You better get down, young man. I know your father, Mr. Callaghan." Jimmy peered down at her from his height and said, "Do you know my mother, Mary O'Brien?"

Jack was doing all the grocery shopping. He really enjoyed it so I didn't pity him. One day he took Brian who was about three to the meat market. It was holiday time and the windows displayed about ten turkeys hanging from their feet. Brian, impressed by the display, said, "Daddy, did you ever see such big penises?" One time Brian had a high temperature that wouldn't go down. Dr. Dunn sat a young Dr. Martin down. He had just been discharged from the army and asked, "Why isn't this child isolated?" Dr. Dunn's response: "You've got to be kidding, Doctor. You've got to be kidding."

Rose LaRose at Fr. O'Rourke's suggestion invited us for Thanksgiving dinner at the rectory. We came, all ten of us, with Jack lugging the high chair across the street. It was a splendid, happy meal and we were introduced to rum pudding. I didn't really appreciate it at the time but it was a lot of work for her. She dimmed the lights and flamed the pudding. The children were in awe.

Sr. Phyllis, the tiny, authoritative principal, crossed the street one day to talk to Jack and me when Eddie appeared and went for her pockets and nearly disrobed her. The nuns had marvelous pockets of unusual depth. They had a variety of things in them like candy, gum, chalk, crayons, keys, medals, endless trinkets. Another nun story: John came home one day and said Sister Veronica told the class to tell their mothers to stop serving cabbage for lunch!

John made his first confession and Fr. O'Rourke yelled at him and made him do it again. Thus confession was not John's favorite thing to do. One time, a month had elapsed and I suggested he go to confession. "I have no sins," he protested. "Well, then," I said, "I can tell you a few."

The dean of the American Guild of Organists was Billy Fishwick. Jack was sub-dean. Billy was from Australia and had a quirky accent and a delightful, upbeat humor. When Billy was around, one could be sure of a fun time. He used to come to the house and tap with his feet to the opening beat of the "Little G Minor Fugue." One day when he came, he saw Jack putting storm windows up on the second floor. He called up to him, "John, come down immediately. That's bad for your technique!"

Nova Bransby was organist at Faith Lutheran Church in Detroit. Her husband was a photographer. She was active in the Guild and a friend of Jack's.

Nova had a lunch for 12 women. It was on a Friday at noon and they invited me. Chicken salad was served. I was the only Catholic present. Should I defer? Should I protest? Should I not partake? I ate every bit of it because I was hungry and didn't want to make a scene. Later my conscience bothered me and I can't believe it but I confessed it. The priest was upset and reprimanded me. I was remorseless.

We were invited to Nova's soirees where Billy Fishwick would entertain us with original music and witty ditties. Nova and I gave a recital at the Wesley Methodist Church. I was pregnant at the time and tried to place a huge potted palm in a strategic place for camouflage. I'll never know how it sounded but I'm glad it was before tape recording.

Before one of my voice lessons I bought 3 cowboy hats and 3 holsters with guns for John, Paul, and Jim. Cameron MacLean and Mark Wisdom, the accompanist, tried them on and played for a while. Cameron and Jesse had a dinner party. A cross section of races and creeds were there. As a blessing before the meal, he had us sing "Auld Lang Syne"—nice memory.

I thought of the Brady house occasionally but tried to dismiss the loss from my mind. The day after Eddie was born Drs. Henderson, Martin and Dunn stood at the hospital room door, Henderson tall, Martin less tall, Dunn short. They startled me. They were in their white coats. Henderson was a bit bloody from a recent tonsillectomy. "We are going to get you, Callaghan. We are doing a hysterectomy sooner or later."

"Get out!" I demanded.

"Don't you want to be tight as a virgin?"

I covered my face with a blanket. They left. I did have fibroid tumors on my uterus. I checked it out with a specialist who said they were benign. I had lost my teeth and I'd be damned if I would lose anything else. At one lesson Cameron asked me why I was studying. What was the purpose? "I love the repertoire, and I always sing. It's something I have to do," I replied.

Whenever Jack had a minute to spare he grabbed a book to read. It was difficult for me to make a comment or ask a question when he was enjoying his favorite sport. After I made a remark, he would put his finger on the page, look up and gaze at me as if he didn't know who I was. I am finally used to the procedure. It was amusing when he read *Don Quixote*; he laughed and laughed through the entire book. I was learning about my husband. He admired the Benedictine's and their motto, "*Laborare et orare*." The Church and Church laws were his primary concern. He read the divine office every day.

My primary concern was my little troop. I'd lie awake at night going over each child's ways in my mind and prayed I'd do the right thing to nourish, encourage and teach them. Enter Lillian. What a happy day when Lillian came into my life. She was young, fast, and fun and the best cleaner in the world. One day I said, "Lillian, we are going to do this and that."

"What do you mean '*we*'? You mean Lillian."

Lillian was black and about ten years younger than I. She told me one day that Kathy asked her what color she was under her slip.

Billy was a great baby and he came so soon after Eddie they seemed like twins. The summer of '48 was hot and we went nowhere except I went up the stairs to the doctor's depressing office. Ann was born July 7, 1948. She was tiny and dear. The same day she was born, Jack received a phone call from Sr. Clement Marie, head of the music department at Marygrove College. She wanted Jack to teach organ there. It was a perk for him. It is strange but every time we had a baby something good would happen; a raise, a new pupil, etc.

37
Iroquois

Msgr. Vismara came to visit me in the hospital. We had a long visit. He hinted that it would be nice if we could live in his parish. I told him about the Brady house. He mentioned other houses that would be up for sale. How nervy I was to keep saying, "The Brady house." Well, Jack's prophecy came true. The Brady's niece wanted to move to another part of town because black people were moving in and her club was far away. Of course the fact that I buried St. Joseph medals in the ground as I passed by didn't do any harm either. Msgr. Vismara helped Jack buy it. Joy of joys! It was ours. By the way, a garage had been built that year on the property.

The house had a center entrance with a lovely tiled vestibule, a wonderful solid oak staircase as you entered; lovely beveled window doors. To the left of the entrance was a 40' living room and behind that a large many windowed sunroom. To the right of the front door was a 30' paneled dining room, bright and sunny with 2 windows facing the front, two large windows facing the side. A small hall to the right of the staircase led to a breakfast room with a large bay window and a built-in window seat. So charming! The kitchen to the right of the breakfast room was too small but who cared? Looking out the kitchen window, I could see the spire and cross on St. Catherine's Church. A toilet and small basin were off the kitchen—the only problem: the back stairs ended at the teeny bathroom.

One bedroom was prettier than the next. All the doors had transoms and huge closets with windows! Two bedrooms faced the front with a huge bath in between. One room had a door that led to a strange place. The other bedroom had a fireplace with blue tiles and a white mantel. One of the back bedrooms had a bay window that looked over the orchard and the cherry trees. What a home, what a sanctuary, what a delight. The children were not impressed and reluctantly left St. Bernard's and their neighborhood and friends.

Oh joy, Oh rapture. I couldn't believe my good fortune to be in the house of my dreams. To the right of our house was a large lot, then a nice house where

Doctor and Mrs. Robinson lived. He was a pediatrician and rightfully so because he was very short and could look down on his patients. He drove a huge Buick with many cushions under him as he took the wheel. Mrs. Robinson was quite a bit taller, a buxom, friendly woman who was often heard whistling as she did her chores and worked in her garden. I met her years later and mentioned how we all enjoyed her cheery whistling. She replied, "Really? I only whistled when I was mad." They were the best. The truth is we always had wonderful neighbors. Some exceptions, of course.

To the left of us on the other side of the driveway was the Ross home: two brothers—one had been unsuccessfully married, the other a bachelor. They admitted they were somewhat terrified that a family with 9 children was moving in next door. They fixed wagons, bikes and had panes of glass that fit their kitchen windows in anticipation of the boy's ball games in the driveway. On a lazy summer day they would sit on their porch with a radio placed on a table between them and listen to the ball games. Eddie was their constant visitor. It was a Norman Rockwell scene. The block was long and about 60 to 70 children wended their way up and down the street.

John and Paul were altar boys and since we were five minutes from the church they were called frequently to serve. Jim too was learning to serve and after we corrected his Apostle's Creed ("He rose from the dead and sat in the right corner..."), he confided in me that Fr. Groth told the servers that they should not yawn. Once you yawned everybody yawned and all was lost, over. Margaret was making new friends; John became a boy scout. Brian was a happy guy. We were in such turmoil when we moved in July that I had never registered him for kindergarten.

There were alleys behind the houses, between the streets, where the kids played, with garbage men and the ragmen and all sorts of characters passing through. A friend of Madge Blaney had moved from the city to Grosse Pointe where there were no alleys. The little boy was saddened and depressed at the loss of his alleys.

The Masserang family lived nearby. The priests loved to go to the Masserang home on Friday nights for cards. The Masserangs had as many children as we did so our children got along swimmingly. Kathy and Judy remain to this day the closest of friends. Mrs. Masserang was short, sweet, laid back and completely adorable. So darling was she that for a while no one wanted to leave or marry. Art Masserang, a deliveryman for Silvercup Bread, was a coach and used our boys on his team. Jack used Art's boys in the choir. This surprised Art because he was certain that none of his boys could carry a tune. We bought our bread from him and marked on the calendar how many loaves we bought. The only trouble: I used the same calendar to mark my fertile and safe periods to abstain from marriage rituals. This method was working well for the Japanese but obviously not for Irish Americans. The bread/birth control calendar was to blame for my conditions. (Maybe)

One day the Masserang children were at *our* house for a change. Mrs. Jehle stopped by. She was loud and effusive, exclaiming how WONDERFUL the Callaghan children were. She went on and on and then grabbed one of the Masserang boys and cooed, "Aren't you lucky to be a Callaghan?" He tried to reply two or three times but his pleas went unheeded. He kept trying to say, "But I'm not a Callaghan." Barb Masserang and I loved to talk on the phone. We saw each other in church and would wearily and weakly smile at each other.

Brian loved first grade. He happily skipped home down the alley as I waited to hear his latest view on the world. One day when he was home only five minutes from school, the phone rang. A woman said, "Your little boy just broke about 30 panes of glass in my garage."

"Oh, no. Not my little boy. What did the boy look like?"

"Big face, big eyes, lots of curly hair."

I knew it must be Brian. "Wait a minute." I put down the phone and told Brian what the woman said. "Did you do that, Brian?'

He smiled and said, "Yes, I did."

"Why would you do such a thing?"

"Because I love the sound of smashing glass!"

Kathy could some times be a pickle, especially if things were quiet. Every once in a while, I would hear this awful gasping or moan, which was very unnerving for me. I would dash to where she was to see what the trouble was. It was Kathy and, most times, false alarms. After so many wolf cries, I smartened up and would call, "Is there any blood?" Troublemaker that she was, Kathy was always entertaining. In order to go to Nichols School to kindergarten, you had to cross Mack Avenue that was a very busy street. Fortunately there was a traffic light at the corner. I made Kathy promise to always cross at the light. One day I checked on her and she was, of course, crossing at a corner without a light.

To go out the back door on Iroquois, you had to go down five steps. To the left of the steps was a shelf where we put the milk bottles, about six quarts a day. One day Kathy and I were talking and she wanted to know who she was and what she was. She never saw Margaret without clothes but with four older brothers and two younger brothers she saw them undressed at times. She thought maybe she was missing something somewhere. I assured her she was made perfectly. I went on to tell her that if your mother is Irish, you are Irish; if your mother is Catholic, you are Catholic; if your mother is Jewish, you are Jewish. I ended up saying, "If your mother is an Indian, you are an Indian." One day Kathy knocked down about twelve milk bottles as she hustled out the back door. "Oh," I moaned. "How could you be so careless, so dumb, so stupid." She looked me in the eye and said, "If your mother's an Indian, you're an Indian."

We were finally in the post-war years. No longer did we go to bed in sorrow; no longer did we dream of bombings. We knew the Nazis hated the Jews but we were horrified about the camps at Auschwitz. Families were reunited, the service men came home, and many marriages ensued. Some neighbors had television sets and they were reveling in "Howdy-Doody" and, in the Detroit area, "Soupy Sales." Industry greatly improved appliances. Jack bought a washer with its own rinse cycle: No more the endless rinsing of endless diapers! Lo and behold, Jack ordered an automatic dryer. I did miss the ritual of being outside and reaching up to the clothesline and pinning the garments but, hey, I got used to it. Some days that was the only way I got out! We followed the Church year with great interest and observed all feast days, plus the usual Advent, Christmas, Lent, Easter and Pentecost. We prayed the rosary and various litanies.

"Mother most pure."

"Pray for us."

"Mother most chaste."

"Pray for us."

"Mother inviolate."

"Pray for us."

One evening I caught on to the response of the little ones. "Play with us, Play with us," they chanted. I said nothing. I rather liked their version. Once I even heard one of the children say during the Lord's Prayer, "...Give us this day our day old bread."

Our young friend, Josephine, who helped Jack and substituted for him, lived near by. She was having a romance and we were all interested in its progress. Josephine had been dating Vincent for 8 or 9 months. In despair she claimed he had not kissed her even once. Fr. Villerot advised her to stop talking on her dates. She did and the kiss came right away.

The first funeral that Jack did at St. Catherine's was for a young man by the name of Wurm. He left behind his mother, wife and five children. One of the young children was Bob Wurm. He was deeply interested in Church music, the organ as an instrument and, at the same time, attending the seminary. Jack taught him organ, devotions and pretty soon he was playing Masses. Frank Janeck, who had been helping us run two parishes, was a student at University of Michigan, majoring in piano. The choirs in those days were men and boys. It was a lovely combination of sound with the boys' purity of sound soaring over the men's harmonies. Bob came often to the house as a repairman, fixing all the many things that needed attention for a family of our size.

As John and Paul grew older, Bob took them camping. Next, Bob became our babysitter. He would arrive armed with stereopticon slides. He organized the gang in the basement and amused them. One fall when Bob returned to the seminary, the rector summoned him and quizzed him about his summer activities. The rector gave him a look of disapproval when Bob told him of his babysitting activities. "Babysitting is not a dignified activity for a seminarian." Bob replied, "Oh, really? It seems to me with babysitting I can observe Christian families and Christian living." The rector had to admit that was a good point.

Bob painted the dining room a strong shade chosen by yours truly. We discussed the shade forty years later. Bob said it was orange. I still maintain it was passionate pink. It turned out so well that Mrs. Collings, who lived a few doors down, had her living room done in the same hue.

Mrs. Claire Wilde lived across the street between our house and the corner. She was a retired English teacher. She would stop by occasionally with a variety of religious periodicals. As she left she would remark that she would return soon to discuss the articles in detail. Thank goodness she never carried out her threat because we never read the articles. She had a cackling laugh and one day she emitted an extra long guffaw just as Kathy was sailing into the living room. "Why do you laugh like a witch?" Kathy asked. We all pretended not to hear that. Mrs. Wilde's husband was a Lutheran and her prayer was constant to the Lord that he would become a Catholic. Once, Mrs. Wilde returned from a trip to New York City with socks and underwear for the children that she had bought at Macy's as *thirds*. They did come in handy.

Andy and Al Welch who were from Boston moved in across the street. They too had a large family. She was tiny, full of ideas, had mega projects, and was a great young woman. Her husband was an engineer at Ford. He took some of our children to the Thanksgiving Parade. Andy suggested I attend a heart smart class with her. We went to a house where we were taught to make a bed in one walk around, thus saving minutes in our lives. Very valuable!

Andy and I had the same doctor, Dr. Henderson. We discovered when she made a visit the Dr. would talk about Mrs. Callaghan. When I visited, he talked about Andy and her physical condition in detail. We got the message and would call each other to see how we were doing.

Dr. Henderson started to take a real interest in our family. He stopped by one day to give a shot to each of the little ones. All lined up and received their shots. Except one was missing—Eddie. With needle in hand Dr. Henderson started the search and found the culprit under the kitchen sink. He opened the door, pulled down Eddie's pants and right there gave him the shot. Kathy and Eddie needed constant observation. They were innovative, creative, busy people. Eddie was fond of accompanying the mailman on his route. Mr. Williams, our deliveryman, called Eddie "my nemesis." Kathy's teacher on the last day of kindergarten said, "I'll never forget Kathy as long as I live." I didn't ask or want to know why.

Lillian was my right hand woman and my salvation. One day she said, "You know, Mrs. Callaghan, you seem like a good woman and if that's true why, oh, why did God send you Kathy and *then* Eddie? What is in God's plan?" I couldn't answer that one.

Jerry the bakery man stopped by three times a week. He arrived at the front door with an enormous basket of delicious goodies. Eddie's favorite word at the time started with "S" and ended with "T." I admit he must have picked up this unseemly word from his mother who was known to use the word frequently. Her husband, Mr. Wonderful, protested but the mother said she was more than qualified to use the word since she was constantly dealing with it. Jerry the baker was nervous with Eddie near the basket because he was inclined to touch, squeeze and pat the merchandize. One morning while Jerry was there, the phone rang and Eddie dashed to answer it. The phone was hung high so the little ones couldn't reach it but the little scamp pulled a chair and answered it with the "S" word over and over. Wresting the phone from him, I said, "Hello." A lovely cultured voice said, "Mrs. Callaghan?" I thought, *Please, God, have pity on me and never let me meet this woman.* I had to confess to my identity.

"This is Mrs. Rawlings, president of the PTA, and we would like Mr. Callaghan to speak on the responsibilities of fatherhood a week from Tuesday."

"Mr. Callaghan isn't here right now but if you call tomorrow I will have the answer for you." I hung up and dashed to the door. Too late! Eddie had crunched a few loaves of bread that I gladly bought.

Jack went to discipline Eddie one day but he scooted out the door. Jack caught him half way down the stairs and gave his arm a good resounding slap.

"Ha, ha. Missed!" said Eddie.

Eddie had trouble with both his eyes. I used to bring him to the doctor's office on Saturday where he did special eye exercises with a stereopticon slide. These were good for me because I had a little quality time with him. His first surgery was at Harper Hospital. There was a young man who was having cosmetic surgery in the room next to Eddie. They each had bandaged eyes and they would walk the corridor together. Eddie was a patient for 5 days. The nurses were happy to see him go. "How long has he been here?" one nurse asked. "Five days," I said. "It only seems like two weeks. We did stop him from banging the bed pans when we approached him with a hypodermic needle."

After Eddie took the hose on the lawn at Wurm's house and sprayed all the passersby, we took him for a ride to the cemetery. He hopped out of the car, perched on a headstone, and said, "So long."

Patricia was born September 29, 1949. Dr. Henderson was out to a movie and wasn't on hand at first; an intern was in charge, but suddenly Henderson was in command. I sure felt better when I heard the sound of his voice. The dearest, sweetest, curly-haired blonde girl entered our lives. The nurses festooned her curls with gauze bows. I was beginning to know the nurses well. This little girl, Patricia, never screamed or carried on. What a delight! I was beginning to feel like an unfit mother because my babies didn't sleep through the night until they were four or five months old. This little doll slept through the night at two months old.

In the back yard at 3811 Iroquois: Margaret (far right) is holding newborn Patricia; right to left are John, Paul, Jim, Brian, Kathy, Eddie with Bill and Ann in front.

Fr. Kowalski, our friend since the Grosse Pointe days, invited us to an Easter party at his brother Richard's house. Richard's wife Margaret was very beautiful, the mother of a son and daughter, bridal consultants at Russell's department store. I enjoyed being with them very much. Fr. K also invited us to a festive celebration where we met his sisters, Margaret, a little sprite, and Agnes, very regal and dignified. There were many other relatives of his who were gracious and fun to be with.

At this time the household words were "Howdy Doody" and "Milton Berle." They were the rage on TV. We didn't have one yet, but there was hope. Mary Martin in "South Pacific" changed the way we cared for our hair by singing "I'm Going to Wash That Man Right Out of My Hair" and literally shampooing her hair every night on stage and twice a day when there was a matinee. The thinking at that time was two weeks should elapse before a shampoo to keep your hair in good condition.

38

Iroquois, Part II

Wonder of wonders, we bought a car from Fr. Fedewa. It was the best car ever, ever made. It was black, of course, with an unused back seat. We bought this '46 Ford in late '48. On zero degree mornings neighbors would struggle starting their cars but not Jack.

Margaret was studying the violin, as was Kathy. After a few lessons Margaret became first violinist and concertmistress—to her surprise and amazement. Gypsy Kate started violin also and Jim worked with Bob Alport, a fine young cellist. Next, Brian played the trumpet, John, the French horn, and Paul, the oboe. Soon an interesting ensemble was forming. We were saving Eddie for the drums. Preston Wells, a band teacher for the public schools, would stop his car in front of the house after school every Thursday. The budding artists and instruments would pile into his car for a trip to St. Bernard's school orchestra. An hour and a half later they would return. What a heroic, thoughtful man! Not only that, he was a handsome version of Danny Kaye. One Christmas Margaret somehow got a hold of 50 cents and bought Mr. Wells a tie at Neisners. And do you know what? He wore it.

John, French horn, Margaret, violin, Jack, accompanying on piano, Jimmy, cello, Brian, trumpet, and Paul, oboe.

With the car Jack could buy groceries, do the errands, drive from St. Catherine's to St. Bernard's, and not have to depend on the streetcar. Fridays at 5:00 P.M. Fr. Fedewa would appear for a visit. He heard 33 nuns' confessions weekly. He lamented the fact that not one mortal sin and very scant venial sins ever came forth. Fr. would occasionally take us out for dinner. In the closet of the front hall I kept decent shoes, a girdle, a nice dress so when the invitation came I would dash into the closet, shut the door and emerge a few seconds later fit for being treated.

Ann and Patricia were the sweetest, dearest girls. Ann was dark haired, thin and very, very serious. Patricia by contrast was blonde and cherubic chubby. Eddie went to kindergarten at Hilger Elementary and was followed by Billy. The kindergarten teacher produced the most astonishing play. The production bordered on professional. The event was so remarkable that I called the teacher to congratulate her. She wasn't in. A week later I walked to school to give kudos to this teacher. One of the teachers told me that that particular teacher had a breakdown and was spending time in the hospital. Is there a lesson here?

We had a piano in the living room and one in the large bedroom upstairs. Summer vacation mornings were spent with Jack sitting beside the piano giving each one a lesson. After each lesson the child would go upstairs and practice and then return to be audited again. One day at dinner we announced that a new baby was coming. Jack was always pleased and welcoming, but did it ever occur to him the responsibilities that put on his shoulders? After this announcement, silence ensued.

Finally Paul said, "This is getting monotonous."

Eddie queried, "How does the baby get in Mommy's tummy?"

Jack said, "The baby grows from a planted seed."

"Who planted the seed, Daddy?"

"I did," Jack admitted. Sex lesson number one!

Halloween was approaching and I received a note from Ed and Bill's school that the children could come in costume that Friday. Right away I knew Ed would be a devil and why not Bill also? Red shirts and pants, hangers for horns and tails made them resemble Satan—somewhat. Ed trotted down the street. I waited for Bill to follow. No Bill. After a search Bill was found behind the garage in a sad mood.

"Billy," I said, "I told you all the boys and girls will be in funny outfits." I walked him to the corner and watched a reluctant devil wend his way toward school.

Fr. Fedewa, Fr. Kowalski, Jack and I went to Ann Arbor in May one year. Ann Arbor held a music festival every year featuring the Philadelphia Symphony under the direction of Eugene Ormandy. The acoustics of the auditorium were superb, the symphony the very best. Fr. K took us to a summer musical "Brigadoon," performed outdoors at Botsford Inn. We'd meet Richard, his brother, and have dinner first. What a sweet memory!

Frank Janeck liked the University of Michigan. He was studying and practicing hard on the piano, his major. He had a buddy from school named John who was lively and full of fun in contrast to Frank who was very serious. John said, "Conversationally, Frank Sphinx." But Frank met a girl and he was smitten.

Eddie's eyes still needed medical attention. A doctor by the name of Windsor Davies, a noted surgeon, condescended to see Eddie in his magnificent office. His desk was an enormous display of mahogany, his demeanor severe. The seat for the patient was 15' or more away from the doctor. He thought he could help Eddie. Another trip to the hospital. Surgery was scheduled for 7:00 A.M. Word came that Dr. Davies would be delayed until 10:00 A.M., then 2:00 P.M., then 6:00 P.M. Since he was on an empty stomach, Eddie was a hungry, unhappy little fellow. After surgery he had a huge patch over his eye. He revived from the anesthetic and looked at me with his good eye and said, "You know, you could die from not eating."

Clare was born in January. I couldn't bring her home from the hospital because one of the babies had dysentery. Most of my stays were in two-bed rooms. Clare was about 2 hours old when the doctor came to me and said he was putting a young woman with me who had just had a stillborn baby so I could console her. They ushered in a young, beautiful, heartbroken girl. It was very sad and even as I write about it my heart twinges. When Clare was two weeks old, I got viral pneumonia. The doctor wanted me in the hospital but there was no room. He came to see me every day until I became well. In the meantime the baptism had to take place within two weeks of the birth. That is what the Church preached at that time.

Josephine came to the rescue and was proxy godmother for my cousin Jean O'Brien. The godfather was August Maekelberghe, a Belgian organist, well revered as a musician and teacher. He was frail and did his organ duties at an Episcopalian church, St. John's in Detroit. He was, however, a Catholic. Jack had been studying with him and asked him to witness Clare's baptism. He was uneasy because he always said his prayers in his native tongue. During the reception afterwards, one of the little ones tumbled down the stairs. "My God," August said, "No wonder you don't have time to compose." Someone narrated this story to me because during all the festivities I was upstairs flat on my back.

There was a group that sponsored a program called the "Christian Culture Series." Fulton Sheen was usually the opening speaker each season. The programs were held across the Detroit River in Windsor, Ontario. I was fortunate to hear the Trapp family singers in person. The Baron was only seen once when he came out at the end to take a bow. Most of the boys were in the service as skiers in the Alps in some capacity, for the war was still in progress at that time. A priest traveled all the time with the family as manager, director, arranger, etc. This, of course, was before "Sound of Music" was conceived. A delightful concert and memory.

Evelyn Waugh was an outstanding English author. I read many of his books. His most famous was *Brideshead Revisited.* English prose at its best. If you read *Brideshead* and *A Handful of Dust*, you wouldn't regret it. Josephine called me and told me that Evelyn Waugh was to lecture in Windsor and she had tickets. The topic was "Three great writers of the 20th century: G.K. Chesterton, Ronald Knox and Graham Greene." A reader never tires of Chesterton, and Knox had just written a new translation of the Missal. Now Graham Greene had written

The Labyrinth Way, Heart of the Matter, Travels with My Aunt, etc. Of all the writers in the world I had to agree with Waugh, Greene was my very favorite.

Waugh took questions afterwards. I asked if he thought that there could be in real life a character like Scobie, the protagonist in *Heart of the Matter.* "Yes, I not only believe in Scobie. I know him." Now you must read the book to find out what his response means.

Fr. Kowalski was sent to Rome to work on his doctorate. The two years he was gone seemed long. Frank Janeck was an officer in the Navy for two years also. Jack was doing some very successful work. Sr. Claretta was head of music at St. Catherine's. She and Jack had great musical ideas. Sister had a great group of singers. Jack had a wonderful men and boys choir. The news leaked out that Msgr. Vismara was very happy with the music programs at St. Catherine's. Sr. Claretta and Sr. Mary Frederick were experts at tableaux. An opera, *The Headless Horseman,* was produced at the CYO Center; very impressive.

Seasonal concerts were held at both St. Bernard's and St. Catherine's. I remember one rainy night Brian couldn't unlock his empty trumpet case so he wrapped the instrument in 2 or 3 baby blankets. Margaret was concertmistress. John no longer bent sideways when he carried his French horn. Paul was always involved as every oboist is with reeds. Jim trudged along with the cello in his arms. After a stint Jack would order a gallon of ice cream from the drug store at the corner to celebrate the success. Teaching at Marygrove was a treat for Jack. The organ was lovely with sweet pipes, installed in an old fashioned, ornate chapel. He had one voice pupil, Rosemary Bonn who graduated from Marygrove with half of my voice music in her folder. On the night of Rosemary's recital, the tuxedo Jack rented was devoid of studs and cuff links. Paul knew of a store that was open after six an Saturdays and ran down and returned triumphant. It started to rain and we were already late. Ten minutes before Marygrove the car broke down. We eased into a gas station, called a cab and arrived to an anxious singer. One look at Jack and she perked up; the recital was wonderfully done and well received.

One of the spring concerts at St. Catherine ended with the "Battle Hymn of the Republic" with boys, men, high school, grade school choirs and orchestra. Jack was in his "glory halleluiah" and every single person there was beyond thrilled. Sr. Claretta, his conspirator in all these programs, also taught piano to Margaret, John, Kathy and Jim.

Margaret had always from the time she could speak had pithy comments to make on life in general. I used to relate these anecdotes to Madge Blaney and

Fran Conen, my buddies. Margaret overheard me. She wasn't pleased and was less open after that.

39

La Boheme

Billy Fishwick, Jack's friend from Australia, the imaginative organist and musician, invited Jack to become a Bohemian, which was a club for male musicians. They met monthly and wore black silk bows around their necks. They looked like French artists. I must admit that Jack looked adorable in his regalia. At the meeting, various musicians performed programs, usually with rare unfamiliar repertoire. They occasionally invited women. It was great fun; one recital would feature a banjo-saxophone combination. Some of the music was so *avant-garde* it would give you a headache. They often performed beautiful pieces by such modern composers as Britten, Faure and Ravel. Some of the members were not professional musicians. I recall Dr. Ginsberg who was hard of hearing and held a huge trumpet like instrument to his ear. When the music became dissonant, he quickly dropped the horn.

They had members from the Detroit Symphony, some of whom formed a jazz band on the side, called Metamorphosis—great music expertly played. The director of the Boston Pops, Arthur Fiedler, was a guest one time. He was always photographed and televised waist up with huge shoulders and massive head. It was amazing to see him at a height of 5'! Arthur Rubenstein was of small stature too. Bruno Walter was a dinner guest. He was a Mahler lover. He sat at the head table, of course. About 75 people were present. We were seated the farthest away. What an opportunity to study that cleft in the chin, the handsome brown eyes, the noble features. I did nothing but gaze. His eyes were so piercing. Oh, Oh, they were piercing right through *me*! I was totally embarrassed and averted my glance and didn't even peek in his direction after that incident. The highlight was when Jack, in spite of all his irons in the fire, prepared a musical song cycle, "On Wenlock Edge." It was a superb piece wonderfully done and well received. A wonderful memory!

The family was a beehive of activity with music lessons, boy choir practices, John, Paul, Jim and Brian; ditto altar boys. Kathy loved school and was a bosom buddy of Judy Masserang. They liked to present shows in Judy's basement. In their favorite skit Judy was singing, "Gonna Take a Sentimental Journey" and Kathy's big number was "I'm As Corny As Kansas in August."

At holiday time spiritual bouquets were popular. Kathy gave me many. An example: 60 Masses, 60 Communions, 60 visits to Church, etc. She did admit a few years ago that she was still working on the prayers she had promised. Kathy was such a troublemaker that one day her father drove her to the police station and parked in front for a short time, then returned home with Kathy not even a bit repentant.

Brian was going to make his first Communion. The day before the big event he asked if he could go to the movies. "Oh no, Brian. You must stay home and think holy thoughts." He took his sad face over to the Masserangs where a baseball game was in progress. Jack Masserang got up to bat and as he swung at the ball Brian approached him and Bam! The next day one little boy in the procession had a big bandage covering the many stitches in his forehead.

Brian was very musical. He was very good on the trumpet and had a Mr. Smith who played with the symphony as a teacher. His big number was "Trumpeter's Lullaby." He had such a good reputation that the Knights of St. John asked him to play taps at graveside for their deceased members. This was followed by a breakfast that Brian gladly attended where he feasted on donuts galore. Brian spent a lot of time hanging around bakeries and thinking about food. Even his similes involved food. On our infrequent rides out Jefferson Avenue to see Lake St. Clair, Brian would say such things as "The clouds are marshmallows, the lake vanilla pudding" and so forth. One time we squashed ourselves into the '46 Ford and headed for Oswego via Canada. As we went through the tunnel, there was an awesome silence. It was dark; it was scary. All at once a voice piped up, "Home," Eddie squeaked. "Let's go home."

St. Catherine School was overcrowded. They even erected huts to handle the overflow. First graders attended half days only. The first grade nun, who was and always will be a saint, suggested Eddie attend for a full day. He was a real student. After lunch he returned and Sister spent the afternoons giving him messages to take to various rooms in the school. What a fabulous idea! She saved my life. Eddie was an early choirboy and altar boy. He was so eager an altar boy that his timing was off as he anticipated the priest's movements. One time at Benediction Ed took the huge cope to cover the priest and accidentally covered his head. It took Father Britz 3 or 4 minutes to extrapolate himself from under the yards of material.

John and Paul were studying with symphony men. Their French horn and oboe instruments were improving. At one recital at St. Catherine's, Paul was to play a solo on his oboe. The morning of the recital Paul was accidentally hit in the eye with a ball out in the driveway. The doctor said no playing for a while. John was scheduled to play a Mozart piece on the French horn. Before the recital Jack made it clear that John was to wash his instrument in the shower and he did. There is a long interval before the horn starts to play; very ornate, very technical played by his father, the longest introduction in musical composition! Aha, the horn finally started and what was that sound emanating, that glubbiddy-glubiddy-glub sound? "Good God!" his mother shouted. I was so startled I couldn't help myself.

The Catholic Church bought a lovely building that was formerly owned by a German company. It was called C.Y.O. (Catholic Youth Organization). Ann studied ballet there and was in a recital. For a talent contest at the C.Y.O John and a friend James Higgins decided to sing a duet, a hymn called "*Jesu Corona.*" When the time for the performance came, the announcer called out, "We have a group, a trio, to perform. I'm not sure what they have decided to sing, but welcome John Callaghan, James Higgins and Jesu Carona."

40

The Summer Visitors

It was a lovely hot summer. The only place for relief from the intense heat was to go to the movies where you could sit in comfort in air conditioning and it didn't matter whether the movie was horrible or not. Sometimes on a Wednesday night you received a free plate! Then we got great news (??)—Jack's mother, father and brother Jim were coming for a visit. They arrived at a late supper hour and in an unhappy mood. It was Sunday and the trip through Canada was hot and tiresome and the worst thing of all not one place in all of Canada served beer on Sunday. I gave them dinner and the dessert was frozen fruit cocktail, a new recipe at the time. I was greeted with gag sounds and Fishy asked me that the next time I served him water he hoped I would keep my fingers off the edge of the glass. It was a good admonition, I admit.

Josephine Schulte, Miss Upbeat and Sunshine, stopped by for a visit. As she left she said to Nana, "Have a nice vacation."

"Nice vacation!" huffed Mrs. C and bitterly repeated, "Nice vacation, Nice vacation…" All at once my heart went out to her. Why was she dragged to a house with eleven children running in and out and a baby crying for attention in the middle of the night? The men had their eyes set on a ball game at Brigg's Stadium and to search out the longest bar in the world that was reputed to be in Detroit. The old girl deplored my cooking and gagged at everything and thrust her plate into the middle of the table. I had spent every moment thinking of how to please her, but let's face it: pleasing Nana was nigh impossible.

Pingree Park was two blocks away and after dinner I fled there, found a swing, and remained swinging until it grew real dark and the stars showed their faces. All was quiet when I came home. We took a streetcar the next day down to the big city. Nana was looking for shoes. At the store she removed her shoe and asked me if I noticed how slender, how lovely her feet were; as she said this, I tucked my feet that were short, fat and ugly behind me. Ever since I had sat on the beach in the 8th grade with Neil, I knew my feet were ugly because he told me so. He didn't actually use the word "ugly"; "odd" I think he said as well as "fat, funny little toes…" Before that moment I had never considered my piggies at all, but he was right and he loved me anyway!

The sidewalk was literally steaming when we came out of the store. The tar on some of the sidewalks was melting. A nearby sign read 96 degrees. We took a taxi home. During the ride home Nan cleared her throat and said, "You know, when one is tired and upset some people make remarks that they don't mean." I said nothing. Jack's priorities were God, Church and job that he loved. To entertain his parents never occurred to him. That night he retired early because he had a 6:00 AM Mass.

Nana was the first to sit on the couch with me. She talked about Jack and how she loved to hear him practice. She reminisced about teaching at St. Paul's when she was a young girl. When Nana toddled off to bed, who came to sit with me but Fr. Jim. His big story was about being very sick. No one could find the trouble but finally the doctors were fairly sure it was his appendix. He was scared beyond scared. He told me not about the surgery but about what he might say under anesthesia. Something vulgar or obscene maybe! The doctor laughed when Jim told him of his fear. No one ever pays attention to a patient, not even a Catholic priest! He was trying to comfort him. I reminded him that he found it impossible to work with his father during school breaks because he couldn't bear his father's constant swearing. Well the surgery went horribly, they couldn't find the damn (oops!) appendix at first, and finally after exploring found it near his back.

My third visitor on the couch was Fishy. He reminisced about living next door to my father as a boy when they lived on Varrick Street and that the O'Briens, Mae, Agnes, Ann and Helen were the thin lipped girls. I asked him about Jack as a boy, was he good? Silly question. He was not only good but sweet, even tempered, and smart. Then Fishy toddled off to bed.

I went to the kitchen to check out its appearance; there on the counter were three cups with three different dental appliances. For a moment I wanted to join mine with theirs but then I had a full set that I only removed when I cleaned them and I didn't want to upstage them. They left the next day. All were happy but I think Nana was the happiest to get out of there.

Let's be serious. Why was I always pregnant? Was I a freak of nature as Fr. O'Rourke suggested? The birth control system that worked for the Japanese women wasn't working even when I put the safe days on its own calendar and not along the bread delivery count which now had a calendar of its own. If you think we were playing house a lot, you're wrong. If you think Jack was an insatiable animal—you'd be wrong. The doctor said he thought it might be possible I might ovulate more than once a month. Three months before a birth and three months later, we waited. I know I loved Jack and it was the only way I got attention, but what I really think is that the children were destined to be born.

Christopher was born on Good Friday before the *Tenebrae* and after the *Tre Ore.* I was preparing Tuna a la King when it hit me. He was a beautiful baby with adorable buns. I nearly died, not from childbirth but from the kielbasa by roommate's mother brought her as an Easter gift. Her mother made it and she offered me one. I happily ate it and then the burn set in and the strange pain in my stomach. I tried to smile in appreciation. You know I can still recall the incident that occurred so many years ago. Bob Wurm, our handy man, organ substitute, baby sitter and friend was Christopher's godfather. Clare and Christopher, just as with everyone else born to us, had their own identity, their own uniqueness. Clare was a very girly girl—very serious, sensitive and a little shy. Christopher as a tot loved to make believe he was playing the piano. He would bang for a while and when he stopped we would clap and make approval noises. He would play again, each time shorter than the one before so he could hear the sound of approval sooner.

Fr. Kowalski let us borrow a record, "*Symponie*" by Honneger. It was deliciously vibrant and exciting. As we sat and listened to the record, Christopher who was five years old at the time came into the room, stopped, listened and started to dance. It was his own spontaneous choreography. He gestured here and there; he stepped this way and that, all to the exciting tempo of the music. We stayed quiet, not moving, not interrupting, hardly breathing, until the masterpiece of a dance finished. At the end he stopped and silently left the room. A great memory for both of us to share!

I was becoming weary and was smoking a lot. The work was an endless, 24-hour drudgery. I stood at the kitchen window and gazed at the steeple of St. Catherine's church that was in view two blocks away. "Take me, Lord," I prayed. "Get me out of here, O Lord, I am beyond weary, take me to you, assume me." Can you imagine anyone having that much gall? But it was a lovely thought being brought out of the kitchen over the steeple and straight into the arms of the Lord. I would sit on the landing going up the back stairs and grieve and grieve and pray I could pull myself up from the depths. "*De Profundis Clamavi, Domino.*"

Ed was an altar boy and tripping the priests in his anxiousness to serve. Kathy loved school and read a lot when she wasn't starting trouble. When Billy was in the 4th grade, the sister called her room "Happy House." One day she called me and said Billy was having trouble with his reading and would I mind if he remained after school so she could help him. Mind? God bless this woman; she saw him every day until he was on his way and getting good grades.

John was an altar boy and since we lived so near the church we received many calls for Masses, weddings, funerals and other devotions. Paul liked to fix things. He was very aware of me. In truth, he was the only one who knew I was alive. God will bless him always for helping me into my nylons in between contractions on my way to the hospital. He even cut my toenails and treated my ingrown toenails. I talked to Margaret as if she were my age, woman to woman. The same was true with John and Paul. Jimmy was full of pep and energy. His deportment was poor and Sister said he could take the entire classes' attention away from her as she taught. He was on a weekly report.

Now some of the nuns thought, "Oh, dear, sweet Callaghan children, aren't they lovely?"; others remarked to the kids, "Just because you're a Callaghan, don't think you are going to get away with a thing." When Jim was in the upper grades, he studied piano with Sr. Brigetta who was determined to bring culture to the east side of Detroit. Recital time was coming and his number was to be "Scotty Capers"; well, it was not coming along nicely. So Sister Brigetta with wisps of red hair escaping from her starched bonnet ordered him to the convent to practice. He went to the room opened the window and escaped.

The older boys were being taught how to play the liturgies: Requiem Masses, about three different Latin Masses, the responses and so forth. I can't help repeating over and over how much the nuns at St. Catherine's aided me in my quest for learning for my children. I admit I liked the nuns. I liked being with them. Sr. Basila had a happy class. She started each day by giving every child a baby aspirin and sprinkling them with holy water. The bottle of holy water was in her desk drawer.

Mother Mary Richard was the principal. She ran a good ship or so it seemed. She was medium height with a sweet pleasant face. The real rule of the school was Mrs. Williams. Mrs. Williams was the school cleaner, busy body, and reporter to the principal about all that was going on. Mrs. Williams was black and a lovely person. She had a daughter, bought a white grand piano, and had her daughter study with Jack. Mrs. Williams was a real asset to St. Catherine's school.

Sr. Claretta was the music teacher. She was homely and Irish (Maloney was her name). Sr. Claretta and Jack got along beautifully. They schemed up all sorts of great programs. Sr. Mary Frederick was a cohort and she and Claretta were expert at assembling tableaus. Sr. Claretta had high school chorale groups. She taught piano privately and John, Paul, Jim, Brian, and Kathy became her students. Margaret was her favorite but Sister told me that when Margaret was upset, she set her jaw and there was no reasoning with her. Jack spent many hours with Srs. Claretta and Mary Frederick. As a result they presented outstanding programs in the high school.

It is true I was busy. The work was non-stop: breakfast cleaning ending just in time for all to return for lunch, care for the babies, then dinner. The kids started to set the table, clear the dishes and wash and wipe them. We celebrated all of the Saint's days, high holy days, feasts of the Blessed Mother, plus the kid's birthdays at which time they chose whatever cake they wanted. I was too busy to think of myself, no more singing except an occasional Mass. I never left the house except to go to Mass on Sunday, and slept until the consecration bells woke me up. I would lie awake at night ruminating about priorities. I reviewed the previous day in my mind. I could hear an echo of my screaming. My standards were slipping. I was becoming a shrew. I can't, I must not, say no all the time. After a baby I would think when I got home things would be different. I would be better organized, a more thoughtful mother. I know no mother could be more caring.

The excitement of the new baby when I got home would last a few days and then there I was back in the endless drudgery and giving 100% was not enough. Some nights I would just get to sleep and it was time for the 2:00 AM bottle. I liked the 2 o'clock event because it gave me time to study and play with the new baby without any interruptions. Then back to bed with my mouth full of plastic teeth, my legs throbbing and feet stinking. I started to smoke a lot. What an insidious habit. But I would quit soon and meantime it was a source of comfort.

If I had a moment, I'd sit on the back landing and have a talk with myself. 1) God would never give me a burden I couldn't carry; 2) I had a husband I loved deeply and was anxious for his success; 3) I was strong, healthy and possessed a lot of energy; 4) I should count my blessings instead of sheep. My dream of a home was a place for peace, comfort, sanctuary where people would hurry home and be safe and secure in the womb of the family.

Kathy was excused early from school to help me make way for lunch, to clean up the debris left from breakfast. His majesty would arrive at 11:30 AM. Lunch was served: soup and egg salad sandwiches or french toast, scrambled eggs for fourteen and make it snappy! The Lord and Master donned a robe and swung his necktie to the back of his neck. A slight flourish of his arm, then a larger high flourish: "Napkin," he demanded. "Napkin." I would have left him then, but I had no money, no clothes, not even energy and my desperate love for him began to dwindle. He left for school to teach looking neat—that he was.

"Keep your sunny side up. Hide the side that gets blue. If you have nine sons in a row, baseball teams make money, you know. Keep, Keep your sunny side up, let your laughter come through so stand upon your legs like two fried eggs. Keep your sunny side up."

41

Therapy

Instead of a complete breakdown, I signed up at U of M for an extension course in French. It was held at the Rackham Building in downtown Detroit. Monday from 7 to 10 PM Jack delivered me and picked me up. I began to do my ironing at night after the wee ones were tucked away around 8:00 PM. I couldn't wait to put them down then around 1:00 after the "Steve Allen Show" I would float from bed to bed: *Aren't they sweet? Aren't they adorable? What a dear, dear family!* Ironing was an occupation I enjoyed because you accomplished something, swaying back and forth in different rhythms, making each wrinkle disappear, putting the articles on hangers or folding them ever so neatly. There! A visual accomplishment!

Now I put the French text on the ironing board, read the lesson, and while ironing put the text to memory. Twenty-five people were in the class, one man a lawyer and musician whom I knew from the Bohemians. He noticed me and we sat together. He was boning up on his French because he went to Paris often. Our teacher Professor Kalla was from Rio De Janeiro. He told us one day was more beautiful than the next in Rio. The breeze was always sweet, the sky always *bleu.* One day he couldn't stand the beauty any longer, so he came to Detroit where in January it couldn't be uglier. I knew my lesson and when Professor Kalla asked a question not one person raised his hand, so I did. After a few lessons my friend on the way out of class told me I was not to raise my hands at all times. I asked him, "Why not?"

"You startle him. He does not expect anyone to answer." All the time I took the class I assumed I would get credit but I discovered at the end this was not so.

Professor Kalla said that young people should learn a different language. Why? Because their focal facial muscles are not formed yet and are flexible. Bob Wurm had bought a chalkboard on an easel and gave it to the kids. It was in the basement so on Tuesday nights I gathered my group of flexible muscles and started a French class. "*Paris est la Capital de la France…*" The gang was very compliant.

At the ten-minute break at class I told the professor of my endeavors. He was quite upset. Didn't I realize I had one of the worst accents in the class? I was chagrined at his opinion and not wanting to ruin the kids for future linguistic adventures I eventually cancelled my class in the basement.

Josephine Schulte was a dear, sweet friend. I know I mentioned her before but she was a dear young woman; head of the Sodality. She studied with Jack and helped by substituting at the many services. Her father, Cap Schulte and Josephine lived in a house not too far away. Josephine's mother had died so there were just the two of them. He was a great collector of tools and began helping to mend some of our things. He taught me never to throw away a nail or screw or anything that looked as if it belonged to something. He was a big German and because of age he shuffled his feet. One time as he was going out the door he wanted to know if I knew that the size of a woman's mouth was the same size as her vagina—odd fellow.

One evening Cap Schulte shuffled up the back stairs and into the dining room where I was swaying to my ironing. He was growling and I was starching and ironing my criss-cross organdy curtains that I dearly loved and considered worth the effort. I was just about to put the starched ironed curtains on the rods when he whimpered, "I can't go on without some money. Mr. Callaghan owes me money. It's not fair. It's not fair." Eddie was playing some kind of game running around the table.

"Don't ask me about it. I don't have a penny. You must talk to Mr. Callaghan, not me." Just then Eddie came around the table and as he passed, Cap gave him a good kick. I went ballistic. I grabbed the curtain rod, held it high and went for him in one of the few rages of my life. He didn't shuffle out, he scurried out and fortunately I missed him and I never saw him again. Josephine looked like her father but other than that you wouldn't know they were related.

Margaret was on the list of Mass players. The services were in Latin and she had the Requiem and a few others in her repertoire. At the end of Mass the priest sings, "*Ite, Missa est.*"The response is "*Deo gratias.*" Some of the chants are simple while on some special occasions they are quite florid. One day at the end of Mass the priest, Fr. Complo, burst out with a grandiose "*Ite, Missa Est.*" Margaret just turned off the organ and left. I was proud of her. The sisters were pulling Margaret aside and suggesting that she might have a vocation and to think about it. She thought, but not long. Margaret, John, Bob Wurm, Josephine, Frank Janeck were all involved with services at St. Bernard's and St. Catherine's. Jack was busy from dawn to 9 or 10 at night with services, rehearsals, organ practice, choir practice, private lessons and, don't forget, grocery shopping. I ordered so much "Glo Coat" that the grocer wondered if I drank it.

Fr. Kowalski was sent to Rome to earn his doctorate in Theology. He returned home after two years; it was good to have him home and still stationed at St. Catherine's. We had such wonderful priests: Fr. Hayes, for example, was an excellent homilist. One young man was sent to St. Catherine's, newly ordained and full of fervor. His first appearance at church was the last Sunday in June at 10:00 AM Mass. The temperature was 94 degrees. No air conditioning in the '50's. If you wanted to cool off, you went to the movies. This new priest's name was Fr. Cunningham. He was very handsome too. His sermon was at least 45 minutes long and the congregation was wilting rapidly. He had his notes and by golly he was over-prepared if there can be such a thing. Once he shouted, "Blood on the streets of Jerusalem." Then he repeated the phrase. He calmed down and after that his homilies were fine. He and Jack had a spat over the importance of altar boys versus choirboys. He had an enemy later in drink but he helped the poor, became pastor of an inner city parish, and founded an education program after the 1967 race riots in Detroit, Focus Hope, with a unique participation of inner city kids in businesses and in the community.

Years later he came to our church seeking funds for his school and he gave me a big hug. He demanded to know why Jack was garbed in pink and orange velvet and was he going sissy, or what? I told him the pink on his robe was for his Master's degree in music and the orange for Syracuse University. He laughed and said he knew all that but he liked to tease. God bless Fr. Cunningham and his Focus Hope, which is still going strong despite his recent death.

42

Visiting Oswego

The trips to Oswego in the summer were a great distraction. One summer we went home for Jack's brother's ordination and first Mass at St. Paul's Church in Oswego. The trip home was exciting with eight children aboard; Bill the baby in a bassinet. Mother had bought a baby bed when I went home for Brian's birth. Some of the kids stayed at the Callaghans. It was a thrill to hear the organ and even more thrilling to hear Jack on a lovely instrument again. It must have been hard for him to leave the treasure in the first place.

For me the summer visits were precious because of time I had with Mother and Dad. Mother and I would talk for hours, non-stop. Being sort of a recluse and without a confidant, it was therapy for her to recount, recall, reminisce (some things I'd rather she had forgotten), or talk about the latest books she had read. After the hours we would call time out and later continue where we left off in our conversations. She loved to talk about God always taking care of the orphan and she was so grateful that God gave her Paul because he took great care of her. Of course, my father could be quite stubborn and she didn't know what to blame it on: his Irish-ness or his German-ness or maybe it was a combination. They were always the great lovers and outside of the drinking episode, which we never discussed, it was a great marriage. Since Dad was a gregarious and a hail-fellow-well-met kind of guy, it was hard for Mother (who was so different) to understand his ways.

One time they were at a wedding and Dad had the opportunity to sit for a while and talk to the "other side," can you imagine? You would think Dad was in politics the way he acted. He spoke to everyone literally and he attended all wakes. Paradoxically, he had no close friend but Mother. Uncle Bill asked him to join the Kiwanis Club. He did so reluctantly but once he did he enjoyed it. In fact, they had a dinner dance and I sang a favorite song of his, written by one of the Firestones of Firestone Tires. It was the theme song for one of the "Firestone Hour" radio programs:

A garden sweet, a garden small
Where rambling roses creep a garden wall.
Where dainty phlox and columbine are
Nodding to the trumpet vine.
I look upon each flower dear
And thrill because at last you're near.

We talked about the mystery of death and how strange no one has come back to tell us about the other side. I told her about my fruit man's philosophy. He intends to lead a good clean life and abide by the golden rule. Then if there is a heaven he'll go there and if there isn't one everyone will say, "That Joe, what a good guy." After hearing that story, Mother adopted the idea as her own.

I would slip over to Virginia Dean's, my former Latin teacher, for a Scrabble game and she always beat me. I wonder why? However, one day we were at the park playing and a bumblebee joined us. It didn't bother me; remember my being covered with bees at Chautauqua? Virginia was bothered and accepted any word I put down and we hustled away and I won by default! In our friendship we must have played hundreds of games of Scrabble. Of course, Fran Brown, who lived 5 houses away, and I were always together. She took the kids swimming at Fair Haven State Park. Fran was a teacher and to describe her as bossy and dictatorial would be only the tip of the iceberg. We parked and she roared to all the boys, "TAKE YOUR CLOTHES OFF IN THE CAR." This they did and emerged as four little nudes. Fran and I had to hold each other with laughter. Well, they did as they were told, didn't they? Margaret, of course, had her suit on under her dress as did Fran and I. Margaret had her own adventures with her Uncle Jim, Fishy and Nana Callaghan, going to Boston, Stony Creek and getting her first major sunburn.

Brian loved Oswego. He loved it at Nana Callaghan's but while he was there he wondered what was going on at Nana O'Brien's across the bridge and on the Westside. He spent most of his time crossing the bridge. "Big Paul," my father, worked at Neal-O'Brien Lumber. On Friday nights he didn't come home until 9:00 PM. Mother depended on Dad to take over the evening entertainment when the children were visiting. Friday night was hard on her. After the dinner chores she would regale them with her repertoire of stories.

One Friday night she said, "How about one of you telling a story?" Silence. Then Brian volunteered. Mother said he went on and on for over an hour and was very interesting with plots, sub-plots, and plenty of characters. He enchanted his siblings and grandmother and suddenly it was 9:00 o'clock and Big Paul was driving in the driveway. I am so grateful that Margaret, John, Paul, Jimmy and Brian spent such quality time in Oswego. For me it was true bliss to sit at the kitchen table at 162 West Third Street. One time my mother served me vegetable soup. I raved how delicious, how comforting, was the soup. Mother was miffed. "It's just a can of heated Campbell's soup."

"Yes, Mother, but it was your hands that opened the can. You served it in a dear familiar bowl on the table of memories, in the kitchen of my childhood." No wonder I found it delicious.

43

Back to Iroquois

Ursula Butler lived across the street from St. Catherine's Church. She was interesting to meet. She had a column in the parish bulletin. The authors were Edith and Gregory who were living in the church steeple. Edith and Gregory were very observant and being birds could remark on all kinds of things and give their terse and critical opinions that mere parishioners couldn't do. She called me one day and asked if I could provide a musical program for the Ladies Society Tea. Of course, I would. I lined up Ann, Patricia, Clare and taught them "Catch a Falling Star," "Side by Side," and "Over the Rainbow."

I taught them gestures and a few dance steps. I went to Hudson's department store and bought three identical white cotton blouses with red and blue polka dots and, of course, with a pocket in which to put falling stars. The day before the performance, Clare ran a temperature and started to wear a strange set of bumps that were later diagnosed as chicken pox. I called Dr. Henderson and bemoaned the fact that no one I knew in the area had chicken pox. "It's air borne," he said. He slammed the phone receiver; he always did. Now it was down to a duet. I couldn't help thinking about the Duncan sisters performing in Vaudeville when I was about 10 years old and their little Eva and Topsy routine. Ann and Patricia were the hit of the afternoon and Edith and Gregory gave them 4 stars for their performance.

Mrs. Wilde would stop by once in a while. She had the boys over at times to help her. She paid them in pennies. They really should have done her chores for free. After all they were Christians. She told me John took forever, Paul would not listen to suggestions, and that Jimmy was ok. Every Saturday she called on the phone for Brian. After a few months I asked him, "What do you do for Mrs. Wilde?"

"Well," he said, "she cleans out her refrigerator and I eat the leftovers. Last week she had a Dairy Queen. Can you beat it?"

My precious boy, a garbage disposal?

Out pastor, Msgr. Vismara, traveled to Rome one summer and died there. Suddenly the parish was in an uproar. I stopped Mrs. Wilde to tell her the sad news and she laughed and laughed and couldn't stop. I remember when I heard of Fran Brown's brother's sudden death in his dorm room at Niagara University, I reacted the same way. I guess laughter and tears are exchangeable emotions. At that time in Italy embalming wasn't practiced so when they brought Msgr. Vismara home he couldn't lie in state.

Dr. Henderson was very interested in my comfort when I was spending my annual visit to Eastside General Hospital. In those days a mother stayed for 10 days, so I was there for a while. Kevin was born July 11 and it was hotter than hot. Margaret was visiting in Oswego and my mother joined her on the train ride back home. What a joy to see her pop into the room at the hospital.

One night Dr. Henderson stopped around 9:00 PM after a delivery. I was reading a book. He said, "You should not be reading by such poor light." He disappeared and returned with a lovely lamp. He got on his knees and then his stomach in order to plug in the lamp. I was thankful and he was pleased. The next shift came on and one of the nurses came into my room. It was a triple room but I was alone. "What's going on here?" she roared, spying the lovely lamp on the table.

"What do you mean?" I replied defensively.

"That lamp doesn't belong here and you know it. How dare you do such a thing?"

Without waiting for a reply, she whisked out and returned with the head nurse. "Well, if you really want to know, Dr. Henderson put it there!"

"Well, he has his nerve!"

The two got on their hands and knees and unplugged the lamp and marched out.

Lillian took care of the kids. It was such a strain on her. She lost her hair and when I got home from the hospital her hair was all on ends because she ran out of Peach Pomade. Her hand was bandaged from a third degree burn from hot grease that spilled. She looked as if she should go to the emergency room. A few weeks later she returned for the Baptism party looking very beautiful. We were so pleased at each other's appearance and Lillian said she never could remember me wearing hose without runs.

"Raisins or popcorn?" she would ask when she came to clean; it was usually both.

Lillian went to a big party on Belle Isle the 4th of July and the next April had a baby. While she was recuperating from the baby, Quintine took her place. She smoked almost as much as I did. She would smoke as she vacuumed and pick up the ashes with the machine as she went from room to room. One day at lunch she confided in me that working for me did Lillian a lot of good. That was a funny thought. Then she said, "You served her good nutrition." It was so upsetting to hear that. What kind of a life did she live? One day when Kathy and Eddie were challenging, Lillian said, "Mrs. C, I know you try to be a Christian woman so what was God thinking when he sent you Kathy and then Eddie? Yes, sir, what was in the Maker's mind?" She worked for the Williams family on the next block. They had fourteen children. She quit them because she said, "Mrs. Williams doesn't try; at least you try."

I saw Mrs. Williams infrequently but when our paths met we exchanged feeble smiles and waves. Mr. Williams was a cop and very juvenile in attitude. He put the siren on the top of his car so he could hurry home for lunch. He repaired our wiring once. At least he was handy. The basement had a foot of water and he stood in it as he did his repairing. I fled to my bedroom and prayed. He survived and did a good job. One noon when the Williams kids came home for lunch, they found their mother under the kitchen table. Three weeks later the hospital released her. The next week she started a job at the hospital that had released her. She did office work and as far as I know got her act together. Her problem, I think, was trying to please her mother, her sisters, her aunts, her husband and her children and that mind set will put anyone in the hospital. I was lucky; I just wanted to please my Lord and Oh, yes, my husband, too.

We were slow in recognizing the fact that Msgr. Vismara had dropped dead in Rome. Even the funeral left us puzzled. Fr. Kowalski was sent to teach at Marygrove. A new pastor, Msgr. Donnelly, head of the seminary, was to be the new pastor at St. Catherine's. Three new assistants came aboard: Fr. Britz, young and handsome, tall with a cleft chin and a humorous outlook on life; Fr. Complo, fresh from ordination; small, wiry and eager to work for the Lord, an aspiration he has never lost; and Fr. Trepsa, tall, heavy European accent and drooping disfigured eye with a cigarette holder dangling from his lips. These three men became very chummy and did not hide their ethnicity: German, Italian, and Latvian.

I remember many of Msgr. Donnelly's sermons. In talking about youth, he said, "You can trust your children, but you can't trust human nature." The sight to behold every morning was Margaret, John, Paul, Jim, Brian, and Bob Wurm all scurrying off to play Masses. Jack was playing at St. Catherine's and in the early days would run down the street to Mack Avenue to catch a bus to St. Bernard's. I would fill in at St. Catherine's in the middle of the Mass, usually before the consecration. I would dash up into the loft and Jack would go off to St. Bernard's. These switches unnerved Ursula Butler. To hear playing and singing and then all of a sudden hear another voice interrupted her meditations.

Fr. Britz was involved with the youth in the parish at the time Elvis hairdos and pointed shoes were popular. They were strong, tough, blue class guys, mostly Italian. They followed Fr. Britz around like sheep. I can see him now with a biretta cocked to one side of his head wearing a black cassock followed by ten or twelve teenagers in procession from church to school. The guys are smiling and pithy remarks are coming from Fr. Britz's lips. One day Fr. Britz called me and he asked me to straighten out Mrs. Hunt and her family. I told him I was too involved with my own family to help anyone else. John, Paul, Jim and Brian had paper routes. There were no profits because the Dairy Queen was at the corner.

Mrs. Wilde was a former schoolteacher. One day when I was visiting she read me some of the papers she cherished that her former pupils had written. Mr. Wilde whom I never met was a Lutheran and her only wish in life was that he would become a Catholic. He died a Catholic. I felt so sorry for the man. It seems as he was gasping his last wheeze he nodded yes to becoming a Catholic. He was laid out at Bourgeoise's Funeral Home with a rosary in his hands; Claire was a happy widow.

The choir consisted of men and boys. Women were not preferred: Boo on the Church! You could not eat meat on Fridays. There was no argument about money in our family; there was no money to fight about. Sometimes Jack would have to go a few days early to get his salary because we were down to zilch!

Dr. Proctor, a well-known ear, nose and throat surgeon, removed Jim, Brian, Kathy, and Clare's' tonsils. Eddie at one time had a severe throat problem. Dr. Proctor was to see him and I brought Kathy along because I didn't trust her. The doctor was not impressed with Eddie's throat. He decided to check Kathy as long as I had her along. Lo and behold! Hers were as bad and needed immediate attention. Jack's hearing was bothering him but Proctor said all musicians think they are losing their hearing.

Fr. Patrick was stationed at Arch Street in Boston. He had problems hearing confessions. He went to a specialist in Albany by the name of Dr. Kopp who operated on his ears. It was a great success. We traveled to Albany and Dr. Kopp thought Jack was a good candidate for surgery. We stayed with friends of Chuddy's in Albany by the name of Callaghan. After the surgery the doctor said that Jack's bad ear was infected so he operated on the good one! Jack wasn't moving much so I took a cab back to the Callaghans, and next morning at seven I returned to Jack's room. I found his roommate in great stress over Jack. He said,

"I never saw anyone so sick. He vomited all night long and no one came to help him." That was my first lesson: never, never leave a relative in a strange hospital in a strange city over night. Jack could hardly walk. We weaved up and down the hills of Albany. The doctor was disappointed. We came home disheartened.

44

A Growing Family

The troops were growing like weeds. Margaret played Masses for Jack. She was first violinist in the orchestra. She had good grades and good friends. John was talking about going to the seminary and becoming a priest. Paul was a good student and he could fix things including my ingrown toenails. He studied oboe with one of the symphony men. Jim was studying cello with a parishioner, Bob Alport, who was married to a musician, Harriet. Bob would come some evenings, set up his cello and play for hours. I really didn't deserve that. Jack, of course, was in the feathers!

Brian was very musical. His piano, trumpet, organ, all were great. He had a gravelly voice. I took him to Dr. Proctor who said he had a growth on his larynx, that he removed. It was a joy to watch when he played Leroy Anderson's "Trumpeter's Lullaby." He was a very serious, young, blue-eyed boy holding his trumpet not straight forward but at a slant.

Kathy went on a field trip to Shrine of the Little Flower in Royal Oak. She brought home for me a plastic covered prayer to St. Girard, the patron saint for fertility! One day she started to tattle on a classmate and Sister told her to mind her own bee's wax. Bill was not quite so shy and he and Ed were as close as pages in a book. One Sunday when everyone was at church, Ann, who was three at the time, wanted to go out to play. I said it was ok. It was January and about freezing. I put her snowsuit on and said, "Don't go away." I was used to putting on snowsuits, boots, mittens, scarves, etc. to let them go out to play and usually in fifteen minutes they were back in. This time it didn't happen. I put on my coat and looked. No Ann. I went down the driveway. No Ann: not in front, not in back, not in sight anywhere. Only a mother to whom this has happened can know the pain that ensued. I ran to Colling's house nearby. Mr. Colling's got his coat. Another neighbor, Mr. Dobson, got his coat and we started to look further and further. Mr. Dobson got in his car and started to explore the horizons.

About thirty minutes later, he returned with good news. He spied a police car on Van Dyke about five blocks away. The policeman was outside his car and one had a child in his arms. He told the police where she lived. Sure enough they drove up. Tears sting my eyes as I recall the sweet, dear serious little girl who was in the policeman's arms. Very serious but not that perturbed. "Your little girl said when I asked her where she was going on a frosty Sunday morning, 'Why, I'm going to buy ice cream for dinner.'" I can't help but think of Mary and Joseph panicking when Jesus was not to be found.

Fr. Kowalski was living in a great apartment in the Cathedral rectory while he was teaching at Marygrove College. He called and wanted Jack and me to talk about married life for a group that met in the church. I said I'd ask Jack. Well, I didn't because I was mad at him for something and as a result I was not speaking to him. This attitude was useless on my part because with all the noise and carrying on in the house he failed to notice. When Fr. K called the next day and wanted to know what Jack thought about talking to young married couples, I said, "Well, to tell you the truth, I am not speaking to him."

"Well, if you do, call me back and let me know."

I took a course in Creative Writing at the Rackham U of M extension. Jack drove me down for a while but then I discovered I could take a bus. When the children went to bed, Jack would sit in the hall on duty. He would read books and proctor at the same time. I met a woman about twenty years older than I at the bus stop. She was heading for the same class. I enjoyed her company immensely. She lived in a posh section called Indian Village. She was a woman of wealth and breeding. She said she was bored, bored to tears. She was so sick of lunch parties and bridge games that she had to do something else so she was starting to get her feet wet with creative writing. There were about 25 people in the class. Our teacher was semi-interesting. I became a prolific writer. I wrote late at night. I wrote getting meals and actually had a bit of food on my paper from being on the drain board. I wrote at the ironing board and on top of the dryer, in the sunroom, everywhere.

As a result, I presented a paper a week. Not many presented writings but one man got our attention. He was a tall, black man with a melodious voice. He was writing a scenario for a movie! Pretty ambitious. It was all about dancing clouds and chariots of angels scurrying about. It sounded great. I wonder if he ever published it; well, at least it was good therapy for us. After a while the teacher started by saying, "We are not—do you hear me?—*not* going to read any of Mrs. Callaghan's material for a while." At the last class, a woman got up and read a superb short story, the plot and dialogue excellent—I still remember some of her terse passages.

There was a Catholic dinner for organists and their pastors. What a brainstorm that was! Msgr. Donnelly was to pick up Jack about 6:00 PM. Jack was not quite ready when his boss arrived. The rest of us rag-tags had just finished dinner. The youngest dashed for him and hung around him and hugged his knees. Jack descended the stairs in sartorial splendor but Msgr. Donnelly was dotted with crumbs, splotched with peanut butter and who knows what else! I refused to let them leave until I restored him to respectability with a damp cloth.

The highlight of the year was Mother and Dad coming for Thanksgiving. Dad would do all the rituals required for fixing a turkey. The ceremony of his carving was awesome. Mother had a mole near her nose and had to answer a hundred questions about it. Mother loved diamonds and wore two or three on a finger. Clare was impressed and asked her how many times she had married. Mother said the gang trooped in early in the morning. Patricia said, "Nana, you are sleeping on the wrong side." They were devoted to Mother and Dad the first week but Mother said in the middle of the second week they wanted to know if Nana and Big Paul were ever going to go home. Mother said years later that the children's personalities never changed; they just got older.

A Thanksgiving pose on the porch at 3811 Iroquois with Mother and Dad, Jack and me (holding Kevin, no.13) and the other 12.

There was no Tooth Fairy in Oswego but there was one in Detroit and since teeth were in and out all the time we were busy dropping change where it could be found. Kathy was bringing home some very interesting characters from school. John (in private) as an 8th grader bemoaned the fact that all the fathers of the other kids worked in factories and why didn't his? Jim was on weekly report. He was acquiring a little group and he was their fearless leader. I observed John one day as he was coming home from school, doing all sorts of jumps, hand tricks, etc. to attract the girls who were giggling at his actions.

Margaret was beginning to like high school. Boys were hanging around. I remember one, Tony Alessi, who was the most handsome boy I have ever seen. I kept encouraging her to go to the Blue Ribbon, a dairy soda place two blocks away: a great hangout. I had such fond memories of hanging out at a soda counter in Oswego. Delores Murphy, Fran Tocco, Annette "Sweetie" Fontana were her best friends and I liked them as much as Margaret did. "Sweetie" used to love to lie on the couch and put her feet up, have some cigarettes and go home where all the above was forbidden. The sisters were after Margaret to be a nun but no go in that department. John at the end of 8th grade announced he would like to be a priest. I was surprised and so was Jack. What a great idea, to have a son a priest; the crowning prize! He would follow in his Uncles Jim and Chud's footsteps. Naturally we agreed. The seminary had great teachers and he would get the best education. Mother Superior reported to me that she saw Margaret in the front seat of a convertible with Busty Calvaruso. She told me that Italians do not make good husbands and I should be more watchful.

By this time Margaret had a full plate, playing Masses at different churches, playing violin at St. Catherine's and St. Bernard's; being a cheerleader, student, and the right hand of her mother. I can hear my voice even now, calling "Margaret, Margaret" just as I can hear my mother call, "Paul, Paul!" Without Margaret I would have died on the vine.

Msgr. Donnelly stopped by one day to visit. He said, "Now that Paul is in 8th grade and John is liking the seminary, Paul should consider entering also." He had observed Paul for some time and thought he had the requirements. I agreed to that but I had never once heard him say he wanted to become a priest. Msgr. Donnelly admitted that when he was in 8th grade he had no thought of a vocation. His pastor stopped him and told him, "I think you have a vocation. I'm signing you up in the fall at the seminary." Msgr. D was surprised and said, "I never thought of becoming a priest." His pastor told him he was going to be a great priest so Msgr. Donnelly entered the seminary. "I went, became a priest and I try to be a good one and, not only that, I am happy that I did it."

I told Paul a few weeks later what Msgr. Donnelly said. He was reluctant but on serious reflection was willing to try. The boys because of their proximity to church were called frequently to serve. They could be scrubbed and ready in ten minutes. One time Brian's surplice caught on fire because he was too close to the tall candles at a funeral. Msgr. Donnelly beat out the blaze. Brian also took evening services. One night there was a crisis between St. Bernard's and St. Catherine's. Brian was sent to St. Catherine's. He was unfamiliar with the Marian Hymnal. He dashed up the stairs to the organ and started to search for the hymnals to be used. He couldn't find them and he didn't know which hymns were required. He hadn't asked and his father hadn't told. Fr. Britz came out on the altar and announced the hymn, "Mother Dearest, Mother Fairest." Brian was in a panic now and was looking frantically for the book. He looked down after a few minutes and held his arms in the air and shrugged his shoulders denoting NO HYMN. Fr. Britz announced the hymn, "Mother Dear, O Pray For Me." More painful minutes go by and more shrugs from Brian. "Hail, Holy Queen?" Britz queried. Finally in despair, Fr. Britz said, "For heavens sake, Brian, pick a hymn and we'll sing it!" This Brian did but the rest of the service continued hymn-less.

After Dr. Proctor removed the polyps from Brian's larynx, he changed into a lyric soprano and then into a beautiful lyric tenor. One summer he subbed at St. Anthony's Church, which involved a tedious hike. He played Masses and funerals and had quite a few weddings on Saturdays. Some required a soloist who sometimes did not appear. In such cases, Brian became organist and soloist. One Saturday the pastor of the church came up to the choir loft and wanted to know where Brian's suit coat was and Brian admitted he didn't have one. One Saturday Brian came home with $50. That was more than his father had made that day. Jack was impressed.

I must be truthful and tell you the children seldom whined, begged or complained. They did request a TV and devised a plan by using Patricia as a lure. The bouncy blonde curls and adorable face captivated her father. So after he got home from rehearsal one night, she approached him and putting her arms around his neck and in a tremulous voice asked, "TV, Daddy?" A week later a Muntz TV appeared in our sunroom.

Kevin was a good but rather skinny baby. I didn't mind now the middle of the night cries because then I would have what is called these days "quality time" with him. I went to confession and the sinister tall foreign Fr. Trepsa was on the other side of the grille. "Father," I said, "I am so upset. I have 12 children and my heart is heavy with the responsibility of these dear souls."

"You should never stop having children," he hissed. I just got up and walked out.

I thought and pondered for a week and came up with a scheme. I called the rectory and asked for Fr. Trepsa.

"Father, this is Mrs. Callaghan. I wonder if sometime you could come to dinner?"

"Well, so nice to ask me. Let me t'ink. Your home is an extension of the rectory and I will be 'appy to come."

The date was made and I said nothing to the children about having a guest. The doorbell rang and Jack answered. There he was, over six-foot tall, with a full-length black cape arranged over his shoulders, a cigarette at the end of the longest cigarette holder I ever saw. He was right out of a horror movie. Aha, I thought, Wait until the little ones climb on him, assault him, pull his ears, and torment him. I was thrilled by the prospect. The usual hassles before dinner stopped. There was an uncanny silence. The stinkers tiptoed to the table, never uttering a word, but gaped in awe at our guest. Damn it all! My scheme was a failure and old Trepsa, I bet, could not see where there ever would be a problem. When Fr. Kowalski, Fr. Fedewa, and Fr. O'Rourke showed up, the kids dove for them; teased them and wrestled with them. In fact, Fr. Fedewa used to say, holding his arms out, "Go easy, guys. I don't have my tennis shoes on." Well, you can't win 'em all.

45

Third Floor

When Msgr. Vismara blessed 3811 Iroquois, he went from the basement up to the first floor, did all the rooms there, and proceeded to the second floor where he distributed more holy water in each room. Then he went up to the third floor, a large area with bright windows and walls and beams of solid oak. I learned later that some priests stand in the living room, spray a few drops of holy water, a short prayer and that was that.

Jack thought it was time to utilize the third floor and have it made into a dorm for the guys. An extra radiator was found in the school. Heat had already been piped in and all we needed was a radiator. My sweet, joyful friend, Sodality president and sub for Jack, Josephine, had a boyfriend Vincent who was "handy." Paul was the only handy person and he was not yet ready for prime time. Vincent and his brother-in-law worked with much interference from Eddie, Bill and Christopher. It made a wonderful difference in our lives.

Once a week I would call up to third floor, "I'm coming!" The response was always, "No, no, give us 45 minutes and then come up. OK?" I think the boys liked their own dorm and their own hangout away from everything.

Eddie was forever losing his eye glasses and one late fall day, after I had changed the linen in one of the bedrooms, I gazed out the huge bay window that overlooked the cherry trees in the yard and there residing on a branch was a pair of glasses visible now with the leaves almost gone. So, there was one pair accounted for. The mailman one February day, when the snow had thawed, rang the doorbell and informed me that there was a pair of unmatched boy shoes lying under the living room window.

On our infrequent rides in the car one had to be vigilant because some of the little people liked to remove a shoe and toss it out the car window. We religiously followed the Church calendar. There was always a feast to celebrate: Mary's birthday, St. Joseph, St. Patrick. We recited rosaries but the best was reciting litanies: "Mother, most chaste; Mother, most pure; Seat of wisdom; Cause of our joy; Spiritual vessel…" The older kids would reply, "Pray for us." But I distinctly heard the younger ones, especially Ann and Clare, saying, "Play with us."

John and Grace Holland lived in the neighborhood. They had a daughter Kathy who became a close friend of our Kathy. John was a social worker, Grace, a nurse. John also did radio and TV work and narrated at Church events. He was a lovely soul and full of whimsy. One day he seriously told me that it wasn't *will* power I needed; it was *won't* power. He told the story about two Salvation Army girls who won a trip to Florida. They had never been there before and on arrival sallied forth to buy bikinis. They rushed back to their hotel rooms and eagerly tried on their suits. As one of the girls surveyed herself in the mirror, she asked her friend, "How do I look?" Her friend studied her and said, "Your navel, what's wrong with your navel?" The girl re-glanced into the mirror and said, "That does it; in the future you carry the flag and I'll carry the drum." John was a joy to have at parties and Grace always had an elegance and charm about her.

The Catholic Youth Organization took over the Deutch Haus, a huge building on Mack Avenue once owned by Germans but now defunct. It was bustling with activities and only two blocks from our house. One Thanksgiving when Mother and Dad were here we went to the Church CYO bingo there and my dad won a huge turkey. I can't tell you how happy I was when they came to the house: there in one house, 3811 Iroquois, were my dearest and most treasured people. Dad's Thanksgiving ritual was wonderful. The turkey preparations began with a salt and water cleansing and checking inside to see that no ugly things were left behind. Mother would do the dressing with sage, onion, celery, eggs, etc. The outside of the turkey was oiled and salted and since Mr. Turkey was usually over thirty pounds, he was put in the oven with the bearer staggering under the weight. Dad donned a bath towel around his waist where it remained for most of the day.

Chuddy was stationed in Boston one holiday and a Franciscan friend of his was attending a meeting in Detroit. He would stop by. This young athletic priest came for dinner. My dad ushered him into the living room and the priest sat on the couch. I don't know to this day what happened but as soon as he sat the entire couch collapsed. He was unhurt but as startled as we were. I guess you could say it was the straw that broke the camel's back. He made a hasty retreat and we never saw or heard from him again. The next morning my father gave me some money toward a new sofa, which also was short lived. Iroquois was a world all unto its own.

One day we got a call that Uncle Bill and Aunt Louise were in town and would visit us. They brought with them their best friends, Kitty and Larry Lyke.

Bill and Louise were very close to my heart and I am eternally grateful for the way Uncle Bill helped my father. Now I had a rocker that had lost its rock. It just had legs and was closer to the floor than one would expect. Kitty Lyke chose this chair to sit in. It never occurred to me to warn her and she was so startled when she sat that she really shrieked. When they headed back to Oswego, Uncle Bill left thirteen silver dollars on the mantel.

Fathers Kowalski and Fedewa came occasionally to dinner and also Jack and I went out with them. I still thought that parents were responsible for each soul that came into their lives and it did hang heavy on me because I felt so ill equipped. But I had a desperate overpowering love for each one. I guess the heart, like the womb, can encompass all.

The crazy, hazy days of summer were endless. It was so hard to go anywhere but go we did after much whining, wheedling, and whimpering. Jack took us to Waterworks Park. It was right by the St. Clair River off of Jefferson Avenue. Jimmy got into broken glass in the pool and had to have tetanus shots and one day Annie started to walk into the deep part and Jack and I went fully clothed to capture her. Also after much whining, wheedling, whimpering, and downright begging, we went to Belle Isle and even though Jack hated picnics we had one anyway. Brian climbed out on a limb of a big tree once and lost his balance and splashed into a shallow pool of water. It was pretty hilarious. We also had a rainy trip to Boblo, a beautiful island with rides.

It continued to rain on the boat and on the rides. It really stormed on the return home. Just as we got off the boat, the sun burst forth and it was lovely the remainder of the day. At least Eddie impressed us by mooning Canada. Elvis was hot in those days and Jim did his best to emulate him with the DA (Duck's Ass) hair in the back of his head. He wanted shoes with pointed toes but his feet were so wide that the effect was anything but "pointy"!

46

Double-Header

It was 1954 and Kevin was no. 13 and I was you-know-what: baby due in February. I seemed to be carrying the baby under my left rib. I checked a book out and found out that is where the spleen is located. "My spleen, my spleen," I would moan. December came and I was in my usual panic over Christmas gifts. By now Uncle Bill was sending toys to us. One toy was a little broom. Clare loved that broom and kept it near to her for months. Religious Christmas cards were to be chosen, etc. One evening in mid-December Jack wanted to go to St. Bernard's and with Fr. O'Rourke and Rose La Rose have a game of pinochle. I was uneasy, and believe it or not, I turned down the offer. Enter Fr. Fedewa—he and Jack were visiting when I came in from the dining room where they were seated. Fr. Fedewa had just returned from a Christmas party and was laden with candies, cookies and fruitcakes. He wanted to leave the stuff for the children. I sat and listened to them talk and they seemed far away. All at once I said, "I feel strange." Father took one look at me and literally dashed out the door lickety-split.

I called Dr. Henderson and told him my feelings. Since I was in no pain and not due until February, I was reluctant to call but right away he said, "Head for the hills." By the time I arrived at East Side General, I was in labor. Dr. Henderson was always there if he could be. One night, when Ann was born, he spent the night in case he was needed. He was a wonderful doctor. Once I said to a pediatrician, "Dr. Henderson is like a father to me."

"A father?" he snorted. "He knows you better than your father ever did."

It was about 11:00 in the evening when a baby girl was born. Then Dr. Henderson became quite animated, almost hysterical. "Double-header!" he yelled, waking up most of the patients on that floor (many of them were laughing about the commotion the next day). A baby boy came into the world. Dr. Henderson called for incubators. "Oh, oh," I said to the nurse, "should they be baptized?"

"No," she said, "they are tiny, but perfect." Mary was 3 pounds, Joe 4.

Dr. Henderson told me that the staff was worried because they were getting no heartbeat. That was because Joe was on his stomach and, rib-to-rib and curled under him was Mary. After they popped me into my bed, Dr. Henderson said, "Mary and Joseph—they have to be called Mary and Joseph." I was so stunned I agreed. I wanted to see the babies but the doctor said, "In the morning." Around ten o'clock the next morning the reporter and photographer from the *Free Press* came. The first time I held the twins was when the photograph was taken. You can be sure I cherish that picture. Then who padded in from having delivered a girl and landed in the bed along side of me was my lovely neighbor, Andy Welch. I think it was number 8 for her. She looked like she had come in from a movie and proceeded to open a file and started to work on a recipe book she was writing. She confided that she never had labor pains, just "sensations"—what a gal! It was a real perk to have her share a room with me.

When Jack got home the night the twins were born, John was pacing the living room. "Boy or girl?" he asked.

"Boy *and* a girl" was the answer. Then Jack went up to Margaret's room and gave her the news gently: "Twins, Margaret."

"No, no," she yelled and beat her pillow. "Not twins, not twins!"

Gifts started to come: bushels of apples, four frozen turkeys, Christmas gifts, etc. Fr. Fedewa was glad he had left in the nick of time because driving me to the hospital to have Eddie was traumatic enough for him. Fran Brown came to spend Christmas with us every year. I think out of fifty years she missed only a couple and that was because she was ill. At times I had mixed emotions when Fran came to visit. She had come by car, by boat, by train and, finally, by plane. But 1954 the train was the choice of travel for us. Fran could be loud, even abrasive and demeaning beyond brassy, and she had a nerve-wracking effect on me at times. On the other hand, we played Scrabble, did crosswords, went shopping, attended movies as well as reminisced about the times she took me to the silent movies and had to read the lines to me.

On New Year's Eve we two saw out the old year and the New Year in and since there was no one else we kissed each other. Fran was a close friend of Neil's family and she relayed messages to me from him. So through the years we kept track of each other's lives.

I staggered home the evening of the 23rd, babyless. Joe and Mary had to be five pounds before they could come home. Fran had worked her heart out, to say nothing of Margaret. Christmas Eve was strange. Kevin cried in his bed; he was cutting teeth. I was on the couch and couldn't get to him. I called Nana Callaghan on Christmas day.

"Gee, Nana," I said, "I never dreamed I would have twins."

"Well," she said, "You certainly tried hard enough!"

Anyway, no one was more welcome the Christmas of 1954 than Fran Brown. We ate so much fresh turkey, candy, fresh fruits, all gifts from family and friends. We were sated to the max. Fran took over much of the work and had the keys to THE DESK, given to her by Jack himself. The desk contained candy, cookies, treasures and some money. The last gesture of Fran's was to put the 4th turkey in the oven, get in a cab, and head for the train station.

Detroit Free Press photo of 13 children getting ready for Christmas 1954 and preparing for the arrival of the twins, Mary and Joseph.

Joseph came home the second week of January; a feisty five pounds, he took residence on top of the buffet in the dining room. Two weeks later, Mary joined us. She was enthroned in the living room. Grace Holland came to my aid and every day she helped with the two new members. My stomach muscles were shot and I began to do TV exercises with Bonnie Prudden, a gorgeous chick who without batting an eye could place her right foot over her left ear, or something like that. Christopher and Kevin enjoyed this daily program because it gave them an opportunity to walk up and down and sideways on my prone body.

One day I was on the phone with my neighbor Barb Masserang, also mother of a large family. I said, "I just finished working out with Bonnie Prudden."

"Oh, I like that program a lot; in fact, I watch it every day."

"Do you think the exercises are too hard?" I asked.

"I don't know," she replied. "I just *watch* the program."

Barbara was right. She was short, a little chubby and adorable just as she was.

Joseph was very wiry and strong. He turned from his back onto his stomach and back again when he was only two months old. The entire family was amazed by his prowess. Mary was like a baby doll. I thought life would be a nightmare but things went very well with the exceptions of sleep loss. I would keep a chart on the cupboard: Joe-3 oz. @ 1:00 AM; Mary 2 oz. @ 1:45 AM; 4 oz., then 3 oz., then 2 oz. But they were very good and they thrived.

The parish sponsored a family from Holland who were housed not far from where we lived, actually in a better neighborhood. There were twelve little Dooers and the children of school age attended St. Catherine's grade and high schools. Mrs. Dooers stopped by to see me one day. She was not a happy person. She confided to me that she was very brilliant in addition to being a great intellectual. She asked me if I had a clothes dryer. When I replied yes, she moaned that she didn't have one. Well, I tried to console her by telling her that, after all, she had only been in the USA a few months and in time she would have it all. Our visit was cut short by some emergency or other in my house.

One day I walked by her house, a lovely brick house on an acre of land. She was sitting on a rocker, reading a book. The girls were dashing around doing dishes, laundry, ironing, cooking, and so forth. I tell you I was impressed. The boys were cleaning, gardening, cutting the lawn, sweeping thresholds. The church got Mr. Dooers a job with the Blue Ribbon Dairy but his salary was mediocre. A year and a half later, Mrs. Dooers had enough abuse from St. Catherine's parish and they left for California where she had contact with people of influence. A few years later I was talking to the pastor and asked about the Dooers. He asked me not to even mention their names.

We went to Albany for a second ear surgery. This time hopefully the correct ear would be done and it would be a success. Chud had a wonderful Irish friend who lived in Albany; her husband had died. Her name was Mrs. O'Rafferty. She came to Oswego when she was sixteen years old; she wasn't pretty but she had an Irish brogue with a lovely lilt and she was interesting. She had worked as a servant for the wealthy homes in Oswego. She married a railroad man and had a family and ended up in Albany. She was very good to us. Dr. Kopp, the same ear specialist from before, was to operate. Dr. Kopp had operated with great success on Chuddy. This time Jack wasn't so desperately ill but the surgery wasn't a great success either. Mrs. O'Rafferty loved politics. She asked us what we thought of Sergeant Shriver and did we know Gov. Rockefeller woke up every morning feeling Happy. Happy was his mistress and later his wife. We took the train home. Hearing loss is a great cross that Jack has to bear. Ironic it is that his love is music and he is unable to hear!

A certificate came in the mail good for one dance lesson for two people. One summer eve Margaret and I walked about a mile to Warren Ave. where we ascended some stairs to a dance studio. They were very gracious knowing darn well we wouldn't sign up. I don't know what Margaret's partner said. She was reluctant to share experiences with me ever since she heard me tell Fran Conen, my friend, about some hilarious incident involving Margaret who frowned and didn't think it was that hilarious. Margaret and I also went swimming at the junior high school a block away. We were the only white people there.

47

UJ

Jack's brother Jim was having a nice career in Syracuse. He was superintendent of music in the diocese as well as pastor of holy Family Church in a suburb of Syracuse. He was very hard working, conscientious to a fault. He was prone to depression, which occurred usually during Holy Seasons. He was tortured at Christmas and Easter especially. He'd come home to Oswego, head upstairs and sleep around the clock. He was a fine singer and it was a delight to hear him sing the Mass. At Mass if the little ones were noisy he called them up on the altar to play while he gave his sermon. He was called "The Red-Head" and was a charismatic leader. Margaret was the apple of his eye. He took her to camp out on Lake Ontario; when he took his mother on trips, he often took Margaret too. Mrs. C had only one granddaughter and that was Margaret. After working incessantly, he would drive to New York City, register at a good hotel and party hearty. One trip I was invited. I went to Oswego where Jim picked up Nana and me and we drove at a scary pace on the New York State Thruway to New York City. He said many rosaries on the way. After a while Nana and I were saying acts of contrition, clinging to each other in the back seat.

After registering in the hotel, we took a cab to a plaza overlooking Central Park. We dined in an elegant room. We went to the ladies room and couldn't figure out how to flush. After a ten-minute struggle, I stomped my foot. I hit a spot on the floor that did the trick. Jim brought about ten neckties loaned to him by his brother Bob. One lunch he forgot his tie and the maitre d' supplied him with one and he was acceptable.

We went to a place called Round Table with singers and a small combo. We went to another place and heard the Australian Jazz Quarter; a group, mixing violin, viola, French horn and flute, a stunning combo. The Tropicana had poor food but a thrilling floorshow with the most beautiful girls, tall, sassy and talented. Jim had seats for us to see "West Side Story" which had rave reviews. When it was time to go, Nana said she felt poorly and would be unable to go. Jim couldn't believe it. Poor Nana, she was exhausted; the more tired she was, the more eager I became. Jim called the house doctor who said it was just too much excitement and he was going to give her a shot and she'd be all right. She fell asleep and I must confess we left and went to a hotel that featured a Hawaiian Room. Jim greased the hand of the maitre d' and we were almost a part of the show. Unfortunately, these men rushed out with long sabers and they started tossing them around. I felt the whiz of one as it just missed my cheek. I was calmer after that and we left with big leis around our necks.

The next place was the African Room. We were seated in a booth. In our sight was a small stage maybe 9' by 12'. The floorshow consisted of a one-act play with a man and woman in great distress. They banter back and forth; he draws a gun and points it at her. She stands there waiting to be killed and then he shoots himself and drops dead at her feet. What a great presentation that was! We were sitting in the booth and Jim said, "I wonder what it must have been like when Mary was conceived by the Holy Spirit." We were contemplating that marvelous moment when a woman asked us where we were from. Jim, who always called women "dear," "dearest" and completely disarmed them, told her I was from Detroit. She insisted that we join them. Jim and I were the only white people. Congressman Diggs and his brother ran a funeral home in Detroit. We sat at their table; after a nice visit Jim made them promise to visit me in Detroit.

The next club we hit was Jim's all time favorite place and there was a guitar player there. Jim did what he had to do and we were seated close to the stage. Jim sent the waiter up to the artist with money and a request. I think it infuriated the artist and he refused to grant the request. I realize that now but at the time I was mystified why he wouldn't grant the request. The next tactic was Jim calling out, "Up a Lazy River" over and over. There were about 50 patrons in the club. Jim said hello to a tall thin man at the next table and asked, "What date is this?"

With a crisp British accent the man replied "August 2nd, my dear man."

"This woman here is my sister-in-law."

"Oh, really?"

"Yes. And she has 16 children."

"Tsk, tsk..."

"You don't believe me, do you?"

"My, my..."

Jim reached in his pocket and withdrew a rosary. He stood up and waved the rosary in front of the man's face. "I believe, I believe!" said the Brit. It must have been 4:00 AM when we finally said good night. Jim removed his tie and put it around my neck and I did the same to him with my lei.

A night at the Copa with the monsignor.

I tippy-toed into the bedroom, threw my body, lei and all, on the bed. Nana heard me and jumped out of bed; she ran to the window and put up the shades. The light from the rising sun was a stab of pain. "I'm hungry," she announced, went to Jim's door, and repeated her announcement. A muffled sound emanated from the room: "Call Room Service." She nagged at him until he got up, dressed and did what she asked. He called Room Service. Do you think Nana was mad? Do you think she was furious? Do you think she never forgave us? Do you think she related the terrible story for years especially in front of us? If you do, you are right. I admit we were rotten and bad, but it was one memorable night. Two days later I was back in the kitchen, but I still have a picture of Jim, Nana and me at the Copa Cabana—Wow!

48

A Neighborhood in Transition

A black couple moved into a house in the middle of the block. They were schoolteachers and drove a Studebaker; Eddie never tired of remembering about its beauty. Christopher liked kindergarten. He had a black teacher and a mixed class. He did love school. One day I asked him if anyone in his class or his teacher was different from him. "Why no," he said. "We are all the same." Don't tell me prejudice isn't taught. HUD was going to build adequate housing in Detroit. They leveled the homes and then never built the low cost housing.

When blacks began to move into our neighborhood, the white people panicked and moved to the suburbs and the only people who made money were the realtors. This didn't bother me because I had the home of my dreams and I welcomed my new neighbors. Then a phenomenon happened. Msgr. Donnelly who was by then a bishop was transferred to St. Matthew's parish because 1800 families had moved from St. Catherine's in one year. He asked Jack to come with him. A new pastor arrived at St. Catherine's. I realized the handwriting was on the wall and I called a Grosse Pointe realtor to help me find a house large enough for 15 children. I thought how odd that they never returned my calls. We also drove out around East Detroit. But most of the homes being built were ranch style. One day we were driving around and checking out the homes. Kevin spoke up. "Hey, Mom, how do people in ranch homes go up to bed?"

Fortunately for Margaret she roomed at Marygrove College. There were only two girls in her high school graduation class from St. Catherine High School who went to college. Marygrove had a small lovely campus, a great place to grow in mind and spirit. Paul left the seminary. Instead of sending him to St. Catherine's, I called Austin High School, located near Grosse Pointe and run by Augustinians. Even though we were geographically far, Paul was accepted at Austin. He was always a good student. He would come home around 3:30, check the latest child, and then study. He was trying out for football but as the fall advanced he would be over-weary so Jack and I decided enough football. The school was noted for the cheering section. The boys assembled in white shirts and did some great coordinated cheers.

I bought a sewing machine. It was delivered one morning, a solid maple wonder, but I knew nothing about using it. I was signed up for lessons a few weeks hence. When Paul came home the day it arrived, he found me sitting and admiring it and dreaming of all the great creations I would do. He opened the machine and an hour later had it going; then he showed me how to operate the damn thing. It is a great memory for me. Of course, I took the lessons. I was known in the class as the hot-rodder; I did do a lot of mending on it and I still have it, as I write, in the basement where it stands in a corner.

Austin had a great basketball team and one year won the state championship. The star was Dave DeBuesscher who went on to be famous in college and the pros. There was a team coming to play Austin and we housed a young man. I asked him if he had any brothers and sisters. "I am one of sixteen," he replied.

"Wow," I said. "How is your mother and what does she think of her big family?"

He smiled and said, "She just tells us to go out and play in traffic."

Jim was always having trouble with deportment and taking the classes' attention away from the teacher. He had a girlfriend, Eleanor Frendo, who lived on the next block. She was a friend of Judy Masserang and the Williams girls. When I first met her, I saw a tiny, sweet, dark-haired beauty. She lived with her mother, a young widow, and her two younger brothers, Freddie and Dennis (who was born after his father had died from an aneurysm). They all lived with her parents, Mrs. Pennunzio, who was very ample, very upbeat and good with financing. Jim was doing well studying the cello with Robert Alport and piano with Sister Claretta.

I received a call from one of the nuns one evening. Sister wanted to know about Kathy. In her opinion Kathy was boy-crazy. I replied that since she was in the 7th grade it was about time. Sister then described a scene. While the class was in Church for confessions, Kathy, exiting from the confessional, proceeded with a lot of clamor to pass by 7 or 8 people until she found Bobby Boyle. She then plumped down beside him. I admitted that behavior was rather extreme and would think about it.

Both the nuns at St. Bernard's and at St. Catherine's had parties for us at the convent. They were a few years apart. All my life I loved being with the nuns. I think I loved them because they could find fun and joy with little things, small events. Once at a Christmas party at St. Catherine's, Sr. Bethany disappeared and returned with a trumpet. She amazed us all by playing a great bluesy jazzy number.

Ann, Patricia, and Clare were like triplets. Ann had poor vision and was serious. Patricia was light hearted with gold curls galore. Clare was inquisitive about everything. Kevin wandered off one day. The police found him in the dime store and returned him to me. "Here's little Calvin," they said.

Jack taught Margaret to drive. One day they were driving along Gratiot, one of many ugly roads in Detroit, and Jack said, "At the next light, make a left turn." Personally, I never made a left turn when I finally learned to drive, and I would scheme circuitous routes to avoid them. Jack told Margaret to activate her turn signal. When Margaret was a little slow in responding, Jack repeated the command. As he did, Margaret grabbed the turn signal, pulled on it and it came off in her hand! She proceeded to present it to her father.

Jack tried to teach me to drive. He took me to the cemetery. We took Kathy along for the ride to keep our eye on her. "Oh my, oh my," she murmured as we passed crosses, statues, angels galore. "I've never, never been in such a holy place." I wasn't ready to learn, I guess—too rattled. But Cyanide (Kathy) made it a fun experience.

One time when Mother was visiting, she asked Kathy to close the screen door which was wide open. "Keeps the flies out," Mother urged.

"Hey, flies, come on in, come on in," was Kathy's retort.

We had lunch and dinner together. There was no McDonald's or pizza delivery. I remember Iacocca reliving in his biography that he had pizza every day fresh from his mother's oven. The kids he knew never heard of pizza. The children ate everything they were served. They never whined and never cried. Some nights after a concert and Jack was in an expansive mood he would send one of the boys to the drug store for a gallon of ice cream. Whole hams, beef roasts, spaghetti and always dessert! One time when Mother was visiting she said, "I'll take over for two hours, do what you want." She told me later she thought it odd I proceeded to bake a cake.

When I first gazed at Teresa when she was born in March of 1956, I found her adorable. She was over eight pounds and a lovely armful. Of course, the baptism was two weeks later. Why? Why so soon? The Church deemed it so. No matter if the mother was weak and still oozing blood. Bob Alport and his wife Harriet stopped by the afternoon of the baptism. Harriet apologized about having the flu and running a temperature. Idiot! Three days later Teresa had the sniffles and congestion.

I called Dr. Henderson and he came by. Yes, he came to the house! He checked her thoroughly and prescribed Neo Silva and I was to put drops in her nose 4 times a day, which I did. Wednesday she seemed the same, but on Thursday she was lethargic and on Friday she refused the bottle. Her temperature seemed ok, but then she seemed cold and I knew something was very wrong. I kept calling Dr. Henderson, but no answer. In my panic I was dialing his office, not his home. I called Dr. Robinson next door. He came immediately and when he saw the baby he asked me if I had any whiskey. We had some left from Christmas. He poured it down Teresa's throat and said she must go to Children's Hospital immediately.

At the door of the hospital someone took her from my arms and left. We stood in line to talk to the doctor. The doctor was quizzing a young black woman who preceded me. "How many children?" he asked. "How many illegitimate?" Wow! When it was our turn, he said his name was Dr. Donnelly and that our child was desperately ill and probably wouldn't last the night; but he would stay by her side. He said I could call him. I sat on the floor in the breakfast room and phoned him every hour on the hour. Early the next morning we rushed back to the hospital. She was in an incubator and breathing with difficulty. Sunday they called from the hospital. "Your daughter is OK. You can come and get her." I was leery and nervous about bringing her home. I was to return for a visit to Dr. Donnelly in a week. He said Teresa had an enlarged heart and the doctors wanted to check her once a month. He said at first they thought she had pneumonia but then decided the Neo Silva might have accidentally gotten into her lungs and that was the real trouble.

Dr. Donnelly and I became friends. He was an intern and was planning on setting up a practice as a pediatrician some place in Pontiac. He had been a schoolteacher but always wanted to study medicine. He had three children and a great wife. She told him to go be a doctor. He took the train every morning to Wayne State Medical School. They lived most frugally but he was a happy man. Teresa started to thrive and all was well except for the enlarged heart.

One day things were going badly. The toilet kept overflowing. I got a mop, pail and plunger. It overflowed into the kitchen. Jack was teaching at Marygrove. He dropped me off at the hospital on his way to teach and I was to take the bus home. The bus was late and carrying Teresa wasn't easy even though the walk from Warren Avenue to home wasn't that far. The children in spite of my pleas had flushed the toilet, and I was ankle deep in shit. In walked Jack and Margaret and one of Jack's pupils in tow. "Oh, Mrs. Callaghan," she gushed, "Such a big family! How do you do it? How many bedrooms do you have? Where are those sweet babies?" I took one look at them. So fresh, so vibrant, so CLEAN! I took my smelly, shitty self up to 3rd floor and didn't come down for two days.

When Teresa was a year old, I went to a special meeting at Children's Hospital. Teresa had an X-ray and we were ushered into a room with, I think, twelve doctors sitting around a table. They were smiling. They showed me an X-ray of Teresa's heart when she was three weeks old: an enlarged heart. The most recent X-ray showed a perfectly sized heart. The doctors were pleased and I was ecstatic.

It was 24-hour chores now, a lot of work. Mary and Joe and Teresa were very good, very fascinating, full of fun. We had a twin stroller and the older children would take turns running around the block with Mary and Joe, who were squealing delightfully all the way. In spite of his romance with Eleanor, Jim attended the seminary. Fr. Britz reported to me he doubted if Jim had a true vocation because he kept seeing Jim with Eleanor in the back of church talking seriously in front of the pamphlet rack. I told Father Britz Jim could still have a vocation because weren't they in Church in front of Catholic literature?

Brian treated Kathy with great disdain. He had always been really cruel to her dolls, using them mostly as throwing objects. Kathy endured this because in her eyes he could be no one but wonderful. All he had to do was put on his big blue-eye sad face and she was at his mercy. An 8th grade teacher asked Kathy if Brian smoked because she thought she detected the scent of smoke wafting from his clothes. Kathy assured Sister that Brian did not smoke and she knew he did.

Ed and Bill were always together; as toddlers they would sit on the steps going up stairs and rock together in syncopation: front to back, side to side. I loved this because I could hear their hums and knew they were for a few minutes out of trouble. Ed had a slight stutter and so did Bill. Bill was very shy. They served as altar boys and choirboys. Ed, of course, was the youngest choirboy; at least that way his father knew where he was and what he was up to.

The boys gravitated to the Masserang house. Mr. Masserang cut their hair and had them on his baseball team. Barb and I talked frequently on the phone, but physically we hardly saw one another. One day she called and said she was not a ratter but Kathy, who was in charge of Mary and Joe, was visiting with Jim McDougal by the side of the Masserang house and Mary and Joseph had narrowly missed death when they wandered into the road and two different cars missed them by a breath.

Hi-Fidelity record systems were popular and we had new records with a nicer sound. Ralph Kowalski bought one system and took Jack and helped him choose a new system for us. He had a nice apartment and he was beginning to collect religious art. Having been exposed to pictures of saints, Madonnas, Jesus, and I admit, a few Buddhas, I was collecting a little art myself. I had advanced from a magazine cutout of DaVinci's "Madonna of the Rocks" to some Winslow Homers. I saw a reproduction of Salvatore Dali's painting of the crucifixion, depicting Jesus suspended over the world globe. This was St. John of the Cross's dream that Dali depicted. I guess it was more than a hint but for Christmas I received an 8' by 10' study of the painting. Was I grateful? No! I pouted, they returned it and bought the much bigger size. And I was appeased. Let us not forget my first purchase ever, and by credit also, in grade school, of St. Therese LeSieux. Ralph was always treating us to a play or to a music concert as did Fr. Fedewa. They lighted and lifted our spirits. There was an artist at Marygrove by the name of Joseph DeLauro, a dark handsome man with a beautiful wife. He sculptured the most beautiful "Pieta" and gave it to Ralph, exquisite in bronze.

I had to rethink my life, my priorities, my *modus operandi.* Every word out of a mother's voice should not be "No, don't do this, do that. Margaret! Margaret!" At night as I reviewed the day's events I could hear my voice nagging, screaming. Is this the way I was ending up, a dirty, smelly, nagging bitch? First, I must decide what was more important besides the endless drudgery. I must lower my standards, but not 100% lower. Lying in the hospital after a baby, I would daydream. When I got home, things would be different. I would be more loving, more tolerant and more like what Fr. Trepsa described. He was the one who said it didn't matter how many children one had and that being responsible for each little soul was not to be taken lightly. I would do my best; not only that, but better than best.

Jim who was in the seminary for two years and because of disciplinary actions washed every window in the huge school decided to leave. Now Brian was a high school freshman at the seminary. He was a good student as they all were but what he loved was the bakery on the way to school, reminiscent of his hanging out at Dockery's Bakery when he was four and being brought home by the police. This had happened more than once and the police were discouraged with me. "What's the matter, lady, can't you watch this little boy?"

Jim now attended St. Catherine High School and the next year Brian joined him. John was hanging in there at the seminary and seemed to be happy. In the mid-1950's TV was really entertaining. The older children and I actually shared some enjoyment together. There was the Steve Allen show and the wonderful crew, Steve Lawrence, Edye Gorme and their singing, along with great comedians: the guests, the banter and silly fun, no *double entendres,* and Jackie Gleason with his many hats. There were beautiful dancers on Saturday nights and some of the skits were LIVE on "Comedy Hour" with Sid Caesar. Imogene Coca and

Carl Reiner were hilarious—pure geniuses. We never heard or saw any of the ugly words and actions we see on today's TV.

I was naïve enough to think my children would have ideas similar to mine. *Au Contraire*. Margaret said, "Mother, you are so opinionated."

"Of course," I explained. "I am 39 years old and I have very definite opinions."

Her opinions were different than mine. They were good and interesting opinions, but different. From there on, I tried to encourage each one's uniqueness and to let them develop their own mental outlooks.

Mother had nervous problems and took Novine and finally went to a doctor. I didn't know about this but Mother told me about it when she came to visit. The doctor gradually got her over the malaise. Since she hadn't been to a doctor since I was born, the doctor thought she should have a physical. That is when she discovered she had an infantile womb. He was amazed that she actually delivered one child. She had always thought it strange that she had only one child and now she knew why. Dad was happy working for Uncle Bill and every Sunday after Mass he would slip down to the office and write me a letter. I have today a box full of the epistles from Paul.

PART III
MOVING

49

Summer, 1954 and Beyond

In the summer of 1954 Fran Brown drove by car to our place for a visit. It was nice to do some summer fun and she drove me home to Oswego. I brought Ann with me. It was July and she spent her birthday in Oswego with gifts, prizes and trips to the beach. It was such a joy to see this serious little girl having fun.

One time Margaret and I were headed home on a bus. One of the passengers from the rear passed by our seat. He was a handsome blond young man. He went over, bowed, and gave a super smile to Miss M.

"Who was that?"

"Oh, a boy I met. His name is Michael Guzicki."

She had met him at a young adult dance at the church and they started to date. He had served in the Marines and was attending the University of Detroit and working toward dental school. Margaret's brothers and sisters made it difficult during the courtship. One evening as they were saying their goodbyes on the porch, a pail of water fell on their heads from above. One night, Joe asked Mike if he was going to marry his sister as she was descending the stairs. Liz Wurm, Bob's sister, said one day, "Boy, Margaret is lucky to get such a catch."

"Excuse me! *He's* the lucky one!"

One summer Jack decided we would take the car and drive to Interlaken, the music school and camp near Traverse City. Margaret was to be in charge, poor thing. I could not believe that the two of us were going anywhere and it was his idea. The radio station for some reason didn't work and his favorite station wasn't coming in. "There's something about me and good music," he moaned. The car started to send puffs of steam up through the hood. It was raining hard so we spent a less than lovely night at a cheap hotel in Clare, Michigan. The next day the engine cut up again. We headed back home and got as far as Flint. We got to a garage where we were told we would need a new carburetor. After a four-hour wait and minus our cash, we headed home. We can't win; we were doomed to be without good music. Oh well, I knew at that moment the concept of a second honeymoon was not his goal. I can tell you, Margaret was overjoyed to see us back.

Patrick Gerald was born August 30, 1957. He was a truly beautiful, chubby, blond baby boy. Fr. O'Rourke had always said, "Not an idiot in the bunch!" I thought, *Of course not, but now I know we beat the odds.*

"Rose Tattoo" had been a popular play on Broadway and was made into a film with Burt Lancaster and Anna Magnani. Plays into films are usually good because of the interesting dialogue. The movie theater was about a half mile from the house. One hot steamy, sultry night I asked Jack if we could go see the film. "Not up to it." A phrase I heard often. He worked from dawn to dusk reading, teaching, practicing, praying. I was on a 24-hour duty but needed a distraction. My, I must have been blessed from the Lord with energy. Anyway, I arrived at the show just in time for the 9:00 PM performance. It was funny, sad and since she was an Italian actress, Anna Magnani did not shave under her arms; this was evident and amusing. At 11:30 Mack Avenue was deserted. What a pathetic street at that hour on a hot humid August night. The only energy was coming from the lights of the many bars on the street. How odd that I could feel so lonely when I was involved with so many lives.

Bob Wurm's mother, Eugenia, worked at Grinnell's, a music and furniture store. Eugenia called me and said she had a customer who had left a huge home for an apartment. She had just purchased a complete French Provincial dining room set and said she would give away her set to anyone who would want it. It was walnut, 144" with all three leaves. Eugenia asked me if I would be interested and if I could go to her apartment and see it. This is true; that as a favor I would come and look. The set was ornate, the china closet with a wood, not glass, front. The backing on the china closet was thick walnut. The buffet was 80" wide and a smaller buffet was 45". Out of the kindness of my heart I relieved her of the set. I thought I was doing her a favor. I can't believe I was so ignorant! That was 40 years ago. It has had quite a journey. For many years it was 144" and remained that way. Each year a new person was added. Sixteen places every night and sometimes 19 or 21 when Nana, U.J. or Jim's three were living with us. Mega birthday cakes, Thanksgiving, Christmas celebrations galore—you name it.

A few years ago I was on my back under the table and looked up: there had to be 1,000 gum wads arranged in a startling pattern. I know who the guiltiest one was but I won't mention her name. Baby diapers were changed on it, and babies were set as a centerpiece in the table's middle. Flowers from Jack's garden were displayed constantly.

Eugenia's customer came from a wealthy family who lived in Indian Village on Burns. Her father had been fastidious and abhorred dirt. He had a real fetish. I have thought many times about him. And when gobs of peanut butter were evident I couldn't help but smile. Since the set came into my life, it has lived in Detroit (3811), Birmingham (the old rectory, yuck), Manor Road in Bloomfield Township, and now Warwick in Beverly Hills. Jim put castors on the table about ten years ago. So, on February 5, 1999 I am glad to have it back all refinished and glowing. It belongs here.

One day a young man delivered a modest box of Florida oranges to our door on Iroquois. He was amazed at the goings on in the household. "Who was so thoughtless as to send you such a small box of oranges? Why there isn't enough to go around."

"Listen," I said. "I'm grateful for anything anyone wants to send."

"Wait until I tell my wife about this family. All she does is whine and cry about our three little ones."

I ran after him and shouted, "Why don't you tell your wife you love her and take her to a show!"

50

Neighborhood in Transition, Part II

The carpeting at 3811 was wearing so thin that the last time Margaret and I scrubbed it on our hands and knees our knuckles bled. The *Detroit Free Press* was our daily newspaper and the home decorating column was written by Edith Crumb (believe that name or not). I phoned the paper and was immediately connected to Edith herself. I told her my predicament of having 17 children and what did she think I should do about the floors? There was a moment's silence and then she offered, "Sawdust…sawdust" and hung up. I can't believe I did this but I covered a 40' living room and 30' dining room in linoleum. In the 9 years we were on Iroquois we had 3 kitchen floors laid in linoleum one on top of the other, and as a result people had to step up in order to enter the kitchen.

Jack's pupil, Frank Janeck, who was my first visitor on Lillibridge and who helped Jack as a substitute so much, had graduated from U of M. He received his BA in piano music. We went to his recital and he did well. He then received his master's in music history. He then went to the Navy and was a commander on some kind of battleship. He always came at Christmas time and sometimes brought a girlfriend. He talked to Fr. O'Rourke about marriage. Father told him to make a list of pros and cons on the girl. I told Frank that if he had to do a list, he couldn't possibly be in love with the girl.

Msgr. Paddock, pastor of Holy Name Parish in Birmingham, called us one day for a recommendation. Jack suggested Frank Janeck. Frank had an interview and accepted the job. He had a boys' choir and a mixed adult choir. He had a romance with a girl and he brought her to our house two or three times. She was lovely, so what was the problem? The problem was that Frank had polio as a child and it left him sterile.

The new pastor at St. Catherine's, Fr. John Foley, was ok. Bishop Donnelly asked Jack to come along with him to St. Matthew's parish. In the meantime the family was involved with St. Margaret Mary's parish. Paul had it for a while and was followed by John, Margaret, and even me. I did a Christmas Mass with a girls' choir. Jim and Eleanor were in the loft. Can you believer it? The girls fouled up the "*Adeste Fideles.*" A girl named Philomena decided to sing alto. The only trouble was she didn't know how to harmonize. Usually, Christmas music is a no-brainer. People love the familiar. It is hard to torture "*Adeste Fideles*" and I felt sorry for Jim and Eleanor sitting there, holding hands and attending as a couple: their first "special" night. I pulled on Philomena's coat as she happily prepared to depart.

"What in the world inspired you to sing alto tonight?"

Apparently innocent of the horrid sound she had caused, she said, "I was just filled with the Spirit!"

St. Margaret Mary's church was not big in liturgy and special rites for holy week, or so it seemed. Margaret and I were on for many complicated rites for the week before Easter Sunday. At 9:00 AM I called the pastor to go over the program for the Easter vigil, the blessing of the sacred oils. When was the "*Exultet*" to be sung and Oh, yes, the litany of the saints? When would the priest sing it? What? We were to do it ourselves? I hung up and yelled for Margaret, as I was wont to do anyway. I told her the bad news, grabbed two hymnals, and raced upstairs with her to the bathroom. The litany is very beautiful, easy to sing and a joy to perform—if you know it. We stumbled over a few saint's names, Margaret seated on the toilet seat and I on the edge of the tub. Our waterloo came when we were supposed to sing "*Ut nos metipsos,*" a Greek phrase the chanters were supposed to blend in with the Latin names. It became funny as we struggled. We had a good laugh and so what if it was a fiasco! *Au contraire.* We did a credible job with a few slight hesitations.

Taking care of St. Bernard, St. Catherine, St. Edward, St. Margaret Mary parishes, along with Marygrove teaching, chorale work at two high schools, private lessons, and maintaining an organ repertoire, was beginning to get to Jack. He never griped, never complained; he just kept on working nonstop. The food bills were growing, the light, heat and house payments increased. Sometimes he would go a week early to ask for his paycheck to keep the boat afloat.

One day when things were getting grim, one of the nuns at St. Catherine's, Sr. Mary Frederick, called and asked if I could help her out. They had an excess of food and could we use any of it? We certainly could. Jack brought home fresh beets, carrots and potatoes. One of the perks of being visible Catholics is to know nuns.

One time, the day after Christmas, the gang of us descended the stairs to discover our gorgeous tree standing completely bereft of needles. We couldn't believe our eyes. The Holy Spirit had zapped me and I called Sr. Mary Frederick. I told her our predicament. "Oh, we have loads of trees. What good church wouldn't? Have Mr. Callaghan come and pick one up." He did and in no time we had a new tree brimming with baubles. I had advanced from pasting stars on windows and doors and mirrors to clumsily applying blue crepe paper over the mantel. Fran Brown had, bit by bit supplied us a gift a year of the Hummel Nativity set to go along with all those stars! And my mother one year embroidered a hanging that became a permanent display in our home:

"Oh, thou, who clothest the lilies
And feedest the birds of the air
Who leadest the sheep to pasture
And the hart to the waters side,
Who hast multiplied loaves and fishes
And converted water to wine,
Do thou come to our table, as giver
And guest to dine."

The threads have worn and Margaret has reworked the flaws and now it is twice as beautiful to me.

51

Opportunity Beckons

Our young friend, Frank Janeck at Holy Name in Birmingham, was in a serious accident in France where he was motor biking with his brother. He was six months recovering in a hospital in France. Msgr. Paddock again called and asked us to recommend an organist. We drove out to Birmingham to check out the church. It was new, built well, and modern, but not the pathetic buildings that were popular at the time, the late 1950's. The windows were pentagon shaped and Margaret Cavanaugh had done the stain glass window work. She used light colored glass and they were a delight to behold. Joe DiLauro, a sculptor who taught at Marygrove, had done a huge crucifix on center altar with a triumphant-faced corpus. A mosaic on one side of the cross depicted Abraham about to slay Isaac; on the other side Melchisedec was breaking bread. But unfortunately the organ was terrible especially compared to the beautiful instrument Jack had at St. Catherine's—a three manual affair with well chosen stops, a treat for the ear and receptive to Bach.

The town of Birmingham reminded us very much of Oswego, a small community with a quaint downtown. We went to lunch at a little restaurant called Machus, which also contained a bakery. When I saw they had an adequate Kresge's, I was smitten with the place. We pleaded with the Holy Spirit to guide us in our decision.

After much deliberation Jack decided to try Holy Name for a year and commute every day. The people were nice. He had a nice men's choir and a fine boy's choir and a women's choir also. In the meantime we got our home on Iroquois ready to sell. Anyone who has moved knows what a miserable job it is and just remembering brings tears to my eyes. Jack brought home the news that the priests were moving from the rectory to a house on Woodland. We could have the house on Greenwood Street, rent-free. The offices could be used for extra bedrooms. Etched on the wall was a painting of "Road to Emmaus," a scene of

Jesus revealing himself to the apostles after the Resurrection; good kitchen and adequate dining room. The only appliance needed was a refrigerator.

Visualize Patrick at 1 ½, Tess at 2 ½, the twins at 3 ½ and Kevin at 4 ½ years old. Christopher was 6; Ann, Patricia, Clare were dear little good sports. Ed and Bill were in grades 6 and 7 and Kathy would be at Immaculata High School in Detroit. Brian as a junior and Jim as a senior would attend Shrine High School. Paul was a freshman at Siena College where his Uncle Chud was on the faculty. John was still in the seminary and Margaret was at Marygrove. Jim had the worst problem. He was elected president of his senior class at St. Catherine even though he had spent two years at Sacred Heart Seminary (mostly washing windows) and he had his sweetheart, Eleanor, staying at St. Catherine's.

The summer we moved to Birmingham: front row (left to right) Patricia, Joe, Mary, Clare, and Ann; middle row (left to right)—Christopher, Bill, Kathy holding Patrick, Ed and Kevin; top row (left to right)—Brian, Jim, Margaret holding Teresa, Paul and John.

The night before the big move we went to buy a refrigerator. We parked across the street from the store. As we approached the store I felt a severe, sharp pain in my head. We entered the store anyway. I could see the refrigerator but I couldn't focus. I said, "Something's wrong with me. We will have to leave." As we got in the car and headed home I started to hemorrhage. At home it became worse so off to the hospital we went. I was convinced I was dying because there was so much blood. I started to pray to myself in Latin: "*De profundis clamavi, Domine*" and "*Miserere Nobis.*" Dr. Henderson came; he had been with me all those years with deliveries and deep care for my welfare. They started to give me blood transfusions, put a blood pressure cuff on me, and all that night a nurse stayed by my bed checking on me. Of course, I knew all the nurses in the hospital. They looked forward to my annual visits. Alice, the head nurse, who was forever bemoaning the fact that more "hillbillies" were appearing at the hospital, kept trying to entertain me. "Callaghan, you won't believe, you know how I hate hillbillies. Well, guess what? Two weeks ago I married one." Another nurse came and told me she wanted to get pregnant but couldn't. Her husband was an airline pilot. The doctor suggested he take six months off; he did and she was pregnant!

Jack came to the hospital and asked how the beds should be arranged in the new house. I tried, feebly, to say which mattress went with which springs. A puzzle, a problem! I started to clear my mind. The next morning a doctor came into the room. He told me his name and asked me what had happened. I gave him a blow by blow. His remark to me was, "I bet you are relieved. You had a miscarriage." I couldn't believe what he said! Dr. Henderson come in and said, "When a woman has a miscarriage, you have to call in another doctor." I told him the other doctor's comments. The next morning the other doctor came in the room and hemmed and hawed and finally said, "I'm sorry what I said, Mrs. Callaghan. I owe you an apology. Please accept it."

Well, I didn't die after all. Jack picked me up. I never said goodbye to 3811 Iroquois but went directly to the house in Birmingham. The neighbors had been wonderful. So many of them looked after the children, sent food, shaped thing up for us. Good Christian action! I was in the house but a few hours and there was a knock on the back door; it faced the school ground and parking lot. It was Msgr. Paddock, 6'3", white-haired in biretta and cassock with red trimming. "I came to say hello."

"Thank you for calling," I said.

"By the way," he said. "Tell your husband he must pay rent because of taxes."

Unforgettable…

Another organist, Jimmy Stevenson, who had ten children, lived rent-free on the property of the parish he worked in. Poor Jack, it didn't work for him. I was humiliated and lonesome for Iroquois. But it was a delight to take the children for a walk in the neighborhood.

52

Birmingham

Fall came and the neighborhood beamed with beauty. Ruth Dolan lived across the street. She was a convert of Msgr. Sheen, a former Lieutenant Commander in the navy. Her husband was a PhD in mathematics. They had three children. They remarked that they had a hard time getting the right formula for their last baby and why was that when they were both math geniuses? I met the woman's choir and liked them immensely. Lauretta Dean was a redheaded alto who was a great asset to Jack, helping with the choirboys and choirboy's robes. She was fun and we became life long friends. A beautiful red head, Mary Murphy, lived near by. She had 9 beautiful children. She pierced most of my girls' ears.

Paul had graduated from Austin High School run by the Augustinians. Most of the students were upper middle class there. The reason the school accepted an inner city boy like Paul was he had a good second year record in the seminary when he left at the end of his second year there. Fr. Pat was teaching at Siena College in Loudonville, NY (a suburb of Albany). It is hard to describe my brother-in-law. He was frail because of health and was left back at the seminary, finally being ordained to the priesthood at the Shrine in Washington, DC. He was multi-talented; a beautiful singer, an excellent preacher, dog lover, photographer. You might call him a snot though. He had a nasty fault of turning against some friends and making their lives miserable. His hero was Cardinal Cushing of Boston. He tried to emulate him in voice and gestures. His next hero was Jack. He and Jack were constantly discussing the Church and her doctrines.

Well, Father Pat was teaching English at Siena. His favorite play was *Hamlet*. His dramatic renditions were legendary. Since Chud was on the faculty, he was able to get half tuition for Paul (and for those who were to follow).

Brian and Jim were good sports attending Shrine High School. Jim was in a musical; Brian played basketball. Kathy got a ride into Detroit to continue at Immaculata High School. Kevin started kindergarten. The twins, Tess and Patrick were in my loving care. Ed, Bill, Ann, Trisha, Clare, Chris were in grade school at Holy Name even though the enrollment there was very high. Ed and Bill had paper routes. Ann and Trisha had a hard time I think because of some of the nasty Birmingham snobs. Clare seemed to rise above class distinctions. Christopher was serious and a good student. Mother and Dad came for Thanksgiving that fall. Dad had his bath towel over his belt and a freshly honed knife and did the honors on his umpteenth Thanksgiving turkey. Our table extended 12 feet and sat 17, plus the high chairs and bassinets. Mother couldn't believe that Jack had left the wonderful organ at St. Catherine's for a no-pedal cheapo organ. She told me Jack looked weary. Weary? Masses, boy choir, rehearsals, private lessons, practicing, keeping up with the liturgies, 4 Masses a day, funerals, weddings, food shopping, you name it. "Weary" described him perfectly.

Lauretta Dean cut some of the boys' hair. They looked handsome. The first Christmas at Holy Name the choir chipped in and Matthew, the tailor, put together a hot suit and accessories, a great thoughtful gift for their new organist and choir director. The men in the choir were very loyal. Their voices could have been better, but they were volunteers.

I went to confession to Msgr. Paddock and admitted that I used God's name in vain, about sixty times a day. Msgr. Paddock kept saying, "Oh, my, Oh, my." I did not go back to him. I had my usual panic the second week of December, wondering if Uncle Bill would send me some money. Choir members, Pat Murphy and Perry Fremont, stopped by and gave me some St. Vincent DePaul money.

Life seemed more manageable on Greenwood; it was fun to walk uptown and it was fun to window shop. The first thing to do on Greenwood was to call Dr. Donnelly. He was the one who remained all night with Tess when she was so desperately ill. Her illness left her with an enlarged heart and I met him often at children's Hospital. We became friends. He had told me he was setting up a practice in Pontiac, about a ten-minute ride from Birmingham. I phoned him and asked if he would like eleven or more new patients. He laughed because he knew who was calling. He told me the location and thus he became a key person in our lives.

Jim was in a musical at Shrine and, since it was near Thanksgiving, Mother and Dad attended. As we were leaving the auditorium, who was standing in the hall but none other than Fr. Coughlin? My father was a big fan of his since Fr. Coughlin was known all over the country as the "Radio Priest" back in the '30's. At four o'clock on a Sunday afternoon, quiet overcame the houses where Catholics lived. All listened to the radio, absorbing every word. He was an old time orator. My memories as a nine-year-old were that I had to be quiet and listen to a raving, maniacal voice whose message escaped me. But my father's encounter with him that night was a highlight of his Thanksgiving trips to our family.

Jim gave my mother a ride home in his car that night. She told me later that a young girl jumped into the front seat with him. He roughly ordered her to get into the back. "The front seat is reserved for my grandmother." Mother liked that.

Edward was in 7th grade. The choir contained men and boys. They were vested and sang from the sanctuary. The women's choir sang from the choir loft. I started to live a little. It was ten steps to the church. We joined a club called Catholic Family Movement. We met often and it was most enjoyable tossing ideas back and forth; a nice group of people. We followed a study guide and assistant pastor, Fr. Maloric, was our chaplain. The thing I liked best: at the end of the meeting, we had a goal to achieve, maybe, be kinder, be more prayerful, more patient with our children, etc.

Kevin started kindergarten and Margaret and I worked on making him look less skinny, less wistful looking. It was down the street, down and up a huge hill, which to him was a huge hill. The class wrote a cookbook. Included was a recipe for French toast for 19 people. Ed had a paper route; it seemed he always had a paper route. In fact, he still does: he delivers the *New York Times* to his father every day. He also loved to ice skate but one day he had a temperature and I kept him home. Two days later he was no better. I checked him about 1:00 AM and he had a temperature of 103. I called Dr. Donnelly who said that it couldn't be 103. I took it again and it was 103. So the doctor said to give him tepid baths. I had a reluctant patient who kept saying, "What's going on here? The late-late bath?" After quite a tussle I did the deed and an hour later he was a little better. Dr. Donnelly came to the house. It was the feast of the Epiphany. He was in a read hunting hat, red gloves, red socks, a real wonder to behold, a truly wise man.

Ed was in so much pain that Dr. Donnelly put him in the hospital in traction. The doctor was amazed to receive a report from the nurse that Ed actually moved to a different position. He became the talk of the hospital. He came home but was not yet ready for prime time.

One evening I was cleaning up and not making much headway when the doorbell rang. It was about 11:00 PM. I was at the stair landing holding a wastebasket loaded with odds and ends. I left it on the landing and dashed to answer the door. There were two IHM nuns looking at me. One was Sr. Alice Clare. "Mrs. Callaghan," she gasped with a laugh, "we thought this was the rectory. I was just saying, 'Look at all those milk bottles. Msgr. Paddock must drink a lot of milk.'" We stood and talked briefly. All at once she said, "Give me shelter. Give me shelter."

"Of course, Sister."

Just as they entered, Mary and Joseph frolicked down the stairs spilling the contents of the wastebasket at the sisters' feet. Oh, well. There was a stack of diapers on the chair in the living room. Sr. Alice Clare started to fold diapers while the other nun went around neatening up the staircase. It was a joyous visit and I hated to see them go. I learned later that IHM nuns could not enter a home unless they were seeking shelter.

Joseph was unpredictable. I heard reports that he was on the priest's seat in the confessional. Someone saw the light go on; it goes on automatically when the priest sits on his side of the confessional. They entered only to find a four-year-old Joseph in charge. Another nervous parishioner was leaving after a visit in Church and happened to look up to the choir loft. There was Joe walking on the rim of the balcony! About 2:00 o'clock one afternoon the doorbell rang and a small boy stood there and handed me a note. He told me he was in first grade and that the note was from Sister. "Dear Mrs. Callaghan: I am very upset and I think you should know that your little boy is sitting on the rim of the basketball hoop in the playground. I fear for his life!" Joe had quite a few houses he visited daily. These homes contained freezers full of candy bars, ice cream, etc. Mary and Teresa were lovely little girls and Teresa was always singing. One fair, one brunette—such a lovely sight to behold. Incredibly, the first grade nun left the convent the following year.

Life in the old rectory was easier; for one thing the laundry was on the first floor. I learned to drive and could go shopping and get out for a while; taking Patrick and Teresa for walks uptown was a joy as the neighborhood was an old time tree lined town filled with pretty homes. Margaret was getting ready to graduate from Marygrove; John was still in the seminary, Paul was at Siena, Jim was a senior at Shrine and Brian a junior, and Kathy was at Immaculata. The most helpful condition, though, was the kids had lunch at school! No more cleaning the kitchen in time to set up for lunch and then to set up for dinner.

One evening at the old rectory, we had an incident. Teresa locked herself in the bathroom. When we lived on Iroquois, all the rooms upstairs contained transoms and when someone was captured in a bathroom that someone was rescued by an adult hoisting a small person up and through the transom and setting the little one free. The rectory bathroom had none of that convenience. We called in to Teresa: "Honey, see the knob?" while twisting and turning it from the outside. And "See the button on the door?" Honey, do this and do that? Teresa was two years old and finally said, "Oh, shut up, honey!" That did it. We called the fire department and they rescued her. She was calm, quiet and completely unruffled by the ordeal. But we were not.

On another evening during the holidays when Paul was home, I decided to go to some ceremony at Holy Name. It was to be at 7:00 PM. Yes, I was going all by myself to church and I had use of the car. On the way out of the brief service, I met Katie Kuebler who lived near by. I offered her a ride home and she accepted. I parked in front of her house and we sat there and talked and talked. We did gab quite a while I admit. It was a quiet evening and only occasionally did a car pass. Then we noticed a police car driving up and down a few times on the street. I lowered the window and called out the cop, "Hey, officer, can we be of any help?"

"Yes," he replied. "We are looking for a missing person." "Oh, really?"

"Yes. A woman named Mary Callaghan."

"Good grief," I exclaimed. "I'm Mrs. Callaghan."

"Well, your husband is looking for you."

I asked Katie what the time was and she said, "10:00." I didn't realize it was so late but I really was starting to be angry. The officer filled out a lost and found ticket and I had to give my age. "40," I grumbled. When I arrived home, Paul and Jack were there. As soon as I saw Paul's face, I knew it was he (the Worry Wart) and he alone who started the whole to-do.

John Holland was a noted MC at Catholic functions and commentator on radio and TV for religious events. One day the TV station was doing a short video and they needed a man to play a dirty drunken bum. John was chosen. The scene was in a courtroom. The upshot was the old drunk was given a stiff sentence. The viewers were appalled. The studio phone rang instantly and constantly with people taking the video seriously and speaking on behalf of the drunk whom they knew as John Holland, great guy! The studio reminded the callers that it was just a play and not a real trial. John was also a square dance caller. After Christmas I got on the phone and called neighbors, new friends and old for a New Years Eve Party. December 31 that year was bleak and a little icy. Everyone came including Fr. Kowalski. John Holland did a fabulous job and all had a merry time.

Around 12:30 the guests started to wend their way home. We waved them a fond farewell. Suddenly there was a bang on the door and everyone returned with the exception of the family across the street. The city of Birmingham was a sheet of thick ice. The couple across the street went home on their hands and knees. It was riotously funny at first; then Fr. Kowalski was furious knowing he would have to spend the night. "It will be a hot day in July before I return here," he said. Because there weren't nearly enough beds, couches or cots for everyone to sleep, a number of the men/boys stayed up all night playing cards. Fr. K was delegated to the only sofa where he tried to sleep, roman collar and all. August Conen, organist at the cathedral, lay on a cot under the cuckoo clock that greeted him every hour and half hour.

Since there were already 17 sleeping bodies in the house, you might say it was crowded. Fran Conen, my best friend, asked, "How many are there here?"

"I don't want to know and don't ask again!" I said.

Two faces peering at him awakened Fr. K early. "Are you an altar boy?" they asked. One couple tried to leave about 8:00 AM and was able to get to their house about 9:00 AM. The radio announced that bit-by-bit the roads were drivable. It was a memorable adventure. I thought how lucky Msgr. Paddock had installed toilets that didn't flush audibly!

53

Manor Road

Suddenly it was time for Margaret to graduate from Marygrove. Uncle Jim came for the event. It was beyond hot. Fr. Kowalski introduced the speaker who spoke endlessly and was boring, boring, boring! Fr. K said he was very Gaelic. We thought he was very bad. At any rate, our precious girl had her degree and a nice boyfriend, Michael Guzicki who at that time was in dental school. In her junior year they had talked to us about getting married. We pleaded with them to hang in there until Margaret graduated.

We (or at least I) wanted to get out of the rectory. The people who bought Iroquois on land contract were not paying their monthly installment. A few homes were up for sale but you have to have some money to buy a home. That March was as ugly as March usually is; Lent was in progress. One day I received a phone call from a Mrs. Campbell. She said there was a house for sale with nine bedrooms and she wanted us to see it. She drove us down a street I didn't know existed, Manor Road. The homes were spacious and we saw a huge dirty yellow house perched on a small hill. We left the main road and drove up the driveway and entered the back door.

The Byron Farwells and a dear little five-year-old daughter who told us there were many beautiful cardinals in the neighborhood greeted us. Mrs. Farwell was pleasant, charming and smiled a lot only it was evident Mr. Farwell was just baring his teeth. His shirt was unbuttoned at the neckline and curls from his chest pushed out at us. I wondered if he arranged them that way. We stood in the kitchen on cheap gray tiles with many of them missing, so walking was a challenge. There was a lovely bay window in the adjoining breakfast room, then a spacious dining room overlooking a sloping lawn. The room to the left of the dining room was a bright sunroom, and to the right of the dining room was a 35' living room painted pink with a tiled fireplace with a stereo wall over it. The room was book laden. In the vestibule was a closet. The wallpaper contained many quizzical Japanese maidens. Off the side of the living room facing the driveway was a porch that used to be screened. The floor of the living room was covered with a thick, dirty, pink embossed wool carpet probably the original when the Tudor-style home was built in 1926.

Off the living room was a beautiful paneled library with many shelves for books and two windows facing the fenced-in yard that was centered by a huge elm tree. About a third of an acre of land lay behind that. Four windows looked down a hill past houses to the Rouge River. Looking out the windows gave me a strange feeling of having at one time stood in the same room gazing at the same scene...weird! One of the library doors led to a huge room with laundry appliances. It was originally an old fashioned pantry. The plaster had fallen everywhere and looked dangerous to walk in. A small half bathroom was next and now we were back in the kitchen.

There was a small hall between the living room and dining room and that's where the enclosed stairway began. Plaster had fallen off the walls on either side of the stairs, and on the landing were French windows, ceiling to floor. The second floor had a sewing room that could be used as a bedroom. Two bedrooms with adjoining baths followed. The master bedroom had a room off it: two sides in 6 pairs of glass on each side. Another lovely sized room; a very large bathroom in the center hall so there were 6 bedrooms in all. Off the hall were more stairs and a landing that led up to three spacious bedrooms and bath on the third floor.

Byron Farwell was an architect for one of the car companies and was on his way to a promotion in Switzerland. Mrs. Farwell was non-committal. There were no payments from Iroquois. Mrs. Campbell praised the house as perfect for19 people—and it was. We said nothing nor did we discuss it with her or each other. Mrs. Campbell called many times and each time we said it wasn't financially feasible. One day she came to the house and had a talk with me. "Isn't there someone you know who could lend you $6,000 for a down payment?"

"Actually, no one," I said as I searched my mind for someone I knew who had *real* money. Jack got busy and evicted the people who were not paying for Iroquois. Mrs. Campbell persisted. One time after she left, the Holy Spirit (I think) told me Fr. Kowalski belongs to the Birmingham Country Club and pals around with Ford executives. He always seemed to be with people of means. Maybe-just maybe—he would know somebody with means and contact them for me. It wouldn't hurt to try, would it? It took a while to get the courage. When he answered my call, I told him the situation immediately and said, "Would you know anyone dumb enough to lend us $6,000?" He was brief and said, "I'll look into it for you." I hung up and sat in a chair amazed at my gall in calling him.

About 15 minutes later the phone rang. I answered it and it was Fr. K. "I found someone," he said. "In fifteen minutes."

"Fifteen minutes!" I yelled.

"Yes," he said. "I found someone dumb enough to lend you the money. *I* will lend you the money."

I was overcome. It took a while for this to sink in, bless his heart. Jack was more than surprised when I told him the good news. I immediately called Mrs. Campbell and we got busy making plans to buy 86 Manor Road in Bloomfield Township. Isn't it amazing how life can change in fifteen minutes?

Mary O'Brien Callaghan

All of us at once: I am seated with Patrick, Jack with Bridget, and ascending behind us in pairs are Teresa and Joe, Mary Cecilia and Kevin, Clare and Christopher, Ann and Patricia, Bill and Kathy, Brian and Edward, Paul and Jim, Margaret and John.

Postlude

That's as far as Mother got. She didn't get to narrate the next 40-some years that brought incredible change and, in some cases, overwhelming events. As you can see from the picture above, the cute little girl sitting on her dad's lap is Bridget Louise, child no. 18, last but certainly not least of Mother's births. It's no irony that Bridget looks quite a bit like her Grandmother, Nana O'Brien, when she was a gorgeous young lady (see picture of Nana O'Brien in Chapter Five). And so some things come full circle. Bridget was also several months away from becoming Aunt Bridget to her sister Margaret's first-born son, Michael Guest (Guzicki), Jr. Yes, it was at 86 Manor Road that the last birth and the first wedding took place.

Many weddings and birth announcements were to take place over the next 20 or so years. Grandchildren arrived and Grandma Callaghan welcomed each one with warmth and joy. Holy Name school filled up with Callaghan children as well as Brother Rice and Marian high schools. Those schools continue to welcome grandchildren and great grandchildren. Many of our siblings went on to graduate from the University of Detroit, Marygrove College, and other fine colleges and universities, earning bachelor's, master's, some even advanced degrees, such as CPA's and PhD's.

Mother did not sit in a rocking chair, knitting outfits for her grandchildren. She dedicated herself to three projects: 1) renovating and/or re-decorating each of the 17-plus rooms at Manor Road, 2) establishing quality music programs and choirs in three different parishes: Madison Heights St. Vincent Ferrer, Auburn Hills Sacred Heart of the Hills, and Walled Lake St. Owens, and 3) creating a cadre of piano students who would visit for lessons during after school hours. All of these projects were in addition to taking care of a huge brood, some still in diapers, others going through adolescent angst, and still others in between. In the early 60's, there was a time when everyone was living at home fully occupying all 9 bedrooms, the daily meals serving at least 20, sometimes more. In fact during one two year span, Mother not only had us to take care of but she also took care of her mother-in-law and her brother-in-law at the same time.

Probably the greatest testimony to how well she lived her faith, hope and love was how she handled the tragedies and disappointments that entered her life. The death of her daughter-in-law Eleanor devastated her and she shook her fist heavenward more than once, but she took on three more babies and a grieving son and provided for them. She had to bury the one woman closest to her throughout her life, her mother. She provided long-distance care for her father by inviting her aunts, Ann and Helen, to live at 162 West Third and take care of their big brother, a job they did well with much help, of course, from Larry O'Brien and his family. Her father died peacefully at the age of 93. Mother was also instrumental in rescuing her brother-in-law, Msgr. James E. Callaghan, from the debilitation of clinical depression by demanding that the Diocese of Syracuse provide dignified, quality care for him. They complied at her insistence.

The greatest challenge to anyone's faith, though, is the death of one's own child. Mother had to endure two such tragedies: the deaths of her daughter Ann and of her son Brian to brain cancer. The grief at times overwhelmed her as it did all of us. Yet she never despaired: she got up every morning, did her chores, taught her piano students, bought Christmas and birthday presents for each of her surviving children as well as her grandchildren and great grandchildren. She remained active in Holy Name parish, supported her husband's work there, and even took upon herself the task of visiting extended care facilities, playing the piano for the patients and leading them in song particularly on special occasions such as Thanksgiving, Christmas and Easter.

She did this work well into her seventies despite struggling with rheumatoid arthritis and emphysema. She endured knee replacement surgery and a gall bladder attack all in the same month and lived to brag about it. She even kicked her cigarette habit, probably the most physically difficult thing she ever had to do. Despite all this, her sense of humor, her love of music, her passion for good literature and art, never waned, in fact in many ways kept her going. She attended her children's and grandchildren's high school and college graduations, concerts, football, basketball and baseball games, as well as their weddings and baptisms, first communions and confirmations. She even organized an annual Fourth of July family reunion that everyone to this day attends ("Be there or be square!"). And of course she hosted a Christmas "Grandma" party for all her grand and great-grand children. And for all her daughters, daughters-in-law, and grand daughters she emceed a "witches" party on Halloween with much cackling, giggling and male bashing throughout the entire afternoon.

To say that we miss her is an understatement. Even now we somehow expect her to arrive at any moment and "shake things up." But of course that is not to be, even though we can hear that distinctive melodious voice of hers singing, laughing, joking, cajoling, and praying with our inner ears, with our memories and imaginations. Dad keeps on practicing two and three hours a day, sitting in as a substitute organist at Holy Name, playing family weddings, orchestrating his magnificent garden, and even giving an occasional organ recital, but we know he misses her more than any of us put together.

Mary Anne and I had the great good fortune to visit Ireland this past Easter vacation. The tour guide we had, Noel McCaffrey, triggered a distant chord in my memory. He was very much like the tour guide Mother described when she and Dad went on a visit to Ireland during the 80's. I was convinced that it was the same fellow. And sure enough it was. We showed Dad the pictures and he remembered Noel and his personality and antics. I was disappointed that Dad took only a cursory look at the pictures we brought back until I realized several days later (Ok, so I'm not real quick on those kinds of things) that the trip Mother and Dad took to Ireland was one of the highlights of their life together and that the memories were just too painful. I then began to imagine some of the grief he must feel every day.

I happened to be teaching my students at the time a unit on rewriting and revising and was taking them through an exercise designed by Steven Dunning and William Stafford called "letter poem." The students make lists of famous (or not so famous) persons who are dead, of famous persons who are alive, and of some objects (such as a winding river) or events (such as the 911 tragedy). As often as I can, I try to do these exercises with them. On this particular occasion I thought of the incident with my dad and I decided to imagine my mother writing a letter to him:

Dearest Husband Mine,

I'm the only one who knows
How much you really miss me,
How hard you strive to quell
The pulsing pain of my departure.

I'm the only one who knows
What your daily rituals are,
What they really mean:
The steps you take to smother gnawing aches,
The relentless, lonely grief you feel.

And I'm the only one who understands
How those dawn-to-dusk routines of yours
Keep you going, keep you from the brink of
Caving in to pity and despair.

I'm the only one who understands such things
Because even on this side of time, your love,
Ever true and strong, tugs at me.

I'm the only one who knows how you sense,
How you feel me present in each of your routines.
You know I wind and coil my very being
Within each thought of yours, around each move you take,
Within each waking moment every day.

The faith we shared glows within your daily Mass;
You hear the music of my voice within the Bach,
Dupre, and Franck you practice every morning,
You hear me echoing behind each note, each complex chord,
Rising and falling with each precise arpeggio.
I'm still your most avid, loyal fan.

The very soil you turn within your garden,
The very seeds you plant,
You know are full of me and will blossom with the
Self-same reds and greens, the amber, mint-green textures that
Radiated from those Lake Ontario sunsets we used to celebrate
So many years ago.

Your love is like God's love, eternal, self-sustaining,
Making all things possible. I'm the only one who knows.

Your loving wife

978-0-595-36553-1
0-595-36553-1

Printed in the United States
36890LVS00005B/118-159

9 780595 365531